In gratitude to my father, David.

THE SEARCH FOR SATYA

By R.A. Moseley

Beginnings

Sunday, 18 April 2032

$\mathbf{L}$ ooking briefly at her watch, she saw that she had enough time to take a diversion into the tranquil surroundings of the walled rose garden. It was her favourite place of refuge as it was designed to offer a secret oasis in the city for the rare few people who had discovered it. It was certainly not marked on the map as a destination for tourists and for this reason it provided a gift for those whose curiosity took them wandering through the back streets of this part of the city. Since the entrance gate marked only a narrow gap in the brick wall, and the welcoming sign upon it was barely noticeable, it was likely that even the locals who walked regularly down this street would not know of its existence. Stepping inside, she could see that there was already a colourful array of roses scattered throughout the garden; the smell of their perfumed scent was noticeably alluring.

After closing the iron gate behind her, she began to wander aimlessly through the garden; choosing a path that was lit by sunshine. She walked at a slow pace and, because she was paying close attention to the details of her surroundings, something suddenly caught her eye. Hidden in the undergrowth of the flowerbed was what appeared to be a small black notebook resting on the ground. As there was no one else in the garden, she stepped across and bent down to pick it up. Surprisingly, it did not look as if the notebook had been lying there for long. Rain had been falling heavily the previous day and yet the cover was bone-dry.

1

She took a seat on one of the many wooden benches that were lined against the south-facing brick wall of the garden and, for some reason, she felt an impulse to open it and see if there was anything written inside. It was only a small notebook but it was a surprise to discover that each page was filled with words. The handwriting was small and neat but, as the book did not carry the name of an author, she could not tell whose it was. Reading on, she quickly realised that on each page was written a poem, and that each page flowed on to the next by an invisible connecting thread.

It did not take her too long to read through to the end, but while doing so she became totally spellbound and absorbed by the potency of the words; she felt they had triggered something deep inside of her. This magical piece of poetic art appeared to be charged with an ancient wisdom; and this wisdom was now resonating deep into the depths of her soul, leaving her with a warm tingling sensation running through her body. This absorbing sensation made her feel empty and as light as a feather. Yet, strangely, she felt full of life at the same time, as never before had she come across words that sang in such a beautiful and lovely way. Sitting there in the silence, a soothing wave of peace filled her heart and she felt with a relief a lessening of the anxiety that she always carried around with her. It felt as if these words were a portal allowing her to view her life with a clearer perspective.

She was only disturbed from this place of intense stillness when her mobile phone began to ring and she hurriedly fumbled through her handbag to answer it. On the other end was her friend who she had been due to meet for coffee in the centre of the city. Although she had had plenty of time on her hands when arriving at the garden, she was now hopelessly late. Placing the book in her handbag and getting swiftly to her feet, she felt a new wave of sadness consume her as she noticed that the moment of bliss had passed. But there was no time to linger so she walked hurriedly to the place where they had arranged to meet.

It was an old-fashioned independent coffee shop that had become a regular meeting place for the two of them, as it was quiet and served great coffee. Pushing briskly through the door, she walked over to the stool where her friend was sat and warmly hugged her. Noticing the empty cup of coffee on the table; she offered to buy her friend a second one and walked over to the counter to place their order.

On her return, they made polite conversation and each caught up on the other's news. It had been a fortnight since they had last met and a lot had happened to both of them during the intervening period. However, it was not long before an opportunity arose to turn the conversation towards the overwhelming wave of emotion triggered by the book of poems she had discovered in the rose garden. Eagerly, she took the book from her handbag and urged her friend to read the collection of poems for herself.

She watched intently to see if the words would have the same impact. It soon became obvious that the book was working its magic and, in seeing her friend soften with emotion, she started to tingle with excitement. Having watched her reach the end and close the book, she then asked her friend a question that to her seemed a natural one to ask:

'What human heart could possibly be graced with such profound and heartfelt insights as this one?'

<u>Part I</u>

Chapter One

Wednesday 10 September, 2025

The digital clock on the old oak chest of drawers had moved a second onwards to 7.23 am and, as it did, there was an eruption of monotonous droning that pulled me from my unconscious state back into the realm of consciousness. Noticing a nagging throbbing sensation in my temple, I remained stubbornly in a motionless state for a few moments before dragging myself across the room to turn off the alarm. I shifted my aching body slowly across to the window where, drawing back the light turquoise curtains, I was dazzled by bright sunshine. Outside it was a clear early autumn morning. Standing in the warmth of my own home it was a sight that briefly led me to believe that it was still summer, and that a sweltering hot day would follow. Deep down, however, I knew this delusion would shatter once outside the front door, as the cold wind snaking down my spine would surely signal the realisation that a depressing winter was well on its way.

I walked across to the plain silk dressing gown that was hanging over the half-closed bedroom door and draped the fabric over my body before padding barefoot across the narrow hallway into the bathroom. It was uniquely circular in comparison to the square rooms in the rest of the house, but its shape was not its only quirk. The combination of saffron wallpaper and a red linoleum floor offered a bold statement within a house that was otherwise characterised by bland neutrality. Under force of habit, I walked across to the sink facing me and doused my face in icy cold water. It was a

7

routine that never failed to stir me from my slumber.

The shower was always the next challenge for my fragile state of mind: the temperature dial had recently broken, which left it permanently set at a level that felt close to boiling. As always, the first drop of scalding water on my bare flesh was the hardest to face, but, after a few nervous engagements with the steaming hot water, my skin adjusted to the heat. When drying my reddened flesh on a coarse blue towel I made a mental note to replace the shower unit, as I had done many times on other days; but, due to my tired state, I soon forgot about it. I moved slowly across to the sink, pulled open the cabinet above, and wiped my hand over the inside mirror to clear the condensation that had built up. Pulling a blunt razor from the shelf, I squirted some shaving foam onto my jaw and proceeded to clear the distinct line of stubble that had formed over the previous couple of days.

Returning to my room, I pulled out from the wardrobe clothes that were appropriate for a professional male. The charcoal grey suit and the white shirt were conventional choices and it was only my favourite green silk tie that provided a more individual, although tasteful, tone.

After returning the dressing gown to its resting place on the door, I moved across to the far side of the room, where, on the inside of the wardrobe, there was an oak-framed mirror. Whilst kneading some wax into my short, dark, ruffled locks, I surveyed the rest of my appearance. The reflection that confronted me did nothing to lift my spirits. Although I was only 33 years old, my face looked deeply drawn and lacked any real colour or vigour. My eyes had black rings around them and it was evident that the lack of decent sleep was beginning to take its toll. My muscles and joints looked stiff and tense and it felt as if they had been wound up tight by the strains of daily life, leaving my body sapped of the flexibility of youth. However, as my eyes drifted downwards below my chest, I was grateful that I had not lost my trim figure. Many of my male colleagues were already displaying the unhealthy consequences of the excesses of their twenties, but I had always led a healthy and

8

moderate life.

My frame was broad and over six feet high; nobody would have described me as slight. I admired my strong, square shoulders and my chiselled, newly-shaven jaw. I also valued my appearance, knowing that, in the company of others, I seemed a strong presence. But my broad frame was set against a pair of misty blue eyes that softened my rigidity, giving those who came into close contact a glimpse of a soft and sensitive character. However, in the blur of the crowd such details remained unobserved, for everything about my appearance had been toned down in order to blend and conform. In fact, the skills of the chameleon were highly important in my world as I had to adapt to ever-changing looks and fashions over time.

Glancing across at the clock on the other side of the room, I noticed that precious seconds were ticking by. This was worrying as my morning routine was planned carefully to give me the maximum amount of time in bed. Moving deftly across the hallway, I began to descend the stairs; intending to grab some breakfast.

It was only when I reached the bottom step that the pungent smells of last night's dinner wafted to my nostrils; the lingering odour of a spicy dish triggering a sickly taste in the back of my throat. More than anything else, the smell left me feeling ashamed, as I remembered how I had prided myself on my standards of cleanliness during the years I had spent in shared accommodation. My neglect of the chores was out of character, but maybe some of the strains from work were taking their toll and affecting my home life.

So I was greeted by the sight of rotting leftovers and grimy work surfaces - a sight that I didn't wish to entertain at this early hour. Making an attempt to ignore it, I swiftly turned my attention away from the sink and let my eyes settle on the opposite side of the room. Pulling open one of the cupboards that stood against the wall, I lifted out a bowl that was hidden behind several chipped mugs. Most of these mugs had not been used in years for, as always, I preferred a red glazed piece that I had been given at a conference many years earlier. After closing the cupboard behind me I saw that

9

this mug was lying dirty in the sink and needed a quick rinse before I could go any further. Afterwards I put the kettle on to make a mug of tea, filled the bowl with cereal, and went across to the fridge to dig out a carton of milk. It had been nestling there for some time judging by the whiff of sourness as I put it to my nostrils.

Noticing the stack of neatly packaged ready-made meals in the fridge, it was hard for me not to reflect upon the fact that, only a few months earlier, I had been spending a lot of time in this kitchen with a deep passion for cooking. But recently I had slipped into a lethargic, disinterested state and had eaten only convenience food bought from the supermarket. It was another sad moment of reflection but I didn't wish to dwell on it, so I poured boiling water into the mug and let my tea brew. After discarding the tea bag into a small compost bin I moved across the room to the window and pulled out a wooden stool from under the breakfast bar. The sun, rising steadily higher out to the east, always shone brightly through the pane of glass at this hour and time of year and I immediately felt uncomfortable under its glare.

When I had finished my breakfast I took a reluctant glance at my wristwatch, slid promptly off my stool and headed towards the front door, where I pulled on my brown leather shoes. These days I rarely bothered to untie the laces as I squeezed my heels aggressively down onto each sole.

Opening the heavy rosewood door, my mood shifted as I laid my eyes on a beloved object sat in the driveway. My sleek, black, jeep gave me the dose of comfort and security, which I so craved at that moment. I opened the door and climbed into the cream leather seat that gave me a handy perch some way above the road surface. Instinctively my left hand brushed the teasing specks of dust off the dashboard. As I turned the ignition the engine immediately responded; positively purring as it did so. I coaxed it into gear before gliding slowly and smoothly away.

The commuting experience was always split into two, starkly contrasting, phases and I had never been able to deal comfortably with the moment of changeover. To begin with, I would be lured into a false sense of calm as I wound through the suburban maze down tree-lined avenues. I would push my spine right back into the soft leather fabric as I coasted smoothly along; with my foot barely having to hold down the accelerator pedal. It was easy for me to slip gently into a calm and peaceful state.

But the moment of changeover was never far enough away, and when it came my briefly uplifted mood was jolted roughly aside. For it was at this moment that the road started to climb gently upwards to a roundabout, which sat above the solitary twelve -lane highway that connected the heart of the city of Sarum to the housing estates that lay to the east. This highway was the focal point of all the surrounding road networks, since it offered the only passable route over the hugely impressive, but equally divisive, mile -wide ship canal that had been built two centuries earlier.

So it was this convergence of traffic onto a single road, with all the vehicles heading in the same direction and with the same desti- nation in mind, which caused the sudden change in my mood. After merging into the queues of stationary traffic, I could not help but let out a frustrated sigh, knowing that it would take another half hour to cover the remaining four miles.

This feeling of frustration triggered a new train of thought about how much Sarum had changed over the years. I knew that the congestion I was experiencing was a consequence of the city's growth. Despite being only the third biggest city in the land of Arasmas – one of the four lands of the globe – it had assumed the title of capital a number of years before, as it held the country's economic heartbeat. It was now very different from the city which had drawn pilgrims with its beautifully carved Gothic 12th century centre of worship, that had once risen like a citadel above the sky- line. The location of this sacred place, on a small mound that rose above the flat and agricultural landscape, meant that, during its heyday, it could be seen for miles around. But today it was shielded from view behind the clean glass skyscrapers that now dominated the city skyline.

Returning my attention to my surroundings, I could see that I was edging ever closer towards the point where the road crossed the ship canal. This nearly always marked the moment where I would grow tired of the journey. Reaching across into the glove compartment, I gave a brief smile as my hands pulled out the disc I was after. MJ was a singer whose songs could always help to lift even the most depressing of moods. As the first tune kicked in, my jeep started to roll slowly across the city's famous cast-iron suspension bridge; an iconic structure which had been built to give the city a defining monument. It had been a product of genius and immense endeavour, created as it was at the same time as the equally impressive waterway running beneath it. However, it had been constructed not only for merely practical reasons, but also to express dominance over the surrounding landscape. Today, though, its gloss had faded; the structure was now impractical and burdensome as it creaked and groaned under the weight of modern traffic volumes.

The canal itself served as an obvious divide between the modern residential estates that spread outwards on one side and the fading industrial areas that lay on the other. It was purely down to the presence of passing ships that the city had spawned industrial activity two centuries previously. I remembered my school tutor once passionately describing to me how these parts were the flesh and bones that had grown around the heart of the old medieval city. He'd explained that, over the course of a century, a whole network of watery veins had gradually evolved and spread their way eastwards from the heart of the city. However, the recent influx of wealth into the city had not helped to prevent these flesh and bones undergoing a long period of slow decay; it had started well before I was born and further large swathes of land had been neglected or abandoned since. All those of us who had to travel through these depressed areas could do was to try to block out the gloomy scene from our consciousness. As I whistled along to my music, tucked safely in the cocoon of my metal box, I had no difficulties in blocking out these images.

Finally I left the main highway behind, turned down a side street and drove into a multi-storey car park. Finding a space within the orderly ranks of metal at this time of the morning was always a matter of pure chance. But my instincts took me up to the third level, where I was able to spot a rare space ahead of me and pulled in. The car park itself was an old, dilapidated building that had stubbornly refused to conform to the city's recent modernisation agenda, sitting isolated and cut off on the opposite side of the inner ring road.

Leaving the car park behind, I had to cross over the carriageway via an uninviting narrow bridge; from here it was a ten-minute walk to the office.

I now found myself caught up again in a world of tension, as I became wrapped up in a mass of people surging single-mindedly down a narrow pavement past a road filled with barely moving traffic. After struggling across to the opposite pavement, and dodging an aggressive cyclist in the process, I took a rest from the breathless rush by darting to my left down a much quieter thoroughfare. This led me across a large green square to another major street on which my office stood. This was a large, modern building made of blue-tinted glass, which stood, gleaming proudly, at a major junction. Passing through the slow-moving revolving door was like taking a step back in time, as I entered a vast and impressive marble-floored gallery. It was traditional in style and was clearly an arrogant show of wealth designed to impress all visitors.

On my right was a large reception desk manned by an ageing gentleman, one of only a few who had lived a full lifetime in this fast growing city. He was a naturally warm being who was always there to greet me with a friendly smile. In fact, I could not recollect ever having seen him wearing a scowl or a grimace in the years that I had known him. He was the longest-serving employee and it was of no surprise to me when I learnt that he was fondly considered to be an institution here. He had already been long established at the company 16 years earlier, when the new office was opened in this building.

It was not hard for me to see why he had been there so long, and I often felt envious of the simple nature of his job. For if he was not sat at his desk half-distracted by some book or newspaper, he could usually be found on the pavement outside smoking one of his cigars.

After we had exchanged our usual warm and polite early morning greeting, I continued across the gallery to the elevator at the far end. I entered alone and pressed the button for the fifteenth and final floor, where our office was located. At their destination, the doors reopened smoothly and I stepped out into a dull grey corridor which had a number of small meeting rooms and offices on either side; these were always kept locked when vacant.

At the far end was a large set of double doors with a small keypad to one side of them; entry could only be gained if the person's fingerprint matched the information in the database. I put my finger against this device, the doors opened smoothly, and I walked through into a large open-plan office. There were about 30 desks that were all set out in small rows and fully equipped with the latest computer equipment. Formerly I had worked at one of these terminals before my promotion to a rather luxurious private sanctuary at the far right-hand corner of the room. This sanctuary was perfectly secluded away from the pressurised environment of the busy office.

Having said good morning to those who were already at work, I stood outside my office for a moment as I still enjoyed the privilege of opening a door that had my name and title embossed on a gold plate. '**Myrkais Demeritus, Area Team Manager**' it read in bold black letters. I strolled into my domain and then placed my hands down on my large but cluttered desk for a moment, as if to gather my thoughts for the day ahead. After hanging my suit jacket on the back of the executive styled leather chair, my first task was always to switch on my own personal kettle and to put some strong coffee into a mug. I then walked back outside to pick up some milk from the fridge at the far side of the office, before returning to the quiet comfort of my sanctuary.

14

It was probably true to say that I'd been very successful at growing a thick skin and a poker face at work: I'd learnt how to cope with the daily strains of working life and office politics so that they did not overwhelm me. However, as I sat there quietly sipping my mug of coffee, the brief moment of calmness gave way to darker emotions, unearthed from deep within me. My brow furrowed as they climbed to the surface. These moments of panic and uneasiness had been plaguing me for several months and they came without any warning and ever more frequently.

My preferred response to these emotions was one of suppression: I would seek to replace these deep misgivings with shallower day-to-day concerns that felt easier to deal with. But unfortunately, I thought, as I set about my first working task of the day, just like the washing-up in the kitchen sink at home, these matters do not simply disappear overnight.

Chapter Two

I was sitting quietly at my desk and, although I'd been in the office barely an hour, I was already onto my second mug of coffee. But the caffeine was doing little to lift me out of my lethargic state and I didn't feel settled enough to be able to focus on my tasks for the day. There was a strong and growing sensation of nervous disquiet within me and, unsurprisingly, I was lacking in concentration. I knew that in an hour's time I would face the senior management team for my latest quarterly review and I felt that this morning would not be a smooth one.

To pass the time I browsed the latest financial news on the internet. The headlines only added to my feeling of gloom: new figures had been released showing that house prices across Arasmas had fallen again over the last quarter. I knew from experience that falling house prices only made my job more difficult. However, because of its continued high demand for housing, Sarum remained the only city to buck the trend. At least this provided me with some good news where my personal finances were concerned, and I felt relieved that I had made the effort to clamber onto the bottom rung of the property ladder three years ago. Purchasing a house in Sarum had been a good decision not only because it provided me with a high - and safe - return on my investment, but, with property prices having risen astronomically in the city, I would not now have been able to afford a house, unless I had settled for a smaller property or one in a less desirable area. I only regretted that I had waited so long and I looked back wistfully at those earlier years when my money had drained needlessly away from my bank account to pay for rented property.

However, browsing the news did not distract me for long and I was soon feeling restless once more. It appeared to me as if time was passing awfully slowly towards the 11 o'clock summons; I was beginning to feel an uncomfortable burning sensation below my collar and a painful sensation on top of my head. I did try to re-focus and concentrate on the smaller and more manageable tasks that lay before me, but even the loud, slow ticking of the clock on the far wall proved a distraction. With every second it seemed to grow louder and more incessant in my mind.

I felt my mouth becoming dry and sore and so I reached over to the water cooler and gulped down a glass of cool liquid. It did not extinguish the burning sensation. I pulled off my tie and undid the top button but there was still no respite. Finally, the time came for me to gather my papers together and to walk outside my private sanctuary into a cacophony of sound. There was always a constant hive of noise that made this office hiss. No-one raised their head as I walked past and I was grateful for this because I knew that I looked awful with my open shirt and ruffled hair. I'd not even cared enough to put my tie back on before leaving.

So it was with a feeling of trepidation that I walked down the corridor towards the lift, stopping at the last of the three doors on the left. Inside, I knew that Marion and Susan, my two powerful superiors, would be sat sternly on the opposite side behind the desk, ready to give me their usual grilling. I turned slowly to face the door and raised my fist to it. Hesitating momentarily, I glanced across to the lift on my right, and then suddenly, without any fur-ther thought, lowered my hand, turned sharply towards the steel doors and started walking. After calling the lift I felt a pang of anxi-ety that quickly diminished, when I realised that my wallet and keys were in my trouser pocket, and not, as I had feared, in the jacket which still hung on the back of the chair in my office. My first thought was that it would be embarrassing to walk out like this and to have to come crawling back later in the day. However, the jan-gling sound in my pocket was a welcome one and within a couple of minutes I was walking back across the ground floor and into the bright sunshine outside.

Although a maze of streets were available to me, I chose to head in a familiar direction, namely, back towards the security of my vehicle. I quickly retraced the steps I had made only a couple of hours previously and, while walking, I felt my composure start to return. However, it was still not strong enough to change my decision and I still felt conviction in what I was doing. Where that would take me though I had no idea.

It felt appropriate to find myself walking into the murky gloom of the car park foyer and I chose to take the stairwell back up to the third level. I proceeded to drop back into the darkness of my car and slid slowly down into the driver's seat. I took a long and deep breath and simply sat motionless with my hands clasped tightly onto the wheel for security. What followed was a long drawn out period of blank silence where nothing happened.

In suddenly glancing at the small digital clock on the dashboard, I knew instinctively what would come next. On cue, the mobile phone began to ring from the passenger seat next to me. Experience had taught me that Marion always gave fifteen minutes grace to those running late for a meeting. Despite the natural temptation to ignore it, I reluctantly reached across and wrapped my fingers around the vibrating object. After taking a couple of deep breaths to calm myself, I pressed to accept the call and put it to my ear.

'Hello, Myrkais speaking,' I answered.

'Myrkais, Marion here. Have you forgotten the meeting we'd arranged for 11 o'clock?'

'No, I had remembered, Marion, but something urgent has come up,' I replied vaguely.

'Well I will be out of the office after lunch. Will you be back in before then?' she asked me, in a distinctly puzzled tone.

'I can't, Marion. This urgent matter is going to take several days to sort out.'

'Several days?' she repeated.

I almost felt like expressing the same question of disbelief for the words had come unexpectedly from my mouth. There was an uncomfortable moment's pause before she added, with a certain hint of irony in her voice;

'Were you planning on telling us what this matter of urgency is?'

Despite the fact that I counted her as someone I could talk with on a personal level, I just could not bring myself to explain what the matter was. Perhaps it was because I didn't know what it was myself. All I could do was tell her that it was a private matter that I needed to go away and deal with. I sensed that her feelings of frustration were beginning to grow, but I could also see that she was using her management experience to hold these back.

'Will you give me a ring on Monday, then, to let me know when you'll be able to come back in and we'll discuss this more then?' she finally asked, in a manner that suggested to me that she had recovered her composure.

'I will do Marion. Thank you.'

With that, I hung up, without allowing her to say anything further. After switching my phone off, I tossed it over onto the seat opposite.

As I continued to sit with both of my hands on the wheel, I found myself dropping into a blissful state of calmness. My eyes lifted over the wheel to the dark void beyond the sheet of glass. I instinctively knew that my behaviour could not be fully explained by a situation at work - one I was not unaccustomed to dealing with. I felt very sure that the prospect of this meeting was the final straw that had simply tipped things out of balance. Then out of the deep silence a question began to form very clearly in my mind: 'What am I leaving out?'

The question came again and again growing louder and louder each time until it felt as if it was literally being shouted at me. Was I going crazy, I wondered? Then the words disappeared and my mind became immediately very foggy as it turned over the question.

Rationally considered, it seemed insane to even think that something could be missing from my life, and I felt a tinge of embarrassment for even entertaining such dark and self-absorbed thoughts. Yet, I could not let them go and nor could I ignore them.

Then out of the dark void the next step I must take suddenly came to me: a clear image of the mountains that lay to the north formed in my mind and, at that moment, I felt very strongly that I needed to go there. These mountains were very close to my childhood home of Monkscaph, and I felt my desire to go there could be explained by a need to return to my roots. As soon as I accepted this as the next step, a deep sense of peace began to fill my whole being and the fog began to shift. Although this was obviously only a brief respite, I felt that I was returning to a state of calm that I had not felt for weeks. I noticed that my fingers and toes start to tingle as the nervous energy that I had been holding inside of me dissipated outwards. I gave out a deep breath and felt a great weight lift from my shoulders. I was startled that this sense of release could come so easily – simply from sitting here in the silence for a few minutes and paying attention.

Having taken this decision I felt a wave of excitement at the prospect of devising a clear plan. Of course, what exactly would happen on my return was still unclear, but, sure of my next step, I was happy to put these concerns to one side. I confidently placed the key in the ignition and pulled out of the parking space. It was unusual for me to be driving on the roads at this hour of the day and so, as I rejoined the road network, I was surprised to see that there was still a large volume of traffic. However, it was not too long before I passed back over the ship canal and drove through the empty, soulless streets of suburbia. Driving through this area, I saw nothing but empty houses and driveways, and was struck by the realisation that the lifeblood of these communities was totally drained during the working day.

Pulling onto my driveway I felt the urge to make haste for what I knew would be a long journey north. However, in walking through the door, I was reminded of the dirty dishes, and I knew I could not leave without first returning some order to my home. Even in the midst of this very strange morning, and despite my rash behaviour, I still seemed to be thinking calmly and rationally. This, at least, was welcome after what had come before.

After vigorously tidying the house, I returned upstairs and packed my possessions, putting them into a suitcase that I had pulled down from the loft. I was unsure what type of clothes I would need, as I knew that snow was not unheard of at this time of year in that part of the country. In the end I decided to try and prepare for all possible types of weather. I also did not know how long I would be away and how many changes of clothes I would need. After putting the bulging suitcase in the car, I decided to brew myself a mug of tea before leaving in order to clear the dryness that still remained in my throat. This was also an opportunity for me to have a few moments of calm relaxation after the hectic rush of the morning. Finally, with the time moving towards 1.30 pm, I washed my mug and was ready to leave.

I had no option but to drive once more towards the city before turning off to join the outer circular road that would take me around and out onto the main highway north. I then travelled at speed, crossing the green belt at the city's northern border and was soon out into the suburbanised countryside – an area that was largely alien to me. A couple of hours behind the wheel had taken me almost half of the distance I had to travel when my eye was caught by a sign at the side of the road advertising a service station that lay a couple of miles ahead. As the information passed through my brain, I was quickly forced to acknowledge that I'd not eaten for several hours and that I was definitely feeling pangs of hunger. The sign had its intended effect, pulling me off the carriageway and into a parking space outside of a large and dull concrete building with an unwelcoming steel frontage.

After walking through to the cafeteria, I strolled alongside the counter looking intently at the pre-prepared meals, which were being kept warm under a heated lamp. Nothing looked appetising, but I picked up a sandwich in order to lessen my hunger. After paying, I took a seat by the window and let my thoughts drift towards the days soon to come, knowing I would soon be enjoying fresh mountain air and stunning vistas. After eating, I looked again at the map to check my route, visited the lavatory, and quickly moved back out into the lingering afternoon sunshine and back behind the wheel of my car.

It was almost another two and a half hours before I reached the foothills of the mountain range that had been calling me: these were the Blue Mountains. When I came to a convenient parking bay I decided to pull in to admire the impressive views. After stepping outside the car I found the clear, cool autumn air refreshing and I lingered against the bonnet for a few minutes longer before continuing with my journey. I remembered from my childhood that there had been a large hotel in a nearby village; a village that was known as the gateway to the mountainous north. Turning off the new road that bypassed the village, I was pleasantly surprised to discover that the hotel was still standing there, just as I'd remembered it. The 'vacancies' sign blowing in the wind was an encouraging omen so I pulled in through the gateway at the side and drove around to the parking area at the rear.

Before getting out, I pulled the phone from my glove compartment, and, turning it on, saw that I had not received any further calls or messages. Taking my case from the boot I crunched my way noisily through the shale and across to the back entrance. Standing behind the front desk was a tall lady of middle age with spectacles perched on the edge of her nose; she looked austere and imposing. Her sharp voice belied the warm welcome that she was offering as I paid her for one night's accommodation. I took the key from her cold, pale hands and took the lift to the top floor of the three-storey building.

The room was comfortable, if a little basic, and I let my belongings drop down to the floor as I wanted to return outside to stretch my stiffened joints in the cold evening air. The village was dead at this time of day, and, because of the new bypass, little traffic now passed through. Although there were many new shops and new developments, the main village square hadn't altered at all. The grass was neatly kept but there were still the same poorly maintained iron benches. I took a seat but soon became restless, and as the twilight ambience deepened further, I decided to return back to the hotel.

When I got back to my room, I took a shower which left me feeling refreshed and ready to go down to the main bar for dinner. Strangely, the place was largely deserted. Noticing a couple of members of staff lingering in a bored fashion, I felt uneasy, and, after paying for a drink, I found a quiet table in the corner where I could sit comfortably without being disturbed. After taking a gulp of the locally brewed ale that I had ordered, I let my eyes rest on the black, lamp-lit street and relaxed in the soft wicker chair.

However, just after ordering a meal at the bar, my state of sleepy calmness was rudely disturbed as my mobile phone began to vibrate from the inside of my jacket. Again ignoring the temptation to turn it off, I clasped my fingers around the casing and cast my eye onto the screen. The three letters that I saw there made my cheeks pale. It was Jen, my partner of more than two years, and, in that second, I realised that we had been intending to go and see a movie that evening. Looking at my watch, I saw that I was already ten minutes late and I knew that she would be sitting impatiently in her flat waiting for me to pick her up. I finally pulled myself together enough to accept the call.

'Hello,' I began, a distinct tone of apprehension in my voice.

'Oh, hello,' she answered. 'I was wondering where you were; the film is due to start shortly.'

'I know Jen. I'm sorry but I only remembered that I was meant to come over when I heard the phone ring.'

'Oh,' she paused. I sensed that she was trying to adjust to my absent-minded behaviour. She continued. 'Are you still coming over though? There's always a later film we can watch or we could just open a bottle of wine together?'

I was having difficulty gathering my story together, and the line went quiet for a few awkward moments.

'I should have phoned you earlier, but I've had a hectic day and so I've been somewhat preoccupied,' my voice trailed off after this last word. After a pause, I continued.

'You see, I wasn't feeling very well and came out of work this morning and I've been out driving for the rest of the day.'

'Driving?' she queried. 'Where on earth have you been driving to?'

'I've headed north out into the mountains,' I replied. Jen had never been to the area and I was in a strange aloof mood that made me feel disinclined to explain further or make conversation.

'And why have you driven out into the mountains?' she asked. I realised that she was no doubt exasperated by the unhelpful one-line answers I was giving to her questions.

'I just need a few days away by myself to think a few things through. I thought the mountain air would be of help,' I continued, in the same vague tone.

'To think what through?' she asked abruptly.

I noticed the strain of emotional concern in her voice and I imagined that she must be trying to figure out what I meant. However, at that moment, I could not find the words to comfort her and explain my undeniably strange behaviour.

'Look, my battery is running out, so I really have to go. I will call you soon,' was all I could think of to say. In desperation I finished the conversation by telling her that I loved her and then ended the call before she had a chance to reply.

After switching the phone off, I returned it back to my pocket and continued with my drink. It was not long before my dinner arrived and I was happy to distract myself from my wandering thoughts. The period of distraction did not last long though for I felt deeply troubled by the defensive way I had behaved while talking to Jen. However, this feeling was too much to consider on top of all the other things that were weighing heavily on my mind.

I assumed that the future of our relationship would emerge over the coming days but for the moment I needed to put it firmly to one side. After a long and exhausting day I just wanted to slip away into a blank state and to silence my mind. I returned to my room at the end of the evening. The strong local ale I had been drinking helped me to drop swiftly to sleep.

Chapter Three

Saturday, 13 September 2025

After leaving the hotel on Thursday morning I travelled north and booked into a remote hostel in the Blue Mountains. I arrived late that afternoon, having spent the day taking a long walk through a beautiful forested valley. It was a walk that had taken me to a lake at the far end of the valley, from which there had been a clear view of Mount Nodwons, the tallest mountain in the range. When I set eyes on this mountain, I had resolved to climb it before returning to Sarum — but that could wait until another day.

The hostel was set away from the main highway along an unclassified road. Arriving, I had grinned broadly, for I saw a beautiful reconverted cottage sitting in isolation surrounded by steep mountain slopes. I was staying, with one other guest, in a smart four-bed dormitory; the rest of the hostel seemed quiet. During Friday I had taken another long walk but was still feeling unsure as to why I had come to this place and I was still none the wiser as to what it was that was amiss.

On the Saturday morning, I woke around dawn after a heavy and deep sleep. The early morning sun was shining through the window onto my pillow, but I turned over onto my back and continued to rest in its glare for an hour or more. In truth, I was waiting for the man in the opposite bed to stir before making my move. Eventually, stirring to life with a snort, the man made a swift movement out of the bed and through the door. The peaceful silence only encouraged me to linger a little longer but soon I too left and went into the stillness of the vacant kitchen.

I made myself a mug of tea and some toast and took a seat in the dining area. My attention now started to wander and I became captivated by a number of pictures that were hanging at various points around the room. Some were of breathtaking landscapes whilst others showed adventurous mountaineers in action. Each picture had a story written next to it that described the scene, and as I read, I found that these tales were full of intrigue, mystery and adventure. This was clearly a perfect hostel for those who loved exploring, but, nonetheless, I was left pondering whether I felt inspired or daunted by these tales of daring and courage.

I was not someone who was a traveller or explorer by nature and my holidays were always sedate affairs. It was, therefore, very surprising that I had felt called to come to the wild mountains: I had grown used to the comfort and ease of my urban lifestyle. Even when I was growing up in Monkscaph, we had usually spent our holidays at a seaside resort about three hours drive to the east of the town, and we rarely headed northwards to this area. I had never been drawn to other parts of Arasmas, nor had I stepped beyond the water-locked border to explore the three other continents that made up the planet. My understanding of these areas was, therefore, limited to what I had been taught in geography class. However, despite this lack of knowledge, I had the impression that the lifestyle enjoyed by most inhabitants of Arasmas offered just the right ingredients to help keep our curiosity dimmed.

As I sat there sipping my tea, with the theme of exploration on my mind, I started to think about the mysterious, largely unexplored continent called Anavrin. It lay beyond Aidni, on the other side of the globe. It was strange that, even in these modern times, so little was known about this small parcel of land that was protected by impenetrable mountains on one side and rough and stormy waters on the other. Whilst the sea route was considered the easier one, I had been told that, to make it safely to land, any willing traveller would have to journey over more than half the globe from the western shore of Adanac, the fourth and largest continent that lay beyond the ocean to the west of Arasmas.

Seeing these images of exploration reminded me that only one Arasmasian had ever written about his experiences travelling to Anavrin. This man, Don Mackinnon, who, nearly one hundred years ago, had taken the treacherous route across the mountains of Aidni, told a tale of a backward mountainous land that contained a few small tribes. Mackinnon had written at length about their primitive state; they were lacking any basic language, living in mud huts and spending their days hunting for food. Our tutor had taught us that Mackinnon had warned that this race was endangered, tottering on the brink of extinction because of the poor soil conditions that prevailed in this region. Unpredictable weather patterns across the globe in recent times have only added to the gloom with today's experts believing that this place must have suffered more than most with tsunamis and monsoon winters running alongside long, dry summers. I remembered reading recently that a group of scientists had reached a startling conclusion that Anavrin must now be a dead and empty place.

Just the thought of embarking on a mission to Anavrin made me want to return to the comfort of my bed. Still, I could see the clear blue sky through the window; the prospect of fresh air and bright sunshine was appealing and gave me a renewed burst of energy.

After I had showered, I was ready to leave, and I left my key on the unmanned reception desk. Stepping outside the front door today I found that it was noticeably cooler and I was glad that I had packed warm clothes. I went and put the case back into the boot of the car before unzipping and pulling out my winter fleece. Stepping around to the driver's door, I looked up at the surrounding mountain landscape and was again impressed by its raw power.

I drove a short distance to the foot of Lake Newgo: a gorgeous sight lying at the head of a long valley; and drove into a convenient car park already filling up with vehicles. Clearly, there were a number of hikers keen to make the most of such a beautiful day, and who were aware of the long winter to follow.

I set out, ignoring the protests from my weary feet, and walked alongside the main road, which ran along the shoreline, arriving after a mile or so into a small settlement that was barely noticeable on my detailed map. Fortunately, here I discovered a small store where I bought food and drink for the day ahead, before heading towards the imposing peaks that sat behind the settlement. After twenty minutes climbing a steep but well-maintained route, the terrain shifted to a grassy plateau, and I was glad for the chance to catch my breath. I felt a great sense of surprise when I came to a point where the land suddenly fell away and I was presented with the sight of Lake Lawdi, a smaller body of water than the one below, with a diameter of about half a mile. I gasped in amazement for the awe-inspiring view had caught me by surprise. Surrounding the lake, steep cliffs made of large slabs of rock rose up as high as my eye could see. Dumbfounded, I scanned the view with an innocent air of wonder. It appeared at first glance that the only possible entrance and exit point was behind me – these cliffs looked immensely hostile and impassable. However, my map informed me of an exit at the opposite end of the lake which I'd wanted to take. It looked like I had quite a steep climb ahead of me.

However, instead of continuing along the path that circled this small expanse of water, I dropped clumsily over some boulders and down onto the pebbly shoreline. Breathlessly, I rested against a large boulder that looked as if it could give me shelter from the biting wind. My busy and chattering mind, which had been active since breakfast, was silent for the moment. Struck by the view, I watched as the brisk, turbulent wind dragged and swirled the water. Meanwhile, gulls soared overhead, swooping suddenly into the water in search of food. As I sat here, I imagined that on a misty, brooding day this spot would leave me feeling extremely vulnerable and overwhelmed, as, even in the clear sunshine, I felt humbled by the rugged power of the natural world around me.

Eventually, soothed by the stillness, I was able to coax my mind back; I still remembered the perplexed feeling I had had on that strange Wednesday morning. My present circumstances were bountiful and my future prospects were promising, so what could possibly be missing from my life? I felt as though I had come up against something as impenetrable as the cliffs ahead of me. There was this persistent, nagging sense of anxiety, but I could not fathom what was causing it.

Feeling frustrated, I got to my feet and picked up some pebbles from the shore. I stood at the water's edge and tried to let myself bask in the tranquillity, listening to the distant sound of water tumbling down the slabs of rock into the lake below. I began to take my frustration out on the pebbles; bending down low, I started to skim them across the surface. Lost in a trance, I had been completely unaware of a tall, languid figure slowly walking around the lake towards me. It was only at the last moment, as he came within my line of sight, that I noticed his presence. For a moment I felt startled but as my eyes turned towards his, and a broad, welcoming smile spread across his lined face, I felt reassured.

'Good morning, young man,' he said slowly; his soft voice floated across on the breeze. Having got my attention, he continued: 'I can see that your feet are standing right on my favourite spot to savour it too. Let me tell you something. I have been walking along this shoreline nearly every day for the past twenty years, and you know, every day it feels completely different.'

The disturbance had made me feel a little agitated, but I hoped that, if I acknowledged him politely with a smile, he might move on, allowing me to return my gaze back towards the water. However, undeterred by my muted response, the man continued talking, explaining, in a long-winded fashion, why he came here each morning. Suddenly, he stopped mid-sentence and turned his attention towards me; he had a look of intent that he held for a few awkward moments.

'What are you searching for young man?' he asked.

It was not the words but the look in his eyes that cut right through me and left me dumbstruck. At that moment, I felt like a naughty schoolboy who had just been caught out by a teacher who'd a gifted knack for knowing exactly what I was up to no matter how hard I would try and conceal the truth from him.

It was a feeling that jolted me back in time; I remembered how my father used to scrutinise and question me in a similar way. However, I quickly pulled myself together and returned to my habitual mode of defensiveness.

'I am just here to enjoy the fresh mountain air,' I responded, deflecting the question away with an air of aloofness.

Yet the stranger continued to probe me, posing deep and testing questions about who I was, where I had come from and what I was doing here. But I stubbornly refused to engage with him, continuing to bat away his questions until the man fell into a deep silence. He seemed tired of playing games with me and I hoped that, exasperated, he would leave me in peace.

Then, from that place of deep silence, he shot a piercing look at me and he seemed to get a fresh burst of energy to come at me again. I don't know why, but he seemed to get a kick out of pushing my buttons. But when he finally spoke, I was shocked at his angry tone.

'I've met many people on these shores, but you are one of the rare few who are simply too ignorant to be worthy of taking on this life as the precious human being you truly are. I can sense that you are waiting for someone to give you the answers to help unblock whatever it is that your mind cannot figure out or let go of. But, believe me, no-one is going to train you and give you the skills of Satyagraha that you will need to unblock your mind. You have to be willing to sacrifice everything in order to develop them, and, to start with, you have to find out what Satya is before you can truly become a living and practicing Satyagrahi in the world.'

I was taken aback by this outburst, but I felt somehow curious as well.

'So what is this Satya that you tell me I need to find?' I asked in a tone that was laced with sarcasm.

The man gave me another piercing look that seemed to express withering disgust.

'You really want to know what Satya is? Well, get out of your head young man, for trust me when I say that Satya cannot be understood through the reason or logic of your mind; although it can be known by the wisdom of your heart. But to truly know it, you have to develop a deep understanding of why you are a human being and not just another pebble on the shore. Yet, at the moment, all I see before me is someone terrified of the overwhelming meaninglessness of his life; you might as well be just a pebble waiting to break down into dust. Ah, for some the freedom to make what they will of their life gives them tremendous strength, but, for you I see that it scares you; I see your busy little mind working frantically to try to make sense of it all. I can see that you don't want to grasp your life and take responsibility for it and that you don't want to risk taking a leap of faith into the unknown, even though it could make your life more rich and meaningful.'

Animated, the man jabbed his finger provocatively at me as he continued:

'Can you begin to appreciate the fact that there is more to you than the person who mindlessly pushes the trolley around the supermarket? Do you realise that every moment of your life you've been running away from this deeper meaning, running away to the safety you find in your creature comforts. Go on tell me. What is the meaning and purpose of your life?'

He paused momentarily but purposely did not give me enough time to even consider how to answer.

'Let me tell you how I see it. There is not a moment in your life when you have not been marching to a drum played by others. The beat goes something like this: you are born; you go to school like a good boy; you complete your education; you find work and step onto the career ladder; you chase after that perfect job; you get married; you buy a house; you have children; you raise your children to be good little boys and girls; along the way you hope to be dealt a good set of cards, so that you will feel more pleasure than pain; you take holidays in places you photograph but never truly see; you retire; you grow old; you die. Think about it and tell me honestly if it doesn't makes you sick to the core. Does it make you sick enough to discover Satya? Yet I see that you are not even sensitive enough to see the suffering that exists within your life right now, let alone being able to take a deep look and understand it. Oh, I know what will happen when we part. You will convince yourself that you know what the distinction is between a human being and a pebble and you will go back to the comfort of your nest; deluding yourself that you are living a meaningful life, even though you've never used your wings to fly. It is only when you go into the silence beyond your mind that you will begin to grasp this, and only then will you finally be pointed towards Satya.'

This strange man did not even let me respond to these cutting remarks; he tossed a pebble into the water and walked off. He left me completely dazed and in a state of stunned bewilderment.

The man obviously knew how to push my buttons; as I started walking again, I could not stop thinking about his words – it was as though they had touched a raw nerve. My immediate reaction was one of indignation: how dare this arrogant stranger speak to me in this way? He knew absolutely nothing of my life, so how could he judge me?

I walked on and, suddenly, the route I had to take was revealed to me: I saw a path that climbed steeply before disappearing through a narrow crack in the rock face. I began to stride up steps which had been deliberately cut into the rock and I was soon puffing breathlessly from my exertions. Absorbed by my feelings of indignation, I entirely forgot that I only had to turn around to enjoy a stupendous view of the two lakes below. The old man's comment that I was not worthy to know anything rankled; I was a success. I had passed all my exams and had gone on to forge a successful career. How dare he offer this stupid opinion? Yes, of course there were others who were brighter than me, but I had proved that I wasn't stupid. Even more galling was the man's withering assessment that I was wasting my life meekly marching to the beat of another's drum. This insult made me really angry; it was an unnecessary swipe and was completely unfounded. I knew that, since I had reached adulthood, I had taken lots of decisions to make something more of my life. Of course I knew that I was more than just a pebble on the shoreline. I scowled and shook my head as I thought about this foolish comment.

When I came to the top of the path I was surprised to find another grassy plateau that gave me a chance to catch my breath before I recommenced my ascent to the summit. In fact it was a long ridge with two distinct peaks. These had been hidden from view from the lake below and so I felt disappointed when I saw the lengthy climb that was still ahead of me. I began scrambling up a less defined path that weaved its way up a steep slope. It was strewn with loose rocks, making it hard to get a firm footing.

As I climbed, I started to think of the things I would say to the man if I saw him when I came down again. I started to think that, even if I didn't see him, I would go back to the lake the following day to challenge him as I remembered him saying that he went there every morning. As I walked, I started to draw up a list of ways to prove him wrong and get him to apologise for his rudeness. All the while, my pride was returning and I felt ever more foolish for having put myself through this period of self-absorbed reflection. There was clearly nothing major to be concerned about and I thought that, since I had a busy few months ahead of me, I would soon begin to forget these few days and these feelings of anxiety.

The future was now on my mind, and I started to think about my application for promotion; this was looming on the horizon and seemed likely to succeed. I also thought about making plans to move in with Jen, as we'd recently discussed, and asking for her hand in marriage. But along with these thoughts, pangs of guilt tormented me as I remembered my conversation with Jen the other day; I thought about calling her that evening to apologise before travelling home. What on earth had come over me that crazy Wednesday morning? As I pondered this question, I began to look at my weird behaviour from a position of greater detachment.

However, absorbed in my thoughts, I was unaware of what was happening around me and I had failed to notice that low cloud was swirling in fast. Approaching the summit, I found myself completely enveloped in mist. I could tell from my map that the flat and featureless rocky ridge was more than a mile in length, but, once I got there, I could barely see more than a few metres ahead of me and the clouds were getting denser by the minute. As soon as I stepped onto the ridge, the path seemed to disintegrate and I quickly became confused about the direction in which I needed to walk. I felt a wave of panic sweep over me. The pride and sense of clarity I had rediscovered on my ascent was vaporising, and I started to feel incredibly vulnerable and exposed.

But then, as quickly as they had descended, the clouds started to clear from around me. I was left with a feeling of exaltation, for they had not evaporated but had merely dropped down into the valley below, leaving me standing above them and surrounded only by clear blue sky. Standing there, seeing puffy white clouds spread out below me for miles around, I felt a sense of wonder and bliss. Only a couple of other isolated peaks also reached through the cloud layer to the sky above and I stared in amazement at the view, feeling as if I had entered into the blessed land of the gods. I moved swiftly to a sheltered spot where I could sit and enjoy this unique experience.

I remained there in silence for an hour or more; the clouds continued to swirl below, giving the odd glimpse of the valley beneath, but they did not clear. I had stopped conducting imaginary conversations with the strange man, although I could still feel traces in my mind of the anger and turmoil that had consumed me earlier in the day. But these pulsing emotions were now channelled somewhere deeper and a sense of peace began to radiate through my whole body, leaving me with a tingling sensation running through my arms and fingers. All the mental chatter that had been absorbing my attention faded out, and, in the quietness that followed, I discovered a tremendous clarity of vision. The answer came to me from the back recesses of my mind, as though it had swooped down from who knows where. As the answer moved towards the front of my mind an image became attached to give the insight some form and content.

The image was of an event that had happened six months previously when I had been asked by Jen to join her at a cocktail party with her colleagues from work. I had been reluctant to join her as I didn't enjoy these formal occasions, but she had pleaded with me to attend. Once there, though, I felt strongly that I didn't belong and was reluctant to engage in conversation. Despite the fact that Jen had wanted me to be there to support her, she had seemed too absorbed with making an impression to even notice my presence, and so I sat sulking in the corner of the room instead. To pass the time, I observed how these strong personalities interacted and mixed with one another. I focused most of my attention on a man in his early fifties who I knew was the top boss of Jen's law firm. I watched him in fascination, struck by the thought that this man looked, to all intents and purposes, dead. His face had a ghostly pallor and was covered in worry lines; he looked haggard and old. Although his hair was black in colour, it was obvious that it had been dyed and that its true colour was either grey or white. His eyes were dull and black around the rims from tiredness. Looking at him holding a drink in his hand and trying to hold a conversation, I was struck by an overwhelming feeling of sadness.

At the same time I was struck by a discomforting thought. This was a man who was, on the surface, a success. I knew from what Jen had told me that he lived on a massive country estate outside the city with his wife, as well as privately-educated children who were now embarking on their own successful careers. Having reached the top of his business, he could easily afford to retire – unlike many people of his age – although Jen had said he stayed in the job because of his strong, even obsessive, work ethic and dour determination. Yet, despite all of this outward success, this man was suffering no less than someone living with a terminal illness. The sight troubled me deeply; my mind could not make sense of what I was observing.

I watched with some discomfort the way in which his colleagues treated him with contempt, offering no respect or genuine warmth. Secret, and sometimes non-so-secret, bullying of this elder statesman seemed to be taking place, as colleagues jostled subversively for the top position. It seemed as if everyone there was crying out for him to fail. As I watched, I saw his colleagues, looking stiff and tense as boards, trying to find the right moment to gather around this poor old man to try to get his attention. It was embarrassing to watch, and it was unpleasant to see that Jen had also been affected by the poisonous atmosphere and dark politics. Her face changed shape and colour right before me, her soft eyes took on a cold and steely glaze, her skin tightened and her shoulders became rigid and hunched. Her antennae seemed to be on a high state of alert as though she was trying to ensure that she stayed in complete control of her environment. The longer I sat there, the more convinced I was that not only did I not belong here with this group of people but that I was strangely glad that I didn't. Watching from the edge of the room, I felt as though I had stumbled upon a scene of utter madness.

After we had left at the end of the evening I said nothing about what I had observed. Yet as I drove us home, a question was troubling me: how could someone have had so much success and yet be suffering so much? This question had disturbed me so much that I had pushed the matter out of my mind for the past six months. For what was most discomforting was not the fact that this man was dying, but that I could see in him a reflection of myself. I saw that this was what I would become in twenty years' time if I continued on the path I was currently taking. The events that evening had shown to me that no matter how much outer success I gained, it would not guarantee the most important thing in life: my happiness.

Returning now to full consciousness, I was able to understand why I had blocked out this insight. But I had not been able to block it out completely, however, and I was now certain that it was this experience that had been niggling away deep inside of me. I suddenly remembered the haunting words the strange man had spoken to me on the shore of Lake Lawdi when he had said about the meaningless path that I had been taught to follow and how it could only end in death. With this, I suddenly felt an overwhelming wave of gratitude for this old man and the way he had helped bring this back to the surface again.

Chapter Four

The inspiration did not end there as, resting my eyes for a moment, I began to slip away into a vivid daydream. The dream began with me walking through a thick forest, enjoying the fresh air and the cool breeze that moved the branches above. After a while I stumbled across a path that took me through a clearing and down to a magnificent waterfall that cascaded down into a rocky pool. I walked over to the waterfall, put my hands into it, and started washing my face. As I washed, I noticed something slip off my face and drop down into the pool. Looking down, I saw, in the water, a veil that was shaped to fit my face. Once it had gone floating downstream, my true reflection was revealed to me in the water.

Then I saw my father standing on the far side of the pool watching me and his presence brought up fresh memories for me. He had been a journalist by profession and had brought his skills of questioning and interrogating into our home. Even today, he still tries to control how I live my life. His presence brought up one memory in particular: the long and difficult transitional year as I finished junior school. I was suddenly right back there, reliving the events of this traumatic year.

Wednesday, 16 April 2003

In the September of 2002 I had moved into my final year at Alnwick Junior School and knowing I was now one of the senior boys gave me a feeling of confidence. The days swiftly passed and soon we were beyond the cold and snow-bound winter months and into the new life of spring. Yet on this spring day, something happened that shattered my confidence.

It was a damp morning and I arrived at school with no knowledge of what lay ahead of me. The trouble began when our teacher said that the time had come for us to decide which school we wanted to move to in the autumn. Monkscaph only had the resources to support one senior school, Allerton High School, and I felt anxious about whether, in the new school, I would be placed in the same class as my friends or whether I would be mixed with children from the other junior schools in the area. I am sure that all of us were concerned about this.

I arrived home that evening with a slip of paper held firmly in my hands and with mixed feelings. The child in me was nervous about the changes that lay ahead and felt a desire to stick with what was familiar. But the emerging adult in me was excited about growing up and stepping into senior school. After placing the form on the kitchen table, I turned and spoke to my mother who had just joined me.

'Mum, I got this form here that I need you and Dad to sign.'

'What's it for?' she asked absent-mindedly, as she continued to roll out pastry on the kitchen worktop.

'It's for you to confirm my application for Allerton next year,' I replied.

'Well leave it there and I will talk to your father about it later,' she answered before asking me to set the table for tea.

After tea, I was sent upstairs to complete my home exercises; this evening I had a short history assignment to finish for the following morning. It was an assignment that I had put off for as long as possible because history was one of my most trying subjects: I had difficulty remembering dates, and our teacher never seemed to teach us anything interesting. Having completed it, I returned downstairs with a warm satisfying glow of achievement. However, seeing my parents in discussion in the lounge, I felt an immediate and distinct drop in the level of my buoyancy. An uncomfortable feeling of anxiety welled up inside of me but I did not know why for it was certain that I would be sent to the school in Allerton. But could I be completely certain? The look they had given me when I burst in could perhaps have caused my anxiety.

'Now that didn't take you long, son, did it?' my father stated, rather abruptly.

This question appeared to me to carry the implication that I must have rushed through my assignment. A part of me always recoiled with wariness whenever my father directed these questions towards me. I was slowly learning how to respond to him, though, and had discovered that I could either answer defensively and hold things back or play the innocent victim and try to make my father feel guilty about his harshness. This time I chose the latter option, protesting with a cry that I'd done the best I could.

'Do you want me to have a look through it for you, though?' he continued.

I gave a weary sigh: my dad never seemed able to trust me. It was almost as though he would rather believe that I'd spent the previous hour absorbed in one of my comic books. But I was wary enough of my father's temper to say nothing, only nodding my head to show my meek agreement.

Before leaving to collect the assignment I pointed at the paper on the table before them, and asked whether they'd signed the form yet. My father was silent for a moment, looking as though he had lost his train of thought; my mother just looked at my father, showing that she deferred to him on this matter.

'Ah yes, the form. We were just waiting to talk to you about that,' he finally answered.

I frowned, feeling increasingly worried. What on earth was there to talk about? Unless...

'You see, your mother and I both feel that it would be in your best interests to enrol you at High Cross Boys School in Studley.'

These words from my father hit me like an unexpected blow.

'What?' I answered back.

My mother turned towards me and spoke next.

'We know that you wanted to be with your friends here in Monkscaph, but, Myrkais, you're now at an age where you need to understand that school is for learning and not just about playing with your friends. We both feel that you will grow much better at High Cross.'

'But why?'

'High Cross is a far superior place for you to study, and, as it is right opposite your father's work, we will be able to get you safely to school much more easily,' she explained.

It sounded like an excuse: I was old enough to make my own way to school now and surely whether I succeeded at school was down to how much effort I put in. I simply couldn't see how it made any difference to them what school I went to.

'Don't I get a say in all of this?' I finally answered, my stern little voice rising with anger.

I saw my mother look down as if she was resigned to my negative reaction, for I was an only child used to having things my own way. I saw her turn and glance anxiously across to my father.

'Don't you dare speak to your mother like that,' he snorted back at me.

I just glared back at them both, defiantly standing my ground in the doorway.

'Go to your room before you feel the back of my hand,' my father shouted, as he began to lift his overweight frame upwards.

'I'll do whatever the hell I please,' I shouted back at him, before storming from the room and out of the front door into the damp and dusky evening air.

Slamming the door behind me, I broke into a slow jog in case my father decided to chase after me. But the street was filled with nothing but silence. I slowed back to walking pace, eventually coming to a halt and sitting down on the kerb of one of the cobbled side streets that ran up the hill. I felt consumed by anger and I threw some loose stones across to the other side of the street. I stayed sitting there for a long time that evening; I was not fearful of returning to face my father's rage but I was fearful of what the future might bring. I felt as if I'd already been punished enough for my behaviour this evening.

Eventually I returned home and skulked silently upstairs to my room. Before going to sleep I sat on my bed stewing for a while, feeling sorry for myself and angry at my parents for their lack of care. What could I do to make them listen to me? It was a question that I would never be able to answer. The next morning it was as if last night had not happened; the whole matter was swept under the carpet. Whilst I felt relieved that my father's anger had subsided, I also felt frustrated that I couldn't discuss the subject of my education with him. I felt totally disempowered and helpless and went to school with the piece of paper in my hand in a gloomy, resigned mood.

The dark cloud remained hanging over me for the rest of that term. I had broken the news to Joe, my best friend, as we walked to school that morning, and, although he showed a lot of sympathy, he could not fully empathise with my situation. It was not long before he and my other friends began talking in excited tones about moving on to the big school together – insensitive behaviour that only left me feeling more isolated and alone.

I remember one evening in particular from this difficult time. My parents had dragged me along to High Cross to give me the chance to orientate myself and to meet some of the staff. I spent most of the evening hiding sullenly behind my father, who I knew was trying hard to keep his annoyance in check. I felt totally overwhelmed and disorientated by the tall, high ceilings and the maze of corridors. It felt a hugely unwelcoming and alien place compared to the small, cosy junior school that I knew so well.

So it was that, with the final day of junior school behind me, I left the school gates one final time with leaden feet and a heavy heart. It was a sharp contrast to the exuberance I'd felt only a year *previously. For the following two months, I felt extremely bored and each day dragged. Yet, ironically, the summer did not last as long as I would have wished. Boredom was the only choice as I sulked my way through each day, spending most of my time numbing myself with computer games. Joe and my other friends would call to ask me out to play, but even they eventually became fed up with my consistent refusals and lame excuses. I was sure my gloom was testing my mother; she seemed too helpless to know what to do about my restlessness and my tearful refusals to leave the house. In the evenings, I would do what I could to avoid contact with either of my parents, knowing that, if I was not careful, my father would soon feel the urge to raise his hand against me.*

Finally my day of judgment came: a day for which I'd been winding myself up like a coiled spring. Looking smart and prim in my new uniform and cap, I stepped outside the house and reluctantly joined my father in the passenger seat of the car. During the journey, barely a word passed between us; I kept my head tilted against the window and scanned the pastoral landscape. Studley was a much bigger and less isolated place than Monkscaph as it had been able to develop more due to good road connections to the south. We crawled slowly through the congested streets and eventually arrived in front of a set of imposing wrought-iron gates.

Opening the car door, I stepped tentatively outside and stood there alone for a few moments. My father drove away grumbling to himself about being late for work. Suddenly I felt very vulnerable. Taking small steps, I began to walk slowly down the long and straight driveway that led to a grand and ancient building. Manicured lawns, already coated with autumn leaves, spread out on either side of me. I kept my gaze fixed firmly downwards as my feet crunched their way through the gravel. Nervously, I climbed a steep set of steps to an entrance, joining a number of other children who were going inside. I immediately walked up to the reception and timidly addressed the haughty receptionist sitting behind her desk. She coldly thrust forward a map and, after checking my name off against a long list, told me my classroom number. She then

promptly sent me on my way, without any sign of compassion, for
there was a queue of boys waiting impatiently for me to move on.

As a vulnerable and confused young child, I inevitably lost
myself within the fast-flowing river of bodies. Roughly pushed to
one side by bigger and stronger boys, I realised, with a shock, that I
was now the baby of the school. Everyone seemed to be in a rush,
and the pace of movement quickened to a crescendo as the school
bell rang noisily. The corridors emptied and welcome silence
descended, giving me a chance to breathe. I looked again at my
map and realised that I was on the wrong side of the school.
Knowing I was late and panicking slightly, I eventually got my
bearings and moved towards my classroom. The door was firmly
closed when I got there, and so, with a gentle knock, I entered into a
classroom full of bodies, all of whom turned and looked at me, their
eyes wide. But my own eyes were focused on an elderly man, sitting
behind a desk at the front of the room. With his receding grey hair
and with thick-lensed spectacles sitting on the end of his nose, he
looked an imposing and stern figure of authority. I took an instant
dislike to him as the prospect of spending seven years within this
classroom dawned on me. He turned his head towards me but re-
mained silent, as if daring me to speak first. There was an awkward
and nervous silence as I turned to close the door behind me.
Disliking being the centre of attention, my face had turned a deep
shade of crimson, but, eventually, I found the courage to speak:

'Apologies for my tardiness, sir.'

'And your name, boy?' he asked in a manner befitting his cold
and stern appearance.

'Demeritus, sir. Myrkais Demeritus,' I replied quietly.

'Well take a seat, Myrkais.' He gestured to the one remaining
seat, in the far corner of the room, next to a window with a view of a
small courtyard.

Having endured and survived these initial moments, I was
beginning to feel a little more hopeful that the situation would
improve and that I might be able to settle here. However, that

optimism quickly drained away from me: the following months were trying and difficult. The class I had joined was made up of a feisty and close-knit group of exuberant young boys who had been together all through their lives at school. I was the only outsider, meaning that the onus was on me to try and integrate: no one else needed to take the time or effort to engage with me, or even to acknowledge my presence in the class.

Confidence evaporated for it was not a challenge that I was willing to face at the moment, and, instead, I found myself becoming more and more introverted, as I retreated into my shell. As my solitary behaviour became habitual, it became harder for me to integrate. Lunchtimes were the most trying period. I was developing a deep fear of standing or sitting in any one place for too long: I worried that doing so would draw attention to the fact that I was isolated and alone. Instead, I tried to keep on the move. Sometimes I would wander up and down the corridors like a centurion guarding his territory. At other times, when I was tired of walking, I would hide myself away in the old library, scanning through books in which I had no interest.

As the days passed, I became more and more paranoid, seeking to dwell more and more in a dream world so I could escape from reality. I just didn't seem to fit in to this place. It was strange. In Arasmas, worship and religious faith had been abandoned long ago, and yet, at the end of most days, I would sit up in bed and pray to be helped through the next. I didn't know to whom I was praying, but I found that when I did the following day would at least go a little more smoothly. Maybe it was only that I would pray when I felt so low that the following day could never match my negative imaginings, however bad it was. I felt cut adrift from my parents: they seemed more and more oblivious to my teenage angst, obviously thinking it was just a passing phase that I was blowing out of all proportion. My pessimistic, 'can't do' attitude was beginning to affect my studies and I was struggling to keep on top of things. It seemed that there were a lot of things which I had never been taught that our teacher would assume we knew, and so he would often move on to the next topic before I had understood properly. But I was becoming too shy to speak up and so would try to quietly muddle through – often without success.

The first term was long, and the winter holidays offered only a brief respite. After our three-week break, temperatures plummeted and the local area was gripped by a lengthy period of cold weather. The grey and leaden January skies above kept me stuck in my depressed state. Even at such a tender age, I knew that life consisted primarily of routine. Some people get drawn into a positive and happy state, others do not. This routine moulds an individual's char-acter or personality and is then worn around as a badge. The more time that passes, the tighter the threads attaching the badge become, until it is stuck as an indelible mark. I had been sucked into this negative routine barely a few months ago, but had already lost the confidence I would need to believe that my new badge could be ripped off.

Then, on a miserable wet morning at the beginning of March, something happened that left me feeling that things were getting not better but worse.

It was my tutor who brought my morale down to its lowest ebb, when, after taking the school register, he read out a short notice. 'One final announcement,' he said. 'The administration department is busy organising a class trip for just before the spring break. It will be a week-long trip to an activity centre two hours drive north from here. On this break, you will develop your orienteering and team-work skills and you will also be able to gather material for your geography assignment in the summer term. The trip is not compul-sory, but the school will provide subsidies to keep the cost at a mini-mum and to ensure that most students will be able to attend.' He put the piece of paper down on his desk and started handing out material relating to the trip: 'This will give you and your parents the information they need. There is a slip of paper inside that needs to be returned by the beginning of next week at the latest,' he added.

I'd stopped listening by this point. As I nervously flicked through the material, a word repeated over and over again in my head; teamwork. My tender little hands were already shaking nervously at the prospect. It was difficult enough for me to cope with each school day let alone being in the company of my classmates for a more sustained period. It didn't even bear thinking about. As the class settled down to algebraic sums and logarithms, my mind was elsewhere. There was the possibility of concealing it from my parents, but I knew how fruitless a prospect that was, especially as a parents' evening was coming up next week. Even at such a young age, I knew that deceit would always catch up with me, and so, by the time the school bell rang, I was resigned to going. Wanting to get it over with, I passed the literature to my father before he had even started the car. One glance at the positive look in my father's eyes confirmed all my fears and I gloomily dropped my head in silence as my father lectured me about what a good opportunity this was for me.

Apart from one difficult evening at home with my parents, who had showed some concern after visiting the school, the next three weeks passed by without any significant drama. Soon the day came, and I boarded one of the two coaches that would take us, and another two classes, northwards. In accordance with my lowly status, I took a seat at the very front, leaving the rear seats free for those boys who held the greatest social rank in the group. Looking to the back of the coach, I realised that it was this short distance between the front and back of the coach that I was so desperate to bridge. We drove north-east, and soon I caught the first glimpse of the spectacular mountains towards which we were travelling. I kept my eyes firmly fixed on the changing landscape outside the window; ignoring the teacher sitting next to me.

The first three days continued the depressing theme of loneliness. I also felt a pang of homesickness: this was the first time I'd been away from home by myself. The daytime was comparatively bearable, as we were kept busy and engrossed exploring the surrounding area. As in the school corridors, I never felt lonely when my body was in motion. I could happily walk all day as long as I was hidden from view at the back of the group. But the evenings proved

*more of a challenge. We were given free time after dinner and I
would always scurry across to a quiet corner where I could stick my
nose behind a book that I'd wisely decided to bring. I had quickly
learnt the art of invisibility and made all my actions unnoticeable.*

    *The moment of transformation came on the third evening, and
the slow process of regaining my confidence and self-esteem began.
It had been nearly twelve months ago since I had let this cloud fall
over me; I was tired of regurgitating the same old sad stories about
all of the injustices that I had suffered. I was also tired of stubbornly
carrying this feeling of anger towards my father for having taken
me away from an environment where I felt comfortable and content. Instead, for the first time in a long while, I was aware of the
freedom I would feel if I could only lay the past to rest and overcome my fears. Something deep inside was telling me that I did
have that option, and suddenly a feeling of empowerment welled up
inside. Despite my youth, I knew that while my father could control
many things in my life, he could not possibly snatch the inner
strength and power of my beating heart away from me – unless I let
him. But how could I use these feelings of empowerment?*

    *My answer came after the evening meal, when the others in
our class left the dining room and separated into their little cliques.
I was one of the last to leave and decided to silently drift up the
stairs and into the empty dormitory that I shared with five others.
There was a mirror on the far left hand wall; I strode purposefully
towards it. Standing in front of it and looking downwards, I noticed
how rigid and tense my body had become. Staring intently into the
glass without flinching, my eyes scanned the reflection before me.
Why had I become so joyless and serious, I wondered. I took two
deep breaths, and then another. Staring at my frowning face, I
allowed a gentle smile to appear. Instantly, I felt more relaxed and
my expression began to mellow and soften. The feeling slowly
spread all through my stiffened joints. Taking a few more deep
breaths, I drew my attention down to my belly in order to create
some inner stability and grounding, and searched here for the courage that could keep me in this relaxed state. Out of my mouth came*

the words, 'I am bigger and better than this fearful child before me.' I repeated this to myself over and over.

I closed my eyes and saw myself stepping confidently out of the shadows, slowly but surely finding open space and basking in the sunlight's warm glow. Taking another deep breath, I held that image and opened my eyes. I looked into the mirror one last time and, slowly and purposefully walked over to my bag, collected a pack of cards that I kept in one of the side pockets, and returned downstairs in a resolute and focused state. My eyes scanned the room like a lion searching out its prey. They soon rested upon three boys sitting together on the opposite side of the room: this was a group I had cast my eyes over a few times before because I felt that perhaps, as they were a middle-ranked clique, they would be more amenable to me than those holding a more secure position in the class. Did I feel ready to befriend them? I felt a sudden wave of insecurity but took another deep breath and strode on regardless. I was aware that I was out of their line of vision, and so was able to take a seat on the couch next to them in a subtle and inconspicuous manner.

I was breathing heavily and averting my gaze from theirs, but I was conscious from their silence that they were aware of my presence. But they soon started chattering again, ignoring me completely. Undeterred, I allowed my back to slide further down the couch and let my posture loosen as I pulled the cards out of the case and began to shuffle them effortlessly. All the while I was trying to hold that newly-discovered smile and soft expression. As I let the cards pass through my fingers, my ears were also half-cocked, straining to hear what they were saying as I waited patiently for an opportune moment to speak up. Suddenly they fell silent. My pounding heart beat faster and my whole body filled with nervous energy; I knew this was my moment. One final deep breath passed through my lungs as I hesitated, before turning to speak to the boy closest to me;

'Excuse me John,' I said quietly. But John and his two friends did not hear my timid voice: they had restarted their conversation that very moment. My split-second of hesitation had cost me. Nonetheless, I boldly interrupted them and repeated my words in a much louder tone. John, aware once more that I was sat next to him, turned around.

'What?' he replied, in a somewhat curt and abrupt fashion.

'I was wondering if any of you know how to play poker,' I asked, showing them the pack of cards in my hands.

'Poker? No, I've never heard of that before,' was his response.

His tone was sarcastic, and I knew he intended to toy with me. Hearing the others giggling at John's sarcasm made me blush nervously and I almost shrank back into silence. But, boldly, I held to my position and pressed onwards.

'It's only a simple card game. Do you want me to show you?'

'Oh, would you,' he replied in as patronising a tone as he could muster. At that moment, I realised that John behaved in this way because of some hidden compulsion that required him to prey on lesser mortals in order to advance his rank among his peers. I do not know where the inner wisdom came from but I knew I could not allow myself to take his words personally and be drawn into this competitive game. Instead I found the strength to believe that I could get past this and move on to a place of friendship. I simply knew that I had to take a risk to make it happen.

So, over the course of the poker game that I had instigated, and followed through on, I began to discover how to behave in their company so that their competitiveness was not fuelled. True, I felt very rusty and clumsy in my social interactions and was uncertain of how to act around the three of them; I was certainly not yet being accepted as an equal. However, there was a hint, a slight glimmer, which suggested that it might be possible for me to regain the sense of belonging and confidence that I had lost. I had reached the turning point.

Chapter Five

Stirring myself from this daydream, I saw that it carried a very clear message for me. I thought I had forgiven my father for having caused this difficult transitional period – after all, his actions had definitely improved my prospects. I believed that he had helped me to grow up and knew that I probably would not have gone on to university and a successful career in Sarum without his influence. But now things were changing, and I saw that it was while I was at this school that my true face had become masked with a veil. My father had held a fixed idea in his mind of what my future should be, and, with my mother's agreement, he had actively imposed these expectations on me. I could not deny that the veil I wore was an attractive one, helping me carry gravitas in society. Of course it was because of this that I had so easily been persuaded to accept it.

So my parents had believed that this veil would give me the chance to lead a happy and fulfilled life, and by implication, if I refused to wear it I would surely be doomed to a life of misery and unhappiness. But this was not my belief: the sad sight of the broken man at the cocktail party, who wore exactly the same veil as me, had made me realise this. The unspoken contract with which my parents had bound me too was now broken. The daydream showed that it was time for me to shake off this false veil and discover who I truly was. It was time for me to make my own way in the world and to walk my own path.

But could the removal of my veil really bring a deeper meaning to my life? Whilst sitting here basking in the warm sunshine and surrounded by beauty, removing it felt like an easy task. The lingering question was how I could sustain this blissful nakedness once I stepped off this mountain peak and went back down to the murky clouds of day-to-day life. The mere thought of it made me cling to the feelings of lightness and joy that I was enjoying; I felt a great reluctance to leave this pure land.

Having eaten my lunch, I finally got to my feet and slowly made my way along the rest of the ridge. I then began my descent. As I did this, the clouds dissolved almost as quickly as they had formed, leaving me unsure whether the experience had really happened – it certainly was surprising that I hadn't seen another soul since leaving the old man on the shoreline. The quietness and peace stayed with me for most of the long walk back to the car. It was getting quite late by the time I reached the road again and it was at this point that I started to think about what my next steps would be. How could I possibly manage to stay in this naked and innocent state and to start living my life afresh? I knew that I would have to explore this question tomorrow before my long drive south to Sarum ahead of my return on Monday morning.

Returning to my car, I took a short drive to a remote and isolated hostel located at the foot of the largest mountain in the Blue Mountains. From the moment I'd been called to these mountains, climbing Mount Nodwons had been top of my list of things to do. I was staying in a large dormitory; it was empty on my arrival, but the receptionist told me that it would be full by the end of the evening. I took a welcome hot shower. Fortunately, this hostel served food and I gladly took a seat, giving my weary legs a rest.

When I had eaten, a couple of large groups of walkers came into the reception, shattering the peace and quiet that I had been enjoying. I quickly retired to the small reading room at the back of the hostel and began to scan through the bookcase, looking for something to read. As I flicked through the row of books on the middle shelf, one book in particular caught my attention, and I went to pull it out. But it was wedged in tightly, and I noticed that, behind it, there was a little black notebook which had been pushed right to the back of the bookcase and hidden from view. Full of curiosity, I put back the book that had popped out at me, grabbing hold of this notebook instead. It looked expensive - the cover was made of leather and a strip of gold ran along the spine. As I looked inside, I saw to my surprise that the pages were completely blank. The paper was cream and lovely to touch. It looked as though it was the most expensive writing paper that you could possibly buy. Bizarrely, hooked onto the back of the notebook was a beautiful fountain pen which was still full of ink.

As I lingered, I found that the sense of inspiration that had taken me over earlier in the day was still alive in me. It told me that this notebook and pen were mine and that I needed to sit down and write. What happened next was hard for me to comprehend: I suddenly found that I was able to describe the feelings I had felt today in poetry. I do not know where these words came from; I did not feel fully in control of the pen as it moved across the page. The poem ended at the bottom of the page, but, before I had a chance to halt, a second poem started on the next. Although separate in form, it was clearly connected to the first in meaning. This flow continued for five pages and it was only when I came to the very end of the fifth page, which was covered in writing to the point that I could not fit another word on it, that the writing came to a natural halt and the fire of creative inspiration went out. I was astonished to find a stream of poetic but coherent words lying before me.

Chapter Six

I had gone to bed early, but, as I was in a busy dormitory, I did not sleep well. There was one man in particular who had come in after I'd gone to bed and filled the silence with a mixture of coughing and snoring. Naturally a heavy sleeper, even I could not help but be disturbed by the noise. As my aching body had not got the rest it needed, I woke up feeling tired and deflated. The bliss of the previous evening seemed to have been dulled overnight and my mood was not lifted when, looking out of the window, I was greeted by dark clouds that shrouded the surrounding mountains with mist and moisture. As I chewed solemnly on my cooked breakfast, I looked out at the deteriorating weather conditions. I was reluctant to leave the warmth of the hostel, but I finally persuaded myself to put on my waterproofs before taking my belongings outside to the boot of my car. I felt tempted to get behind the wheel and leave that very second; the rain was falling more heavily and was running down the nape of my neck. But, at the same time, I did not wish to leave before finding a resolution. So, with a show of defiance, I slammed the boot shut and strode out onto the wide gravel track that snaked ahead of me out into the mist.

Although it was a well-worn path, the route soon became quite treacherous in parts. I took a brief respite from the elements in a sheltered hollow, but the path deteriorated even further as I gained altitude. I had become quite sodden and my waterproof clothing clung to my cold flesh. But it was the strength of the wind that troubled me the most and which ruined all my attempts to find some clarity of thought. Beginning to traverse up a steep slope of loose shale, I was all too aware that one unexpected gust could easily knock me off balance and send me crashing downwards onto the lower rocky ground. I nervously took to my knees to help lower my centre of gravity and literally crawled my way up towards the summit. All the while the mist was thickening and my vision became more and more restricted. I was fortunate that the path was clear, otherwise it would have been easy for me to become disorientated and lost.

The path finally levelled and began to wind around towards the peak. The drizzly rain became heavier and started to freeze into pellets of ice that stung my face. I tried to pull the hood of my waterproof jacket around my face as much as I could, but my nose and mouth were still left exposed. Never before had I been out in such ferocious weather conditions. Yet, at the same time, and in spite of the cold and the stinging pain, experiencing nature at its wildest was exhilarating and I was bursting with adrenaline. There was a cairn at the summit and I clambered up this exposed pile of rocks to stand at the top. Bravely - or perhaps foolishly - I leant forwards into the wind, which was strong enough to hold me up, and emitted a loud yawp. But even I could not hear it: the howling wind had made it inaudible.

After leaving the summit behind and beginning my ascent, my body was shuddering from this mad adventure; my legs had also gone numb and were drained of energy. The wet clothes clung heavily to my skin, making it hard to walk. But at least the path only descended gradually down to the distant settlement of Berris. Ten minutes after leaving the cairn, I was clear of the worst of the weather and the hail was once more replaced by light rain. Away from the exposed ridge I was now sheltered from the wind and could begin to hear my own thoughts again. After another five minutes of walking, I stopped and turned around to have a long look at the summit I had left behind: all I could see was an ugly black mass of cloud that clung to the rocks above me. It looked so menacing that had I been walking towards it now I probably would have decided not to continue. I certainly didn't feel surprised that I had not seen a soul while walking; I wondered whether I'd lost my sanity. But that was behind me now, and ahead the way was clear and the skies were grey. It was only at this point that I could return to contemplation.

The one thing that was immediately clear to me, and which I had not wanted to admit yesterday, was that I could not now go back to the way things were. This was a brave thing for me to think, but I knew that there was no way that I could slip my veil back on and pretend that this had never happened. Yet, at the same time, the prospect of a major upheaval in my life was unsettling, especially when I still didn't know what the alternative would be like. The first thing I had to ask myself was whether I could stick to my daily routine if I was not wearing my veil. Could I go back to the daily grind of the office, with all these ghostly figures flittering here and there, and overcome the temptation to slip back into the old robotic way? I knew instinctively that I couldn't. My immediate reaction was to breathe a sigh of relief; it felt as if I had unloaded a burden from my shoulders.

But this left me with a question: what type of environment would help me in my desire to live in a state of innocence? Looking back through my past, I could find nothing that could serve as a starting point. I then began to think back to my experience the previous day and wondered whether it would not be possible to sustain my discovery by dwelling in the midst of this remote and hostile place. For I knew that silence had been a gift to me over these past few days and that readjusting to the hustle and bustle of life in the city would be difficult. But then there were practical concerns: how would I make money and a living for myself if I hid out in the mountains? I had little in the way of savings and had not paid off enough of my mortgage yet to get any capital returns on my investment. A move to one of the villages in the foothills would also not be ideal as a compromise: for even here the tentacles of busyness had swept in to swamp the area.

As my eyes finally caught sight of Berris in the distance, I felt that a new door was beginning to open. I understood that during childhood there had been two clear options available to me. One

57

path was the one that my parents had helped me along by giving me the opportunity to attend a better school and to have a university education. The other path was the one I would have taken if I had continued my schooling in Monkscaph. I was beginning to see what life would have been like for me if I had taken this route: I realised that my desire for worldly possessions would have been less and that maybe I would be living in a more open and honest way. For, surely, having little or nothing of your own meant having little or nothing to lose. Was this not freedom? Also, those who followed this route were not gripped with the tension affecting those concerned with maintaining and advancing their status. I felt drawn to the wild romantic notion that despite the poverty suffered by those who had fallen off society's treadmill, they had something that mattered more: happiness. It suddenly became clear to me that I needed to stay in Sarum, for here there were still small areas of the city that had stubbornly refused to change. These were little communities that the authorities had given up trying to fix.

As I continued my descent, I suddenly felt foolish for considering this preposterous idea. It felt almost laughable that I would give up my well-paid job and my comfortable, cosy life and join society's underclass. Something from my cultural upbringing was totally repelled by the idea and felt stirred to react against it. Yet, precisely because of this knee-jerk reaction, I believed that the idea must have some merit. I remembered that I had learnt yesterday that I had to get out of my head and allow my behaviour to be guided by a deeper knowledge. There was no way that my logical mind would have come to such a conclusion, so where else could the idea have come from?

But then my thoughts turned to the things that I would have to leave behind. Leaving material possessions and my respectable position in society would perhaps be bearable, although I knew that breaking the news to my parents would be hard. But it was when my mind turned to Jen, the one love of my life and my rock of security, that I suddenly became afraid. I suspected that her love for me was not strong enough to enable her to accept my decision, and deep down I felt that she would not want to join me on this new adventure. Nor would I wish her to sacrifice her life for me; I had to admit that this was a journey I needed to take alone.

I finally arrived at the centre of the village. My clothes were still sodden, but at least the rain had lessened. The cold, grey streets did little to lift my tired spirits, and my nose and cheeks were still raw from the buffeting winds I had endured at the summit. The damp and gloomy weather served as the perfect backdrop against this old mining town, where the roofs were tiled with a grey slate taken from the local quarry. It seemed a tired and worn-out place; its beating heart had weakened since the mines had closed, which must have been at least 40 years previously. No new investment had reached this place since, and I thought about the ironic fact that areas of great beauty are often harsh places in which to live. I think this was one reason why I felt drawn to the city; I had the impression that these people had, at least, held onto their vibrancy and kept the community's heart beating.

As it was Sunday, the main street was lifeless; the shutters were pulled down over most windows, creating an unattractive vista. Only one or two stayed open, their owners obviously hoping to pick up scraps of trade from anyone passing through. However, on a day such as this, very few people were around.

There was, however, one brightly-lit building in the street: an outdated public bar, which, judging by its crumbling brickwork and rotting window frames, was fit for demolition. Opening the door and looking into the gloomy-looking bar area, it took a while for my eyes to adjust to the darkness, although it did not take long for me to realise that what remained of the life of the town had been sucked into this building. I had not seen a soul for some time, and so being around large numbers of people in a small and crowded space was stressful. Regardless, after a moment's hesitation, I walked in. I hurried across to the bar and, looking at the limited lunchtime menu, ordered some soup, as well as a much-needed mug of steaming hot coffee. I found a small table close enough to the glowing wood fire to warm me up. However, whilst the fire was close enough to warm my exposed flesh; it was too far away to dry my damp clothes. The lady at the bar brought my order to the table soon after and I devoured the soup and the huge chunks of buttered bread.

Afterwards, I reluctantly returned to the chill of the outside air. My spirits had been lifted, and for the first time that day the sun's rays filtered momentarily through the heavy low cloud, and the wet grass on the verge glistened with appreciation. I walked down to the banks of the lake that the village had been built upon, and looked back up the rising and twisting valley that was brooding in the misty air. I gave a weary, resigned sigh, knowing that I had some distance to cover before reaching my vehicle at the head of the valley. But, before moving my weary and damp body, I lingered for a moment to watch the light that was being cast down onto the landscape below through the parting clouds.

Part of the mountain I had scaled could be seen rising upwards and away to my right hand side, while, on my left, a shallower peak unsuccessfully strained to mirror its rival. I walked along the verge of a dangerously narrow and twisting road which seemed to go on endlessly up the valley. Cars whizzed down the road, giving me barely any room as they passed, and I was starting to feel anxious for my safety. Though my mind was alert to dangers, my thoughts stayed silent. It was over an hour later that I finally caught a glimpse of the long roof of the hostel building, nestled into a dip on the horizon. With an exhausted sigh of relief, I stumbled down to where my car was parked and opened my car boot. I took out some fresh clothes and a towel before going to the nearby toilet block. I was glad to finally pull off my wet attire and get into something dry, although I also began to think about the five or six depressing hours of driving that lay ahead of me.

The journey home was a long one: I only made it back into the familiar territory of suburbia as the time approached nine o'clock. I only stopped briefly on the way home and I felt both exhausted and hungry as my weary legs finally took me through the front door – I had decided to leave my things in the boot overnight. With this exhaustion, I felt glad that at least the home I was returning to was a clean one.

It was hard to know whether my tiredness or my hunger was more pressing, but I decided that I would not be able to sleep without eating something. Even though I knew that Jen would be spending another night worrying about my whereabouts, I did not yet have the courage to turn on my mobile phone, let alone to call her. Deep down I knew that I would have a lot of challenges to deal with the following day but, in my state of exhaustion, I did not wish to think about them. It was imperative to get a decent night's sleep, so, after eating one of my pre-prepared meals, I turned myself in, feeling thankful for the peace, quiet and luxury of my own bed in my own private room.

Chapter Seven

Having decided against setting my alarm, I woke up late the following morning with the additional rest helping me to feel quite jovial. I sat upright in bed, and composed a list of tasks to be completed. The mere action of setting out plans in clear concrete steps helped to give me the feeling of energy and empowerment that I needed.

The first item on my list was writing my letter of resignation. So, clothed in my dressing gown and feeling purposeful, I went across the hallway and forced my way through the clutter that was strewn across the floor of the second bedroom. In the far corner sat a computer that I'd bought second-hand many years ago. I sat in front of the monitor, and my mind slipped into a blank void; my eyes glazed over as I hesitated. The flashing cursor in the top left-hand corner was teasing me provocatively; as if it was screaming to be put to use. Eventually I randomly pushed a finger down onto the keyboard so that there would be something on the screen, but the single character did nothing to fill the space. However, it did feel strangely symbolic; it was almost as if my every gesture was magnified with significance: each step was important in this process of change. Once I had made this symbolic gesture, my mind kicked into gear and helped my hands to flow freely across the keyboard. Although the reasons I gave did not make sense, the letter did at least convey the essential fact: that I was resigning with immediate effect.

After printing the single sheet, I proceeded to sign and fold it, before slipping and sealing it into a brown envelope. Despite the temptation I felt to simply stamp it and place it in the nearest mail box, I accepted that I had to go and hand it in personally: I knew that Marion was expecting to hear from me today and I didn't want to have to tell her my decision over the telephone. After the promise I had made last Wednesday, I knew that she would be surprised to discover that I was still absent from the office. But I also knew that she always had a management meeting first thing on a Monday, and so I didn't think that she would try to contact me until later that morning. I hoped that this would give me enough time to reach the office before she called.

After a leisurely breakfast, I put on casual clothes. Just before ten o'clock I was finally ready to drive into the city. At this time of day, the journey was a relatively quick and easy one. However, rather than following my usual route towards the centre, I decided to drive around to the other side of the city to a popular tourist spot on the banks of the river. To get to the financial district from here, I had to walk up the steep slope that the old town was built upon before descending down into the business district on the opposite side. Having parked my car, I found that I was only able to dawdle slowly up the hill. This may have been partly due to having done too much walking over the previous few days, but it also displayed the apprehension I felt about what I was about to do. Doubt was still present in my mind. I questioned my own sanity: why was I giving up this well-paid and secure job in exchange for something that was uncertain and unknown? What would friends and family think of me, I wondered. Was I being reckless and irresponsible by giving up a job that had given me status and respectability for so long?

The cobbled stones were painful for my tired legs to walk on, and I felt glad to reach the top of the street, passing the citadel that was Sarum's centre of worship. I had not walked through this quarter of the city for some time and I had forgotten what a charming area it was to ramble through. However, I did not have to walk much further before my eye caught its first glimpse of sunlight reflected in glass as the tall skyscrapers came into view.

The commercial quarter was a striking and impressive sight. However, it felt cold and lifeless, lacking the warmth and quirkiness of the old town. Reaching the building where I worked, I took a deep breath to calm myself and defiantly pushed my way through the revolving door. But I had only walked a couple more steps on the other side when I was again gripped by fear and doubt. I looked at the elevator, but my nerve was failing me and I could not move my feet forwards. I had wanted to be brave enough to hand the letter over in person, but my courage was definitely failing me. Feeling self-conscious, I turned and saw that Trevor was watching me from behind his desk, wearing a rather quizzical expression. I overcompensated for my nervousness by greeting him exuberantly. Grabbing a pen off the desk, I scribbled the name of my manager across the front of the envelope and left it for Trevor to dispatch.

After returning outside, I took one final look at the glass frontage and for a moment felt a distinct pang of sadness as the realisation sunk in that I would never walk through there again. Yet, at the same time, I knew that it was not the building, the job or even the people that I was sad to leave, but the security and comfort that all of this had offered me. Feeling my nerve begin to waver, I nonetheless knew deep down that I had to press on and keep the momentum going.

Feeling enthusiastic, I headed to a quarter of the city centre that I had rarely visited. The focal point of the quarter was a large precinct, created during the middle of the last century. Today the place was largely desolate: most shops had closed down as the then-fashionable concrete slab buildings had become increasingly unpopular and unattractive. The narrow passageways were funnels for the cold wind and so it was not a space where people could spend time in comfort. The eerie squares looked bleak and uninviting.

The reason I had come here was to visit the central library. I wanted to look through the local papers to see what properties were available to rent. The library was another typical product of its era, with its archaic frontage leaving nothing to the imagination.

Inside, it smelt damp; the faded, grey carpet tiles matched the gloomy atmosphere. I honed in on the rack containing the newspapers and was relieved to see that the papers were stamped with a recent date; there were four different publications in all. I took these to a seat at a large table. I had brought a map of the city with me so I could see the location of any available properties. Taking a seat, I felt conscious that this was not likely to be a nice place to stay for long. Although I had the table to myself, I noticed a number of vagrants nearby who were clearly seeking refuge from the cold wind outside; many of them had their eyes closed. I could also see that this place was a sanctuary for them; here, they were able to rest undisturbed and in relative safety, unlike out on the streets.

After scanning studiously through the classifieds, I marked two properties that looked as though they might have potential, then, with a guilty feeling, ripped out the pages and put them in my pocket. Rather than wasting time phoning the numbers on the advertisement, I decided to take to the streets in order to test whether I would feel good about living here. So, having found my walking legs in recent days, I opted against driving and instead began to stroll towards the inner ring road.

It was not long before I had left behind the serenity of the quiet city streets and become entwined in the noise and smog of the westbound traffic that clogged the busy arterial routes. My surroundings were chaotic and disordered: a hotchpotch of large industrial warehouses and bleak terraced housing were mixed together on either side of the eight-lane highway. These were interspersed with large areas of derelict land, laced with piles of rubble, refuse, and other distasteful objects. I could not help but shudder at the sight; a shudder which quickly gave way to a cough as I struggled to bring clean air into my lungs. I paused for a moment and leant against the six-foot steel barrier shielding me from the traffic that was   constantly roaring past. I wondered what on earth I was doing   walking these streets when my car was nearby. But, after taking a look at the map to check my bearings, I took a deep breath and walked on.

I was glad when I finally reached a junction which allowed me to branch away from the main road and into the different housing estates. The road climbed up swiftly, reaching a vantage point from which I looked west and saw row upon row of houses sprawled out as far as the eye could see. The builders of these estates had made no attempt to fit them subtly into the undulating landscape; they had clearly been erected at great speed at the time when Sarum was fast becoming the primary economic hub of Arasmas. It was a completely chaotic and dysfunctional scene, and, for this reason alone, it captured my imagination. The sight of a landscape that was so neglected by the authorities was exactly what I was looking for: it offered the tantalising prospect of freedom from the orderly world that I was used to.

But at the same time, this romantic idea was one that I was still struggling to fully believe, and my doubts began to surface again. For once I'd moved into this web of narrow streets, my instinctive prudishness came to the surface once more. Taking a closer look at my environment I was squarely faced with a scene of decay. I stared intently at each crumbling building. It was clear that none had been built to last and that most would surely have been red-crossed for demolition if only the authorities had the will or resources to clear this land and start again. It was a surprise to me that the inhabitants had stubbornly remained, with many trying forlornly to patch up these brittle homes so the wind and rain would be kept out. Subsidence was also evidently a problem here, for developments on an open hillside could not remain stable for long. As I walked along, I felt shocked by the state of the roads and pavements, which were riddled with cracks and potholes. It really seemed as if this was a part of the city that the world had turned a blind eye to. But the political will for change wasn't there at the moment and I was still wavering as to whether this was a good thing or not.

I turned to my map to help me navigate to the first property on my list. It was, according to the blurb, a stylish self-contained flat, set in the heart of a vibrant community. However, as I stood outside, I wondered cynically if it was the noise of traffic that gave it the feeling of vibrancy: it was located beside a busy main thoroughfare. The house was slightly odd in that it was on the corner of a street, but was free-standing, and not joined like the many rows of terraced houses that dominated the area. Looking down a narrow passageway to the side of the property, I noticed that there was a rusting iron stairwell resting unstably against the wall. This led to a glass door which I imagined would lead into an upstairs flat.

Concerned by the seeming instability of the decaying steps, I stepped back and, walking around to the front of the building, decided to knock on the front door of the house. After I had rung the bell, I felt I was being watched and, as I turned round to face the main bay window, the closed curtains clearly twitched. No doubt the person inside was wary and puzzled by the presence of this stranger on their doorstep. A shadow moved behind the main door, and it was slowly drawn back to reveal a tiny and frail woman who was almost bent double at the hips. Despite her ailing frame, she was perhaps only in her late fifties. Opening the glass door, she cast her eyes over me with suspicion.

'Yes?' she asked in a tart and shrill voice, which was extremely harsh on the ear.

'Sorry to trouble you, but I was interested in the flat that is advertised and I was wondering if you knew how I could get access to take a look around,' I responded in a soft and soothing tone.

'Yes, the flat is mine,' she replied flatly.

'Oh,' I answered, in a surprised tone. 'Is it still available for rent?'

'Yes, for the right person it would be,' as she spoke, her eyes cast across my frame; she squinted with suspicion, trying to look deep into my character. This left me feeling awkward.

'Would you be happy for me to have a look around?' I asked eventually.

'I'll just get the keys,' she said, moving back from the open door.

She put on her shoes and joined me outside, before leading me around the side of the house and to the bottom of the rickety iron steps. Passing me the keys, she muttered something about the pains in her arthritic legs and left me to continue alone. I climbed up the creaking steps, the fingers of my right hand clasped tightly around the rusted handrail. After reaching the safety of the platform at the top, I paused for breath before turning the key in the lock of the glass door and pushing it open. The rotting wooden door frames groaned under the pressure. Inside, the stench of dampness was the first thing to hit me, and it forced me to recoil backwards. For that split-second, the cold sterility of my modern home seemed far more appealing, but, with gritted my teeth, I walked onwards.

After awkwardly lowering my frame under the beams that jutted out from under the sloping roof my roving eye noticed damp patches, as well as the cracks in the roof that were causing them. Shuddering violently with disgust, I stumbled onwards. It was not only the dampness that was causing me concern: there was only one tiny window in this small abode, and it was covered with so much dirt and dust that no light filtered through at all, leaving me feeling uncomfortably claustrophobic. But I reached the pinnacle of my despair in the small dark bedroom; it caused a deep nausea to rise within the bowels of my stomach. Even from this distance, I could see the dirty bed sheets and the infestation of bugs. Automatically, I began manically scratching myself. Taking a look at the stained and worn carpets, I could tell that they were also rife with bugs. At this point it was definitely time for me to take my leave.

So, with a feeling of relief, I moved back out into the fresh air and away from the dark and dank hovel that was behind me. I descended cautiously to the bottom of the steps where the lady had been awaiting my return. Thanking her for her time, I mumbled that I would be in touch and escaped quickly back to the main road. I was beginning to feel a deflated air of despondency: this experience had only filled with me more doubts. Despite this, I had no choice but to continue my search, and so I swiftly walked towards the second property on my list, which was located even further out of the city.

The property advertised was part of a block of flats that stood out noticeably from the low-rise housing around it. The building was constructed from drab, grey slabs of concrete and was not particularly endearing; it was of a similar architectural style and vintage to the library that I'd visited this morning. There were four tower blocks in all, each one rectangular in shape and rising to a height of four storeys. An area of parkland weaving itself around them offered a break from the concrete but looked poorly maintained.

I found the building I wanted and saw from the number chart at the entrance that the vacant flat was on the third floor. Strangely, the steps were outside of the building rather than inside; there was a covered walkway that went around the building on each level to give access to the front door of each flat. As I climbed up the stairs, I felt uncomfortable: it was eerily quiet and not a soul was to be seen. My footsteps sounded noisily on the metal stairwell and it was quite a climb to the third floor. I followed the walkway around to the right flat and rang the bell. I wasn't surprised when no-one answered the door and assumed that the property must be vacant.

However, feeling impatient, I decided to try my luck by ringing the bell of the neighbouring flat instead of calling the phone number on the advert. It seemed unlikely that they would have a key but I thought it was worth a try. Unfortunately, after ringing the bell I heard loud sounds of bawling and screaming; it seemed that my actions had caused a disturbance. A young lady in some distress opened the door with one hand, holding a red-faced tearful baby against her side with the other. A second, slightly older child stood clinging behind her leg and looking up shyly at me. Her eyes were wide open, and she was sucking on a dummy. I felt pity for the mother, for, though she was not out of her early twenties, she appeared to carry the burden of someone twice her age. I felt embarrassed about disturbing her, but still tentatively inquired about the availability of the property next door, asking if she knew where the owner lived.

Surprisingly, my hunch was correct: she told me that she had actually been given a set of spare keys in case there were any problems while the flat was empty. She left me to try and find them and I was struck by how trusting she was of the stranger on her doorstep. While waiting, I had taken a quick glimpse inside. It looked disorganised; toys were strewn across the hallway floor. But I understood that it was not an easy task for her to bring her two children up at such a young age and to keep on top of things as well. Eventually, she returned with the keys in her hand and, so as not to trouble her further, I offered to put them back through her letterbox when I'd finished.

'Yes, that's fine,' she replied, before turning crimson with embarrassment as her youngest child, cradled in her arms, started to cry again. I hurried away quickly so the poor young woman could close the door and deal with her baby's needs in privacy.

Putting the key into the door, I took a couple of deep breaths. The door swung open smoothly and I was surprised to see that the living room in front of me was dark. Perhaps this was because there was only one window, and the covered walkway outside did not let much sunshine in. As my eyes adjusted to the darkness I started to make out some furniture through the gloom. An old settee and an equally old armchair stood in the corner, along with a chunky wooden sideboard. Although it was cold and dim, the room was at least relatively clean and hospitable, and there were possible sources of warmth in the form of two old storage heaters, one on each side of the room. As well as the door through which I had entered, there were also two further doors, which led deeper into the flat. I chose the one on the right first and pushed tentatively, entering into a small space that served as the kitchen. The window looked out onto the park below, although one of the tall buildings opposite blocked out some of the sunlight. The room was quite cool, being north-facing, but it had at least been kept clean – the surfaces were polished to a sparkling shine.

I went back to the living room and through the third door into a bedroom containing a comfortably-sized double bed. There were also a chest of drawers, a wardrobe and a bedside table, all made from pine. On close inspection, the bed did appear to be free from bugs; it was comfortable to lie on too. However, a pervading musty smell hung in the air. I wanted to get some fresh air in my lungs, but could see that the window on the far side was shut too tightly to open. But I was sure that, with the right tools, I could wedge it open and clear the mustiness from the room. Adjoining the bedroom was a bathroom with a rusty tin bath inside. The sink and toilet also looked clean and useable, and for me this was what mattered most.

So I returned outside, feeling more cheerful than when I'd arrived, and pushed the key back through the young lady's door. I felt decisive as I pulled the advert from my pocket, noted the number of the landlord, and pulled out my phone. The phone had been turned off for five days. In the interim, I had received a couple of messages, but I decided not to read them. Instead, I keyed in the number and pressed to make the call. After a slight pause, the connection was made and the phone began to ring. Unfortunately the owner was away on business but I spoke to a secretary, who seemed to be responsible for handling matters in her absence. I guessed that, because the property looked as if it had been empty for some time, she would be keen to help me, and I was right: she arranged for me to meet the owner at the property, on Wednesday next week, to negotiate a six-month contract. I felt hopeful that I would be able to move in the same day.

Resisting the temptation to look at my messages, I turned my phone back off and returned the handset to my pocket. I was feeling satisfied, having completed another of the tasks I'd set myself that day. But I knew that I had saved the worst job until last. That evening I would have to finally get back in touch with Jen; the mere thought of it filled me with dread. So for the whole of the long walk back to Sarum, I was consumed with nervous tension that increased as my mind tried harder and harder to concoct a story explaining where I had been for the past six days. However, even though I walked for an hour or more, I could not find the words to properly explain what I had gone through and what it was that I had experienced at the top of the mountain. It seemed pointless even to try to put it into words.

As the sun disappeared over the horizon behind me, I finally caught sight of the old centre of worship rising upwards in the distance. As I returned to my vehicle, another alarming thought crossed my mind: I suddenly realised that this sleek piece of machinery would also have to be sacrificed. For if I was to make a completely fresh start, then there had to be nothing left of my old life left for me to hold onto – apart from the memories at the back of my mind. But, I thought, as I was caught in the evening rush hour, the daily grind was one aspect of my life that I would have no difficulty letting go of.

But something had changed since my last commute: I was more sensitive to my surroundings and looking at those sitting alongside me in the traffic made me feel more unnerved. Everyone had the same look of pain and agitation; they sat stiff upright with steely, glazed eyes fixed straight ahead, as their fingers tapped on the steering wheel. Had I once been like them, I wondered? It was truly depressing to see these lifeless-looking beings drift past – beings who looked like ghosts to me. But at least they had given me a moment of reassurance before the difficult evening to come.

Chapter Eight

On my return home, I picked out another pre-prepared meal from the fridge and, after placing it inside the electric oven to cook, poured myself a healthy dose of whisky from the cabinet, emptying the glass in a single gulp. I coughed and spluttered for a moment as the burning liquid passed down my throat and my eyes watered ever so slightly. But the burning sensation quickly passed and the alcohol served its purpose: helping me to unwind after what had been an intense day. But it was only after dinner, and another dose of whisky, that I felt able to take the mobile phone from my jacket pocket. I read my messages, but they were only from friends, and so I felt slightly upset that Jen had not tried to get in touch. I also began to wonder whether Marion had received the letter I'd handed in this morning and what her reaction had been. I anticipated receiving a formal response from the office at some point in the coming days.

Eventually, taking a deep breath, I pulled up Jen's number and made the call. After a handful of rings she answered, and I could tell from her tone of voice that she was relieved to finally hear from me. However, I sensed her becoming anxious again when I refused to speak further and told her that I was on my way around to her flat. After replacing the receiver, I kept my promise, walking quickly out of the door. I knew that the alcohol I had drunk may have pushed me over the limit, but I felt safe to drive so I got behind the wheel and put the car into gear.

Only when I started driving did I realise that I still had no idea what I was going to say to Jen. There were simply no words with which I could make her comprehend the decision I had taken. She had taken a massive risk when she started the relationship; how could I possibly tell her that all the sacrifices she had made had all been in vain? Without realising it, I was easing my foot off the accelerator: once again the dark clouds of doubt were sweeping through into my mind. The wave of uncertainty caused me to hesitate once more. But I knew I had no choice but to grit my teeth and get through this ordeal as best I could. I just hoped I would be able to find the words to make it as painless for Jen as possible.

I arrived, parked my car behind her apartment block, then walked around to the front gate. The building was a very elegant and commanding piece of architecture; each apartment had a balcony that overlooked the river. I had never felt that I belonged in such a place and, when I was there, I always felt like an intruder. I pressed the buzzer for Jen's apartment, and then took the stairs to the third and highest floor. As I got there, I saw her leaning against the frame of the open door. She was wearing a tight-fitting purple cashmere top and a knee-length silk black slip-skirt. She looked beautiful and, at that moment, my desire almost overwhelmed me.

I strode confidently towards her and gave her a peck on her glossy lips. She froze as I did so; I felt slightly taken aback, but initially put her reaction down to the smell of alcohol on my breath. However, when I caught a glimpse of myself in the hallway mirror I could understand what it was that had caused her to react so coldly. The dishevelled and unshaven figure I saw was barely recognisable, and the sight immediately quelled my lust and pride. Jen turned away in embarrassment, obviously having seen the shock in my eyes.

As I removed my jacket, an awkward silence quickly descended. Breaking the silence, Jen offered to make us both a hot drink, as she always did when I came round. While she was in the kitchen, I slipped through to the living room and took a seat. She soon returned, holding two mugs of steaming hot chocolate, and, placing the mugs on the table before us, took a seat next to me on the couch. There was another long silence; both of us could sense the distance that had grown between us in recent days, and neither of us were willing to paper over it with false pleasantries. Eventually, Jen nervously spoke:

'What on earth is going on with you, Myrkais?'

Her tone was caring, but I struggled to find words to express my thoughts and feelings with clarity.

'I don't really know what's happening, Jen. All I can say is that things have got to change because I can't go on with this way of life anymore.'

'With what way of life?' she asked, puzzled. 'Has something bad happened to you at work?' she added.

'It's more than just work, Jen... everything has to change'.

'Does everything include us, then?' There was panic in her voice now.

I turned to face her and took hold of both her hands.

'I don't know. I really do love you with all my heart, Jen, but, honestly, I am torn. I can't ignore my needs... but if I go to the place where these can be met I don't think that you will come with me.'

Jen shook her head in confusion, before replying.

'Myrk, I don't understand what you are telling me. What is this place you have to go to?'

'I don't really know yet,' I mumbled quietly. I added 'I have to move away from the life I am living today; hopefully then I will find the answer,' and then my voice tailed off. I was beginning to feel frustrated by my defensive aloofness and inability to communicate; I could see that I was straining Jen's patience. My frustration did not diminish when she started to patronise me, talking to me like she would to a small child.

'Okay so you don't know what you want, but can you at least tell me why you have to run away from the life you are living now?'

I shook my head.

'There isn't anything specific that has caused me to come to this decision, but I admit something has been weighing on my shoulders for some time now.' I pushed myself upwards in the chair, as if suddenly finding the words I needed to take me out of my shell and onto the offensive.

'You see, I am disillusioned and upset with myself for having believed that I truly belonged in a world that is so much more suited to you. You know what I mean, don't you? I am talking about this world and its obsession with power and money... and the need to constantly put across the right image to others. You see Jen, for you it's effortless: it's the world you were destined to live in, but for me, it feels completely false. I need to let it go in order to find a life that is clearer. Do you understand? I want a life that has greater meaning to it.'

'Well what's the alternative, then? What is your true nature, Myrk?' she sniped back at me, almost immediately.

'As I said, I honestly don't know, but if I don't get rid of this veil I will never find out, will I?'

Jen's patience finally snapped:

'So you are saying that you want to end what we have together, after all this time, and for what? For something better? I really don't think you appreciate just how fortunate you are,' she sneered back at me, ridiculing my actions, and pulling her hands away from mine.

'I don't want this to end, and I still want you to be part of my life. But I don't think you will follow me because the person you love is not who I really am.' I knew the moment these words came out that they would not help the situation, and I could see straight away that they had only fuelled Jen's anger.

'Don't you dare try to blame me for this nonsense. I really am not prepared to tolerate your foolish behaviour any longer. Don't you know what I have sacrificed for you over the years? All my friends and colleagues asked what I saw in such a lost and immature boy, which you surely cannot deny you were then. And look what I have to show for it now!'

I could not dispute this: her support had helped me to mature in recent years, but, stubbornly, I refused to show any guilt or remorse for throwing Jen's loyalty back in her face. I felt defensive, wanting to ask her if her love was truly unconditional, but I knew that my muddled thoughts on this would only make things worse.

Jen slowly turned her face away from me, and I could see there were tears now streaming down her soft red cheeks. I knew that after all the years of being the strong, dominant one in the relationship she could not bear for me to see her in such a state of emotional fragility. I knew that the shock had knocked her off balance; even my odd behaviour last week could not have quite prepared her for this. Watching her lift her hand to wipe the tears from around her eyes, I knew that my irrational behaviour must be making it hard for her to digest what was happening.

Finally, I could not bear the silence any further and, shaking my head, I said

'What else can I say Jen? I know I can't explain to you why I have to do this and I know you cannot appreciate that I am doing this because I want both of us to be happy. Jen, you really deserve to be with someone of a like-mind and not someone who has to work hard just to reach your level.'

She still could not bring herself to face me, and answered while looking the other way. 'Don't you get it? Love doesn't come from the head, Myrk, so how can you coldly tell me that I would be happier with someone of comparable intellect. I am happy being with you…'

'But you've already said that you cannot come with me on this journey. That's the problem. It's not a matter of intelligence; it's a matter of class. I've spent too long trying to cultivate an image of middle-class respectability… right the way back to my teenage years. But I don't think that is really who I am.'

She finally turned back to face me, shaking her head and with defeated, resigned air.

'I'm sorry, Myrk, but I really do not understand what you are saying or what this is all about.'

'I know, Jen, but it's so hard for me to find the words to explain why I have to do what needs to be done.'

After another pause, Jen spoke in an ice-cold tone.

'Well, if that is the case then I guess there is nothing else for us to say to each other.'

'I guess not,' was all I could reply. Taking the hint, I stood up and placed the mug, which I'd been holding for comfort, back onto the table. Jen remained frozen and statuesque in her seat and did not move an inch as I went to leave. I kissed her softly on the top of her head and whispered a hushed goodbye; Jen still refused to show any emotion. It was only when I had closed the door that I heard a sudden, anguished cry from inside. I felt torn: part of me wanted desperately to go back and console her; yet I knew that this would not help, and that I needed to leave and give her some space. I just hoped that, in time, I would be able to find the courage and the words to give her the explanation that she needed and deserved.

In the meantime, all I could do was to return home. As I left, I looked up to Jen's balcony, and could see her silhouetted figure watching me from the window. I simply kept walking to my car, got in and pulled away. I was on autopilot as I drove home; I felt dazed, numb, foggy – barely conscious.

It was only when I walked into the lounge of my cold and empty home that I was hit by a feeling of loss and an overwhelming sense of loneliness. It had been relatively easy for me to imagine myself giving up my possessions and my job, but then neither had their own feelings which I needed to consider. Even cutting myself off from friends and colleagues had seemed an easy task to accomplish – perhaps because they were no longer as close to me as once before. I was virtually estranged even from my parents, now only making one annual visit and the rare phone call, and I did not really care about their reaction to my decision. So now my only real bond was with Jen, and only now was the reality of our separation hitting me, along with a realisation of how strong my feelings towards her were. Feeling anguished and impulsive, I walked straight to the drinks cabinet, and grabbed the half-empty bottle of whisky.

That evening, I was unable to resist the temptation of reflecting nostalgically on the experiences we'd shared together. I felt strangely compelled to indulge my feelings of sadness and pity, but this only served to intensify my feelings of loss. I went over to the cabinet in the lounge, and, pulling out photograph albums, began to flick through our collection of holiday snaps. As I did, I remembered vividly the happy times we spent together. I knocked back another glass of whiskey, and the tears came that I needed to help release the pain.

Part II

Chapter Nine

Friday, 19ᵗʰ December 2025

I t was early afternoon and, having just eaten lunch, I was flopped out on the stained floral couch in my flat. Just as I was dropping off to sleep, I sneezed violently, which led to another coughing fit that made me wince. I instantly felt my aching ribs bearing the strain. I sat bolt upright, trying to get some fresh air into my lungs. But each position I tried seemed to cause discomfort somewhere inside me, leaving me feeling restless and frustrated. The heaters, which generated and stored heat during the night and released it throughout the day, had just given their last breath of heat and the room was already beginning to become chilly. Pulling the woollen blanket tight around my body, I lay down again to try and get some rest.

As I lay there, I complained inwardly about the fact that the city was in the midst of an exceptionally cold winter. It seemed to have been going on forever, and I was craving the comfort of my old home. Since moving here three months ago I'd picked up one illness after another, and, without the respite it needed to rebuild itself, my immune system had weakened. I had lost a lot of weight and my flesh had become paler. It was a vicious cycle because I was not well enough to go out and buy the fresh, nourishing foods that would have built up my strength. Indeed, after those few days of living here, I had barely ventured beyond my front door, except to go to the local store to buy the bread and canned soup which had become the mainstays of my diet. Stubbornly, I'd also refused to ask any of my friends to help me out by cooking me a decent meal.

On most days I didn't even get out of my bedclothes, and, even though these had become stained, I had not had the energy to clean either these or my bedsheets for a few weeks now. The initial fuss I had made to ensure that this was relatively clean had been forgotten soon after the start of my first bout of flu. Even my hair had become thick and tangled, as well as lacquered with grease, for I found that I became dizzy and faint if I stood for too long and so was reluctant to take a shower. I was not yet desperate enough to take a bath in the rusting tub. So, at that moment, lying down on the bed or the couch seemed like all I could do to help myself. In my more reflective moments, I knew that I was stuck in a state of limbo between the old and the new Myrkais, and this realisation always left me feeling desperately morose. The mid-winter darkness that accompanied this cold and drab weather only served to squeeze more energy from my body and spirit; I felt overrun by lethargy. All the while, the clarity of the vision I had experienced in September was fading fast.

As I laid there, unable to sleep, my thoughts turned to Jen: I wondered how she had been coping since our relationship had ended. This was a question I had found myself asking a lot because I still harboured strong feelings for her and had started to feel some guilt for the way I had ended our time together. I had never been able to find the words to bring things to a satisfactory conclusion, and now it felt that the opportunity to do so had passed. I had been surprised by how hard our separation had hit me, and I continued to wonder if, by choosing to separate, I had made the right decision. As I lay awake on the couch, I was haunted by the memory of those first couple of days after that horrible last conversation. Now, the mere thought of that time added heat to my fever and made my legs move restlessly.

To help me deal with the grief of our separation, I had tried to distract myself with the moving process; I swiftly forced myself into overdrive. I remember going through the house like a tornado, clearing out all my belongings and sorting everything into three piles. One pile would go to the rubbish dump; the other to charity. The third pile, by far the smallest, contained the things I wanted to keep.

I also put my house and car up for sale, and, because the price I asked for the car was so low, I was able to sell it in a couple of days. The following Wednesday, the day on which I had planned to move, my house was still on the market – although there had been a couple of interested buyers. Since I'd only been living there for three years and was willing to sell for less than its value, I knew that most of the money from the sale would go straight to the bank and that I would not be provided with any significant return on my investment.

So when the time came for me to lock up the house and visit my new landlord, I left with only two suitcases; they fitted neatly into the boot of the taxi that I had ordered for the journey across the city. One suitcase had my clothes inside; the other had some day -to-day items that would be needed in the new place, as well as a few personal objects that I had decided to keep. It was quite incredible that I'd managed to clear out all of my belongings in such a short space of time, but the distraction had helped keep my mind occupied. I'd been so busy that after those first couple of days I hadn't had time to think about the past. I remained excited about what might emerge from the empty space that I had created.

I signed the lease and collected the keys, and the first few days sustained my optimistic mood. I unpacked and arranged the furniture, before giving the house a thorough clean and a much-needed airing. I even managed to get the bedroom window open, having discovered that it had only been sealed up when the frame was repainted. Although living without the distraction of television was odd, I got used to and even enjoyed the silence. Also, having rediscovered my walking legs, I found it liberating to wander through the streets, thinking of how much better it was than being stuck in my motor car – however fondly attached I had been to it. At the end of the following week, I received the news that my house had been sold.

However, it was not long before my exertions caught up with me and my body started to cry out for rest. Unsurprisingly, it was then that I was struck down with my first bout of flu; I guess this was nature's way of forcing me to stop. Only then did a deep and raw feeling of grief start to come to the surface. The spark of optimism I had felt was extinguished by this rising tide of angst. Strangely, although I had watched the spark fade before my eyes, I had felt completely unable to stop it from happening. Even when I recovered from my illness and tried to remember what I'd learnt in the mountains, I could not manage to overcome my feelings of grief for the life I'd abandoned, and the next bout of flu soon arrived to consume all my strength once more. As I lay there on the couch, thinking of this depressing story, I found myself suffocated with regrets. I did not regret my action, but did regret the way I had gone about it – especially having cut my ties so swiftly and ruthlessly.

To drown out these morose feelings, I turned to the one thing that helped to soothe my aches and pains: the bottle of whisky that sat on the side cabinet. Tempted by the sight of it, I got up and made myself a coffee, putting a generous dose of whisky at the bottom of the mug before I put the kettle on to boil. The alcohol not only helped to ease my physical symptoms but also helped to numb my mind, blocking out the horrors of my recent past.

Yet, as I took a sip, I almost wanted to scream at myself for being so weak and pathetic. How could I sit here poisoning myself and yet feel too helpless to resist? I thought wryly about how easy and pleasant life had been when I had been able to hide behind my veil. For I had revealed, and was now having to face, the darkness and the raw, painful emotions of my own heart. If, back then, I had known that making this leap would trigger these feelings of grief, anger and sadness, I would not have been so forceful and would have done things more gently, in smaller steps. Looking back, it seemed crazy for me to have carried out the execution of my old life in little more than a week.

Yet, during this difficult time, something did happen to console me. It had happened a couple of weeks before when I'd had a dream. In the dream, I was standing in the middle of an unlit tunnel. There was a glimmer of light both behind me and ahead of me, but it was only a glimmer; I could not even see the hands that I held in front of my face. I could see that the light behind me was somehow brighter and that it was somehow calling me to turn around and go towards it. It was as if this light was trying to tempt me back to what was familiar and known. Yet, in the dream, I ignored this call and kept on walking towards the light ahead of me. But because I was completely focused on navigating through the darkness that surrounded me, I stumbled and fell over my next step. The sense of panic caused me to wake up sweating, but at least it was a reminder that I had only temporarily lost my way and that the light had not been dimmed.

But I had not yet reached the darkest point. The widely-celebrated end of year festival brought back a lot of fond memories from my childhood: it was the one day of the year when my extended family all came together under one roof. More recently, it had become the one time of the year when I would go and visit my parents. The fresh sea air would always help blow away some of the cobwebs from my city life.

Although my parents' house was small, it had an incredible view. It was set on a long promenade that ran along the shoreline of the sleepy seaside town they had retired to. I don't know why we had become so estranged over the years, but it seemed as if we were living in different worlds. Neither of my parents had ever liked the idea of travelling down to the big city to visit me and, when I started going away with Jen for the holidays, I never seemed to have the time to get up there to visit them. I still kept in touch by telephone though, especially now both of them were completely retired and had minor health concerns. But over the last three months I had not had the nerve to speak to them, and I was sure they would be deeply concerned by my silence. My cowardice over this was just one more cause for regret.

Regardless of whether they had received the news of my disappearance or not, I was sure that they would be expecting me for the annual gathering. But I knew that this year I could not go: I felt uneasy about trying to explain my lifestyle change to my family, especially in person. I was wary of how my father might react and it made me think about the sacrifices that he and my mother had made in order to educate me. How I could possibly justify my decision to throw all that away? Although I wished to avoid the issue, I knew that I needed to make contact and so I wrote a letter, which explained that I was unwell and so was unable to come to the gathering this year. I kept the letter short, but knew that it would prompt many more questions than it would answer. I put my new address at the top of the letter, in case they should wish to write, and ventured out to put it into the post box. With a heavy heart I dropped the letter in the box, and then breathlessly struggled home.

The day of the annual celebration arrived and, with it, came my bleakest mood yet. Not only was it depressing to be alone on this special day, but a persistent illness was making me feel worn down. I stayed in bed for the whole of the morning nursing a sore head. It was only at lunchtime that I forced myself into the kitchen, and was soon sat over a bland, watery and insubstantial bowl of soup. I had still not mustered the enthusiasm to buy food that would give me some substance and strength. Yet my mouth watered as I dreamt of the lavish spreads traditionally served at family gatherings. Juicy chunks of freshly-cooked meat, lashings of gravy and steaming hot vegetables floated before my eyes. I even fondly remembered the condensation that would often mist the windows of the family home, and the feelings of warmth it gave. I now seemed a world away from these happier times, and, after slurping the final drop from my bowl, all I was able to do was drag myself over to the couch and wrap myself up in a blanket. Once again, I reached for the glass tumbler, filled it with whisky and settled in for the afternoon.

This day was my lowest point, but things did not really improve for at least the next couple of months. During this time the flame of my spirit remained extinguished; the harsh and dark winter continued, and I remained in a state of lethargy. It was as if I was in hibernation and was waiting for the warm chorus of the spring birds. But, by the end of February, the first signs appeared that the seeds I had planted in the autumn were beginning to grow.

For one thing, in making my rare visits to the grocery store, I had been pushing myself to take a longer walk than was strictly necessary in order to build my strength up again. It was a struggle though: I'd acquired a rasping cough that seemed to have become permanent and which made me double up. But at least my other symptoms had eased and so my strength was not as sapped as before. I was also starting to regain the appetite that I had lost months ago and was finally buying fresh fruit and vegetables to eat. I even went to a health food shop and stocked up on vitamins and other supplements.

I'd also started to make a conscious effort to fight my laziness by setting my alarm for the morning and making sure that I immediately got up, showered and dressed. Just before the end of February, when the days had become a little warmer, I went out and brought a razor to shave off the thick hair that had been growing on my face for half a year. This gave me an incredibly cleansing feeling, and afterwards I felt fresher and more alive. As well as cleansing myself, I found the strength to begin to give the flat a spring clean; on the warmer days I could even allow some fresh air in. But by far the most important change was the vow I had made to not buy another bottle of liquor. It was good to finally get back to a state of clear-minded sobriety.

These changes helped to cleanse and heal me emotionally as well. I was finally coming to terms with my past, and felt ready to let go. I'd received a lovely letter from my mother, and was glad to hear that both of my parents were in good health and spirits. She told me that they would always be there if I needed them and that they were open to hearing about my difficulties. I decided that I needed to respond and, after I had told them about my decision to leave my old life behind and the events of the last few months, I felt more at peace with myself. I wrote that I was in the process of discovering what I needed to do with my life and that I wanted to find a way to live life more fully, from my heart. I added that I hoped this would not disappoint them or cause them to worry and that I was grateful for all that they had done for me. I closed by asking them to keep in touch.

I signed and sealed the letter, but, before going out to post it, I felt compelled to write a second letter: this time to Jen. The idea surprised me, but I knew that I did need to write some things down in order to feel complete and be able to move on. So I took out a fresh sheet of paper, and, without further thought, began to write down whatever came to me. I wrote mainly of my sadness and grief about the way things had ended between us, and said that I hoped she was doing well and moving forwards in her life. I told her that I didn't expect a reply and that I was writing this letter to help me feel complete. I felt comfortable saying that I did not regret making the decision and no longer felt that I had to try to explain my reasons. After this outpouring of emotion, there were fresh tears on the lids of my eyes, but I felt that the writing of the letter was helping me to complete the grieving process. I was torn over whether I should post the letter or not, but, in the end, I decided that I should, and so I went out and sent both letters together.

It was about two weeks later that I came to a new and important realisation about my journey. It happened as I was strolling through the estate on my way back from the shop. For the first time in months my mind felt clear and sober, and I was able to remember why I had been driven to remove my veil. But I was beginning to understand that the renunciation of my veil was not the right path for me to follow: I had realised over the past five months that I was tied to the objects I had renounced, just as much as I had been holding on to them. If anything, my longing for my veil was perhaps stronger now than when I was possessed by it and I realised that this was why I had been in a depressed state for so long. Despite an initial burst of energy, I had gained no lasting freedom from my actions. I now knew that a healthier solution was to let go of my attachment to the past and I did not necessarily need to renounce it.

But that was history now. Regardless of whether I should have let go of the veil without renouncing it, the truth still remained that my old way of life was no longer serving me and it was the right time to move on. Yet, before I could do this there was one last thing I needed to do. I returned home and pulled out one of the suitcases that I had stored under my bed. This was the case with my most personal possessions inside and, digging to the bottom, I put my hand around the object that I was after and felt a smile light up my face. In my hand was the black leather notebook that I had found in that hostel and decided to keep with me. The fountain pen was still hooked over the back and, eagerly, I sat down and turned to the next empty page. Once again I found my hand moving freely, writing a stream of words that I didn't feel I was consciously putting together. I reached to the bottom of the page but was compelled to continue onto the next and start another thread. As before, my writing came to a complete halt at the end of the bottom line.

Only now could I turn my attention to the future. In my sober state, I began to remember the dream I'd had during my time in the mountains: of the jolly and liberated life led by those who did not strive to be someone who they weren't. I realised, with frustration, that the dream had not matched the reality and that I needed to find a way to contact members of this community, and to start to build a relationship with them. Only then would I be able to tell if my hunch had been right or not. With this thought, I turned my attention to finding work: work that would allow me to get to know members of the community and help me to come out of my isolation.

So, on a mild morning the following day, I rose from my bed feeling strong and purposeful. After breakfast, I boldly ventured out into the early spring air and dared myself to walk further into the heart of the estate. I followed a route I hadn't walked before and soon found myself following a disused railway line that was recently converted into a public walkway. The track skirted the edge of the housing estate and seemed to mark the boundary with another estate to the west. I joined a path that would take me to the heart of this estate: what I was looking for was a shopping street which contained, at least according to the directory in my flat, a couple of employment bureaux that I hoped would be able to find me suitable work. I soon turned onto a long street that was bustling with activity.

It was market day, judging from the brightly-coloured stalls that spilled out onto the pavement. Many pedestrians had been forced off the pavement into the street, oblivious to the motor vehicles that were trying to also pass by. Why cars would choose to drive down there I do not know but a chaotic scene was ensuing. For me, it was an anxious walk because, having spent too long in silence and solitude, I felt overwhelmed by seeing so many people in such a small area. People pushed forcefully past me, swinging bags of shopping by their side, and I was fast losing my emotional balance.

Finally I reached the far end of the street and came to the building I had been looking for. A set of stairs ran up one side, rising above the shops that fronted the high street. The door at the bottom had the name of the bureau printed on it in faded ink. As the door was open, I ventured inside and went upstairs unannounced. But, after reaching the first floor, it became clear that the bureau was no longer in operation: the glass door was locked and all I could see inside were empty cardboard boxes. With a frustrated sigh, I returned back to street level and carried on towards the second bureau on my list. Again, there were a set of stairs to one side of a shop, and again, the name was printed on the door. However, while the door was locked, they were clearly still in business, for, after pressing the buzzer, I was allowed to enter.

I climbed the stairs and walked through an open door into a sunlit room. A young lady, probably in her late teens, was sitting at a desk just inside the entrance. As I entered the room, she raised her weary eyes to me, before returning to the magazine she was reading. She sullenly continued to ignore my presence for a few moments longer before abruptly asking what it was that I wanted, still keeping her gaze half-lowered. I replied that I was looking for work, but she responded with an exasperated sigh, telling me there was a shortage of jobs at the moment. After a brief silence, she gave another frustrated grunt, seeing that I was stubbornly refusing to walk out, as she had clearly hoped I would. Seemingly she had not received training in helping those who came to her seeking advice.

I was bemused by her behaviour, but, after giving another frustrated sigh, she finally turned to her computer screen and typed a few characters on the keyboard.

'I may have found something that might be of interest to you,' she eventually replied. 'Would you be happy doing some temporary work in one of the large factory units close to the city centre?'

I was desperate to do anything, so long as it got me into the company of a different crowd and so I told her that I would. She telephoned the factory foreman and confirmed that they did still need someone. Replacing the receiver, she informed me that I could start the following Monday, before printing off the details. Thanking her for her help, I took my leave and went back out into the hustle and bustle of the main street.

Chapter Ten

Monday, 23rd March 2026

The clock by the side of my bed woke me at an early hour; I had not been awake at this time for many months. Resisting the temptation to go back to sleep, I returned to my familiar routine, dousing my face in icy cold water that helped stir me to life. After showering, I dressed, putting on jeans and a t-shirt before eating breakfast. Neither my appetite nor my health was fully back to normal, but I knew that, if I was to make it through a day of physical work, I would need to eat a solid meal. I left the house and took a deep breath to prepare myself for the two-mile walk that lay ahead, knowing that, to make the eight o'clock start, I would have to walk briskly.

I arrived at a large and sprawling industrial estate; the building was relatively simple to locate, for its large neon sign was fixed to a brick wall that towered above the rest of the units. I walked with trepidation: I'd been starved of sustained human contact for some time and my confidence had been weakened as a result. The feeling of fear in the pit of my stomach took me right back to that morning when my father had dropped me off at the gates of the high school in Studley for the first time. Remembering that time, I walked through the main entrance and reported to reception. I was told to take a seat until John Dursby, the manager whose name I'd been given, could be located. Eventually a small, pugnacious figure came in and walked purposefully towards me. I could tell from his stride that this was a man who would be tough and uncompromising. As he got closer, I saw that his face was hard and worn, and that the cracks were filled with dust, making him look older than he really was. However, his muscular and stocky frame showed no sign of age and, compared to my weak and pale body, he looked as powerful as a titan.

Shaking me firmly by the hand and bellowing a sharp and gruff welcome, John led me through a set of double doors to a large open space where all sorts of complex machinery were whirring away. I could not help but stop for a second, spell-bound by the ingenuity of these creations, and by the minds that must have dreamt up and designed these highly efficient processing machines. I had to walk quickly as John led me across to a number of chutes reaching down to the floor from a large mechanical belt that wound itself around the building.

Three men were busy collecting differently-sized boxes and stacking them onto wooden crates; these were scanned on the belt and then dropped down the appropriate chute. It was an amazing piece of machinery for it seemed able to calculate which box should go down which chute. Stopping briefly, John told me that the boxes were sorted by the postcode to which they were being sent and that my job would be to stack them on the crates, before taking them over to the appropriate loading bay. From there the items would be taken by lorry all over Arasmas. Without another word, he thrust a pair of thick gloves into my hands and forcefully directed me to join and help the three men before striding purposefully away. As told, I found a spare spot and started the task of collecting and sorting the boxes.

Although the boxes were light, I had not worked for much longer than one hour before I started to wheeze breathlessly: the winter of discontent continued to grip me with its icy fingers. But the boxes came down in such a flurry that the morning passed quickly and it didn't seem long before the sirens blared and the machinery slowed to a halt as the workers stopped for lunch. Although the three men working alongside me appeared friendly and warm-spirited, I had been kept too busy to engage in conversation, so I didn't have the confidence to join them in the canteen. Instead, I yanked off my gloves, grabbed my coat and silently drifted away in the opposite direction. Passing through a narrow side exit, I walked outside and took a seat on a bench. It was sheltered from the wind, and I enjoyed feeling the warm sunshine on my body. I put my hand inside my coat jacket, pulled out a couple of sandwiches that I had made the previous evening, and ate them slowly. But before long, I heard the whirr of the siren, marking the beginning of the afternoon shift.

Being outside in the warmth had a nourishing effect on me, but I still felt slightly sorrowful: I was frustrated by how afraid I felt about the idea of socialising with my new colleagues. It really felt as if I had returned to that time at the beginning of high school when I had been so tormented by the acute sense that I did not belong. I could feel my confidence draining as these old wounds were opened again. It seemed as if my decision to take off my veil meant I would now have to relive that painful time in order to start on a new path. While I could see that working in the warehouse gave me the perfect opportunity to do just that, I was still hesitant. I returned home that evening in a sombre and reflective mood. But my mind was active, and I felt compelled to remember the school trip – especially the moment when I had stood before the mirror, telling myself over and over that I was bigger and better than the fearful reflection I saw before me. I knew it was at that moment that I had sewn the first stitch of the veil that I would wear for the following 20 years. But the question I had to answer was how I should now behave differently. How could I possibly feel confident and comfortable in my own skin without having to take on a different personality in order to fit in and belong?

I could not find an answer to this question and so my hesitancy continued for several days. However, although I kept my distance, I started to watch, very closely, one of the three men I was working with – a man called Cipher. His behaviour suggested that he might, possibly, be able to answer my question. The more I watched, the clearer it became that he offered the first confirmation of the emotions I had experienced on that walk down the mountain six months ago – the emotions that had drawn me into this world. Cipher was perhaps five, possibly even ten, years older than me, but, despite this, he had a childlike impish charm and sparkling eyes that seemed full of life. His eyes were so bright and joyful that, in looking at them, it was hard not to be captivated. He always had a spring in his step, and put so much enthusiasm into a job that would, for most people, be a mundane and dull one. It became like a dance for him: he would glide from one chute to the next, holding the boxes like he would a dance partner before gracefully putting them down on the crate. His energetic, bubbly nature always had a positive effect on my two other colleagues, and when he shouted some humorous remark across the room, I could not help but smile.

Yet what I found most interesting was that he was just expressing himself in a natural way; he was in no way trying to impress or trying to be something he wasn't. I wondered how Cipher had been able to retain such light and warmth despite his age. I wanted to know his secret.

It was during the middle of my second week there that the sun stopped shining, giving way to a prolonged spell of torrential rain. This forced me to abandon my usual routine and so I reluctantly joined the lunchtime queue for the canteen. At least I would have the chance to observe Cipher in a different setting, I thought. When it was my turn to be served, I was given a plate packed with steaming hot meat and vegetables. But as I walked towards the seating area, I hesitated, passed up the opportunity to sit near my colleagues and, instead, sat down at the end of a long bench on the other side of the room.

As I ate, I paid close attention to Cipher, observing his behaviour from afar. I ate quietly, timidly cowering away from those around me. But after my first visit to the canteen, I started to feel more confident and so returned every day for the remainder of the week and the beginning of the next. Not only was I beginning to feel more comfortable around other people, but the food was surprisingly good. My body had been crying out for regular nutritious meals, and my lunchtime snacks of cheese on crusty bread were simply not enough.

I couldn't resist the lure of Cipher's companionship for long, and so, early the following week, I plucked up the courage to sit next to him. But to begin with, he paid no attention to me, for he was lost in conversation with a couple of other men sitting on his other side. I was left chewing silently on my food and waiting for the right moment. But sitting there, I was suddenly overcome with hesitancy, realising that I was acting in exactly the same way that I had on that school trip.

On that occasion I had spied out the children who I thought could help me integrate into that particular environment and had simply begun to learn to mimic behaviour patterns that would help me to slot in. Now I was in the same situation, with the same feeling of being an outsider, and I was reacting in the same way. It was embarrassing to see myself repeating this pattern again, as I realised that I had paid so much attention to Cipher because he was someone whose behaviour I wished to mimic in order to feel I belonged here. Feeling terribly frustrated with myself, I hurriedly finished my lunch and left the table in order to get some fresh air. Walking out of the door, I began to wonder what I could possibly do differently so that I would not have to play these games anymore.

The answer that came to me was a surprising one: I realised that I just needed to be straight and honest, and to go and talk about my feelings with Cipher. There was no need for agendas; this was just one human being longing to reach out and connect with another.

An opportunity to talk to him came after we had eaten lunch the following day. I walked purposefully over to Cipher and asked if he had a spare hour after work. He seemed a little surprised by my approach but, at the same time, was open and willing to engage with me, agreeing to join me at a nearby bar. So, after the sirens whirred to mark the end of the day, we picked up our coats and walked out of the gate together. We didn't talk much as we walked. When we arrived he went to find a seat, while I went and ordered us two juices.

When I joined him at the table my awkwardness soon faded: I knew all that I needed to do was look into those warm, bright eyes. Those eyes made any resistance melt; his mere presence put me in a state of comfort and ease. It seemed as though Cipher was doing everything he could to make me feel comfortable enough to share all the things that were sitting heavily on my heart, and so for the next 20 minutes I told him everything that had happened to me over the last few months. I was touched by his genuine curiosity but could also tell that Cipher felt puzzled by the decisions I had taken. But he seemed willing to at least try to understand, for he seemed someone who was fascinated by other people and the lives they lead. I was keen to hear about his life too so that I could begin to understand his world as well. Cipher said that he would be only too willing to reciprocate, and so we arranged to meet up again later that week. The meeting of minds that took place that evening marked the beginning of a special friendship.

When we met later that week, Cipher, who seemed to be a natural storyteller, started to talk about his journey, to which he compared his life. I listened; spellbound.

'I think my journey is built upon the lessons that my mother taught me while I was growing up. For most of my childhood, she brought me up by herself. She had had to do this because, not long after my eleventh birthday, my father and older brother both died. I remember the day it happened; they had gone off together to fish at a quiet spot just outside Sarum. Driving home, they crashed into another car: a young male driver had been recklessly overtaking a car coming in the opposite direction and there was no way for them to avoid colliding. My father and brother were both killed, but the driver who caused the accident came away with barely a scratch. He got away with just six months in prison, and, because of this incident, I vowed never to get behind the wheel of a motor car.

'Anyway, despite all the pain we were suffering, my mother remained a rock for me. I think she regained a lot of strength by helping me through my teenage years and into adulthood. But the most important thing she taught me was to stay optimistic and not to allow life's difficulties to weigh you down. She also taught me the importance of enjoying the simple things in life, which can often be missed if we are preoccupied by our own difficulties and struggles. Her strength was amazing: after the accident, she stubbornly refused to allow the past to become a burden and she was not consumed by feelings of anger and grief about what had happened. Believe it or not, she even forgave the man whose recklessness had caused the accident and quickly moved on from that dark period.

I followed her advice, and my teenage years helped me discover that the reason I was here was not to take life seriously and so I used my sense of humour to help me cope in a very challenging school. I am not talking about a few naughty children ruffling the teacher's feathers, Myrkais, but about gangs of children literally ruling the school. You see, Myrkais: you so fondly dream of the world here being sweet and innocent, but the reality is often very different. So how did I learn to cope? Well, I was never a member of a gang, but I quickly deduced how they worked: they mercilessly bullied anyone who showed the slightest amount of fear around them. I started to understand why my mother had taught me to be optimistic and light-hearted: I found that when I came to school with this attitude no-one would lay a finger on me.

Nonetheless, I left school as quickly as I could, and, after a couple of apprentice schemes that didn't work out, I was offered a job at this factory. I had just turned 20 at the time. My mother was a dreamer, and she instilled in me the importance of having something in your life that you are truly passionate about and which makes your heart sing with joy. For me, my joy is my family. My mother still lives nearby and I also have a wife and a child who mean everything to me. Let me tell you, Myrkais: I have been stacking boxes in that warehouse for the past 25 years, and I have stacked every one with a feeling of tremendous joy because I know it helps me to support my family. That is what has kept me happy, despite how long I have worked there, because I never get bored when I am so full of joy. I tell you this because I was thinking about what you said the other day and I realised that you became bored of your old life precisely because you did not have this feeling of joy. Now if I think about it in this way it makes perfect sense to me. So if you really want my advice, Myrkais, I would say that you need to stop all this thinking and worrying and find something that really pulls at your heart.'

The setting could not have been any more different, but the message that Cipher was giving me was exactly the same message I had heard on the shores of Lake Lawdi. In order to discover my true calling and purpose in life, I needed to forget about my head and follow my heart.

While I had been saddened to hear about how he had lost his father and brother, I was also inspired by his tale of optimism. He reminded me of Ken, a friend from university who had a similar passion for learning and for work. Ken was someone who was more at ease in following this path than I had been. However, whilst Ken did seem to handle his responsibilities in a noticeably relaxed and light-hearted manner, I sensed that he had also always had things relatively easy and had never been tested in the way that Cipher had. But still the question remained: how could I build up my own strength of spirit to help me find Satya rather than relying on others?

From this point onwards, our friendship only deepened. In our regular conversations, we would discuss the two, very different, worlds that we had inhabited since our early childhood. This inter-weaving of our different experiences nourished my imagination and my spirit. Strangely, at the age of 11, we had both experienced a traumatic event that had changed the direction of our lives. But, of course, my trauma seemed insignificant when compared to the tragedy that had hit Cipher's family.

The more we got to know each other, the more I appreciated Cipher's big heart, as well as his natural inclination to take people under his wing. For the first time ever, I actually started to enjoy working; bizarrely, I would probably have chosen to spend my time here even if I hadn't needed the money. The atmosphere always seemed jovial when Cipher was around, and I was finding it easier to let go of my grief about the past and recapture the sheer love of life that I had lost. It was great to feel that I was getting my spark back.

Cipher wanted to help me integrate more fully into the local community. He did this by trying to include me in his circle of family and close friends – all of whom lived on an estate about a mile south of where I was living. This began with an invitation to Sunday dinner at Cipher's house. Here I met his wife Crystal: she was a plump and dowdy lady, a couple of years older than Cipher, with a toughness to her which suggested she had been through a lot in her life. But my first impression was wrong: throughout the afternoon she frequently broke into infectious deep-bellied fits of laughter which softened her whole appearance.

Also at the dinner table was their ten year-old daughter Abbey, as well as Cipher's mother Jane. Abbey seemed to be at that awkward age when children feel insecure around strangers, and remained quiet before asking to be excused. Jane, meanwhile, had the same radiance in her eyes as Cipher. I could see why she'd been such an important presence throughout his life – indeed, she evidently still was. Although it wasn't made explicit, I could sense that there was a little bit of tension between her and Crystal, suggesting that Jane had not quite adjusted to losing some influence over her son's life.

But my concern soon passed as I became absorbed in the conversation; I was made to feel most welcome. I was also invited to join Cipher at his local bar a couple of evenings a week, when I would be able to play some traditional pub games with him and some close friends who he had known for many years. Although alcohol was available, I steered clear of the temptation to drink it; in any case I did not need it, for I did not feel inhibited and was easily drawn into the jovial, noisy conversation.

Thanks to Cipher, I was starting to experience a manifestation of the vision I had had in the Blue Mountains. I felt that my choice to abandon my old way of life was slowly being vindicated. I now socialised with a small group of men who had let go of the burden of expectations and who seemed full of genuine camaraderie and bonhomie. This was so much better for me than being around people whose only love was of competition, and who were always striving to be top dog. The atmosphere I was experiencing now was so different from that at the cocktail party which had triggered my determination to make a change to my life. Yes these people were dreamers, but at least their dreams gave them the opportunity to enjoy their journeys. They also seemed less prepared to clamber over their friends in the process of getting to their destination. This love of life seemed so much more natural; it seemed more human too. However, Cipher could only show me part of what a healthier lifestyle would look like. There was still the unanswered question of what it was that truly called me in life.

Chapter Eleven

Monday, 10th May 2027

Over a year had passed since I had started working at the factory and I was now employed on a permanent contract. Whilst I was still unclear about what my calling was, I was at least settled into a satisfying daily routine. One Monday morning I walked into work joyfully, with a spring in my step: summer was fast approaching and the thought of having longer days was a delightful one.

But, just like the seasons, it would become clear that my routine could not hold indefinitely, and I was soon to realise that the kaleidoscope had been turned, sending my world, once again, into a state of flux. As soon as I stepped onto the factory floor I knew that something was wrong: Cipher was nowhere to be seen. This in itself was a cause for concern since Cipher was always in first. He never took days off, and he had seemed his usual fit and healthy self when leaving the factory on Friday afternoon. Time passed and he still did not arrive, but the morning was a particularly busy one, so I soon let go of my worrying thoughts and became immersed in the job at hand.

Only when Mr Dursby came past on his daily round did Cipher's absence become a cause for serious alarm.

'Have any of you seen Cipher this morning? He hasn't clocked in,' he shouted.

I shouted back that we had not seen him all morning, and Mr Dursby walked off, muttering to himself. He seemed to be having a bad morning, so I waited until lunchtime before going to speak with him. He told me that he had telephoned Cipher repeatedly, but that there had been no answer. He seemed as puzzled as I by Cipher's absence; we were both sure that Cipher would have phoned if he had been taken ill over the weekend. Going back to work after lunch, I was filled with a deep and solemn foreboding.

It seemed an age before the sirens whirred to signal the end of the day. I had long since decided to walk around to Cipher's house in order to put my mind at ease. He lived midway along a long row of houses, on a narrow street just off one of the major routes that ran through the city. At this time in the evening the road was heaving with traffic in both directions. I had never been to his house via this route, and I had to take quite a detour to find a subway that would get me under the main highway. I then had to walk back in the opposite direction to gain access to his street.

The house was crumbling and, from outside, looked cramped, but both Crystal and Cipher had worked hard on the interior in order to make it a tidy and respectable family home. Walking through the gate and up the short path to his door, I could still feel the gloomy foreboding from earlier hanging over me. I knocked on the door several times but, judging from the silence, nobody was home. I tried his mobile phone again but it was still switched off. Unfortunately, I did not have contact numbers for any of his family or friends, and, furthermore, I would not be seeing any of them until Thursday. There was nothing I could do but wait.

The following two days were the same: on both mornings I walked into work with the hopeful expectation that Cipher would be there to greet me with his warm, healthy smile, but each time I was disappointed. On both of those evenings I went home via Cipher's, but the house remained empty and his mobile remained turned off. Although I knew that it might be a good idea to talk to his neighbours, I also knew that his relationship with the neighbours on either side had become strained over a petty disagreement the previous year. Apparently the disagreement had started at a community meeting where Cipher had enthusiastically tried to persuade everyone to club together to buy a set of gates in order to stop vandals from accessing the rear alleyway that ran behind their homes. He had told me that these young vandals had been hanging around more and more regularly, daubing fences with graffiti and leaving behind used needles and other nasty little objects. But while some were in favour of his ideas, others, including his neighbours, refused to pay. The stalemate had caused lasting friction in what had previously been a very close-knit neighbourhood.

Instead, when Thursday morning came around, I decided to phone in sick, in order to see if visiting Cipher's house during the daytime would shed some light on the mystery. But before doing so, I decided to first take a long, slow walk in a westerly direction in order to clear the agitated, negative thoughts that were consuming me. Walking had become my therapy, for the gentle motion helped me to let go of things I was holding on to. So, when I finally arrived at his front gate, I was feeling more at peace with myself than when I started walking. From the outside, I could not tell whether anyone was present, but I walked to the door with my fingers crossed. After knocking loudly without any response, I was ready to turn on my heels without another thought. However, giving the door one more firm rap with my knuckles, I was shocked to hear the sound of hurried footsteps and the latch being turned slowly and deliberately from inside.

But the person now facing me was not Cipher, but Crystal. However, I could barely recognise her, for Crystal's complexion had altered dramatically since I had seen her last. The warm rosy colour of her skin had faded to a lifeless grey and she seemed to have shrunk. Her hands visibly shook as she held open the door, looking weak and vulnerable. She had black rings around her eyes. I had never seen her looking so distressed, and felt unsure what I should say or do next. Crystal also remained silent, and for a long, awkward moment neither of us spoke.

Finally, she opened the door fully, and turned around to go back inside. I took this to be a gesture of invitation, so followed her into the gloom of the main living room. This was at the back of the house, and, for some strange reason the curtains had been kept closed today. We sat near each other, but I sensed she was not able to express the pain that she was clearly feeling. Turning to face her, I tried to find the right words to say.

All that came out was: 'Crystal, can you please tell me what the matter is?'

After a long time she shook her head and said in a soft, but forceful, voice: 'I wish I could, Myrkais, but it's hard to find words that can tell what has happened over the past few days.'

'Is something wrong with Cipher?' I asked, bluntly.

In response, Crystal burst into uncontrollable sobs that seemed raw with emotion. All I could do was to try to console her, and so I put my arm around her shoulders and pulled her tightly into my chest. At the same time, I was hit by an overwhelming sense of panic, and felt terribly pale and weak. As I waited for Crystal to regain her composure, my imagination started to run away with me. Had he been taken seriously ill I wondered...or worse? Finally she turned around, looked me deep in the eyes and, in a resigned sort of way, said,

'He's gone, Myrkais. He's gone.'

'What do you mean, 'he's gone'? Where has he gone to?'

She turned towards me, and, looking deep into her eyes, I knew what she had meant.

'Gone to a better place, I hope...' she spoke vaguely. To me, the manner in which she spoke and behaved seemed to show a reluctance to face the dark truth that had caused all this pain. She continued in the same dreamy and detached tone, speaking so quietly that I had to strain to hear.

'It was all so sudden: one second he was kissing me goodbye, the next he was out the door and gone forever...'

Crystal fell silent again for a few moments before continuing, in a tone of deep melancholy.

'I doubt he told you about the thing that really tore him apart, and which cost him his life in the end.'

So there it was in black and white – a confirmation of all that I had been fearing since Monday morning. Crystal's words seemed to have shocked her as much as they had shocked me; she continued to sob, and tears started to fall down my cheek too. I felt numb and my stomach started to churn as the realisation began to sink in. Surely not, I thought to myself, shaking my head. Cipher was just too young and had too much life in him to die. Crystal seemed to want to talk again, and, taking a deep breath to regain her composure, she started to tell me what happened.

'It happened on Friday evening, after he came home from work. He seemed in a good mood as we sat down for dinner together, but, while we were eating, the telephone rang. Cipher went to answer it and, before long, I saw his face drop; I had never seen him wearing an expression quite like that before. He said barely another word, but replaced the receiver and dropped down to the floor, sobbing his heart out.

Our daughter was distressed by her father's behaviour so we took her up to bed. Afterwards, I was able to find out what the telephone call had been about; brokenly, Cipher told me that he had just spoken to a doctor. He had given the sad news that Cipher's mother had passed away in the night, falling victim to a heart attack. Apparently one of her friends had found her that afternoon. The doctor had told Cipher that he had recently warned Jane that her blood pressure and cholesterol were higher than they should have been but that she had refused to listen to his advice or take his prescription for medication. He said that her high blood pressure had probably caused the heart attack.'

Crystal paused for a moment before turning towards me and speaking with greater intensity.

'Myrkais, I've never seen him in such a state. I hadn't truly appreciated before just how much he depended on his mother. He literally crumbled, collapsing like a skyscraper whose foundations have been pulled out from underneath it.'

There was another long pause as she wiped newly formed tears from her eyes. I stayed silent, but gave her shoulder a squeeze to encourage her to continue with her story.

'He was inconsolable all that weekend; it was left to me to call all of Jane's relatives and close friends to pass on the sad news. As well as trying to give him my love and support, I also had to be there for Abbey, who was facing her first experience of a death in the family. That poor child was so close to her grandmother...I was close to her too.'

Another pause followed. I was struck by the thought that Crystal had lost not only one, but two people who were close to her. I couldn't begin to imagine what she was going through; all I could do was pull her tightly to my chest.

'On Sunday evening Cipher came downstairs for dinner and told me that he was determined to work the next morning – he said he needed the distraction. I very nearly told him to stay at home and rest, but I knew that it was not the time to argue so I simply bit my tongue and allowed him to do his grieving in his own way. But I now wish that I had spoken up, especially when I remember how terrible he looked on that Monday morning, having been tossing and turning all night. But Cipher was a stubborn man; he was determined to do as he wished. But, nonetheless, it was with a feeling of unease that I said goodbye to him that morning and I only let him go once he had promised to call me as soon as he arrived at the factory. But that phone call never came.'

It was then that Crystal's voice suddenly changed from a soft, sad tone to one of impassioned anger. She pulled away from me, and sat upright in her seat.

'Did Cipher ever reveal to you the one thing that disturbed him the most?'

Stunned by the sudden change in her behaviour, I told her that I didn't think he had.

'It was the sight of a person who was motionless and mindlessly sitting behind the wheel of a motor car. It seems a trivial thing to be disturbed by, doesn't it? But Cipher was a man with a big heart; he loved to connect with people and with the world around him – you know this more than anyone. He always told me that he had only discovered this desire to connect with people after he started walking the streets of this city following the accident that killed his father and brother. But, Myrkais, because he never drove – or even travelled in a car as a passenger – he couldn't understand what was going on inside someone sitting behind the wheel of a car. He simply didn't have a clue, and this inability to reach out and connect with these people troubled him deeply any time he was anywhere near traffic, because then all he was able to see was blank robotic faces moving at speed behind a pane of glass. To him, they were not human beings he could connect with. Did he ever tell you that, Myrkais?'

I told her that he hadn't, still feeling puzzled by her change of tone. I was not quite sure why this had bothered Cipher so much and why it had never come up in our conversations. But, before I could think too much about this, she continued.

'I'm surprised he didn't mention it: you two were so close. But he talked about it with me regularly, and it was because I knew what a vulnerable state he was in, as well as how upset seeing people in cars made him feel, that I wanted him to call me as soon as he got to work. Instinctively I knew that the walk there might possibly trigger something inside of him, but I never imagined that it would happen to such an extent.'

Crystal fell silent once again; it seemed to me that she was remembering the fateful events in question. Taking a deep breath to regain some composure, she began speaking again.

'After he left that morning, I sat here anxiously, waiting for the phone to ring and to hear that he had arrived safely. The time at which I expected him to call came and went. It was then that I knew something was wrong: Cipher was always reliably punctual. I decided to leave the house and go to his workplace, following the route he always took. As I came onto the main highway, the first thing I saw was the flashing blue lights of an ambulance. I remember running towards them, but then things became a little blurry. The only thing that I remember clearly is the image of Cipher lying

110

on the road being tended to by paramedics. But they were too late to save him.'

We both cried as we thought of this gut-wrenching image. At that moment, the image felt as immediate to me as it surely had been for Crystal. After another long, deep breath, she was able to speak once more.

'I immediately went home, woke up Abbey and took the bus to where my mother lived. When I got there I told them both the news. I think I must have been in a state of shock, for the reality of what had happened did not fully hit me until later that evening. Even now, it hasn't really sunk in. This morning, I came back to pick up some things; I will be going back to my mother's this afternoon.

'One thing I did feel strong enough to do this morning was to contact the owner of a nearby shop who had witnessed the event. The day before she had told me to get in touch when I felt ready to hear about what had happened.

'You know the place I mean don't you? It's just around the corner from here on the main highway which Cipher had to get across each morning and evening. He always felt irritated by having to take a ten-minute diversion down the main road in order to use the subway that went beneath it – and then having to walk another ten minutes in the opposite direction to join the side road that ran towards his workplace. I guess that sense of displeasure got too much for him on Monday morning, and that he decided to scale the railings and make his own way across. The policewoman who contacted me on Tuesday told me that, because Cipher had done this, the coroner would have to record a verdict of suicide. However, I think it's important that I let you know now what the shopkeeper told me this morning for she gives a rather different version of events.

'She told me that Cipher had indeed climbed over the railings; she had watched him doing so with a sense of concern, and had immediately dashed inside to call the police. She told me that Cipher had looked strangely calm and hadn't suddenly stepped out into the traffic in the way you would expect from a suicidal person. Instead, Cipher waited for a gap in the traffic before walking across, and then, in her words, she saw a car accelerate towards him.'

I interrupted Crystal at this point, having listened in disbelief to her story.

'You mean to tell me that someone killed Cipher deliberately?'

Crystal pondered my question for a moment before responding.

'No, Myrkais, I don't. But I think I'm beginning to understand what Cipher meant when he talked about how, while driving, the motorist becomes completely desensitised from everything outside of their protective metal box and, consequently, doesn't think about what impact they have on those around them. Surely, to kill someone deliberately, you have to see them as a human being in the first place?'

I did not understand how she could speak so calmly and rationally about her husband's death, and could only guess that she was trying to find some explanation to help her to cope with the shock of the news. But I felt consumed by anger and could not help challenging her.

'Did they not stop even after they had knocked him down?'

Crystal shook her head, but said nothing more. What did she really feel about it all, I wondered? I pushed further:

'But surely, now we have this witness account, the police will have to try to catch the individual and bring them to justice. In any case they certainly won't be able to record a verdict of suicide.'

'I don't think that's the case, I'm afraid. From what the policewoman told me, since Cipher stepped into the road himself, it's an open-and-shut case. In any case, I know what Cipher would tell me to do. I'm quite sure he would tell me to forgive, and to not let myself be dragged down by feelings of vengeance and anger; that was indeed what his own mother told him to do after his father and brother died. He would also tell me to think about his life and to honour his memory by bringing Abbey up according to his values and beliefs. Even though I don't yet understand why he did what he did, I at least feel comforted by the knowledge that he did not want to die.'

I was touched by these heartfelt words. I was beginning to see a tender new side to this lady; one I had never been aware of before. I knew she now wanted some time by herself and so I decided that it would be best to leave her and to grieve in my own personal way. I stood up to go, pulling her into my arms as the tears continued to flow for us both. I promised I would help her and her family in any way I could and then walked through the doorway, out into the bright sunshine.

As I walked home, I felt full of emotions that took me right back to my winter of discontent. At that time my heart had ached with anger and grief; now I could recognise these emotions, but I knew that dealing with the pain they caused would not be any easier. Once again, I felt called to get out my notebook and pen from the suitcase underneath my bed. As before, words exploded out of me. This time I covered four pages with my writing, ending and beginning in a flowing pattern as one page finished and another began. When I had finished, I put the notepad back into the suitcase.

Chapter Twelve

Wednesday, 28th July 2027

More than two months had now passed since Crystal had told me the news of Cipher's death. The day of the funeral had come and gone in a blur, and I was aware that I was starting to slip back into a familiar daily routine. It still somehow did not seem believable that Cipher was dead, even though the changing atmosphere at work only served to emphasise his absence. He had been such a presence in that warehouse; no-one could possibly fill his shoes. But at least the feeling of listlessness that I had struggled with for weeks was finally beginning to lift, and I had started to move on with my life. After the funeral, Crystal had decided that she could not bear to stay in Sarum. She moved to a small country town where she hoped to raise her daughter and to begin the slow process of rebuilding their shattered lives. Having lost touch with her, I felt no desire to continue my visits to Cipher's local bar and to maintain the friendships I had formed there. So I was again spending the majority of my free time either inside my flat or out wandering aimlessly through the streets. But at least the long summer evenings had helped me to keep my energy levels high enough, and so I had not sunk too deeply into depression.

It was on one of these evening walks that I felt a sudden impulse to get away from the city for a few days. I thought I would go to the seaside, thinking hopefully that maybe I would get some nourishment from the fresh air. It seemed very important not to just carry on as if nothing had happened, but to make sure I spent some time honouring my friend's memory. The place I was thinking of visiting was near my parents' home; I still felt hesitant about the prospect of seeing them in person and was content to stay in touch by letter as this had proved a healthy way of contacting them for the past year or so. Having made this decision, I arranged to take time off work. I bought and packed a large rucksack the following weekend, and by Sunday morning I was ready to leave. I walked into town to catch a bus – one of two I would need to take to reach the south-east coast

Early that afternoon, I arrived in Ross, a quaint little fishing village. I checked into a small hotel which I had booked to stay at for two nights. The hotel was busy with tourists taking their summer holidays in the village, and so, after taking a walk and grabbing a bite to eat, I decided to head back to the sanctuary of my room for the evening. It had been many years since I had visited this part of the country; I realised I had missed the seaside having not visited over the past couple of years. But being here also brought up memories of happy moments spent with Jen, like walking hand in hand along one of the area's many sandy beaches. We had never actually stayed in the village but its sights and smells were still familiar. Even now, I sometimes wondered how she was doing; had she moved on and met someone else since our separation? She had never replied to my letter that had sought closure.

The following day I felt happy just to be alive. I let my mind rest and felt my body unwind, letting go of all that had been hanging heavy on me. I walked out of the village and strolled along a paved footpath that ran along the seafront. The stiff sea breeze certainly helped blow away some of my cobwebs. Even the tourists could not stop me enjoying a blissful day of peace and solitude. As it ended, I sat down on the beach, watching the fading light and the setting sun that was behind me; I could feel myself coming back to life. Touched by the beauty of the experience, I vowed to get up early the next morning and to head back down to the waterfront in order to watch the sun rising out of the water, off to the east.

I kept my promise to myself, and was not disappointed. The

early morning dawn was incredibly still and quiet; there was not a soul to be seen. I took a seat on the cool sand, and patiently waited for the sky to change colour and for the first rays of light to appear. As the sun started to rise over the horizon, I was stunned into silence. In this briefest of moments I felt able to forget the past completely. I felt my grief dissolve, leaving my body energised and refreshed. Once again I had found that blessed feeling of joy; the same one that had left me that fateful morning at the beginning of May. The experience also reminded me of the beauty I had discovered when on top of that mountain, above the clouds; it had a similar feeling, tone and quality to it. Both occasions had certainly helped to silence my chattering mind.

Emerging from this state of bliss, I turned my attention to a problem that had been niggling at me, somewhere deep beneath the surface of my consciousness. Did Cipher's life really offer me a glimpse of Satya? I could not help but think back to what he had told me at the beginning of our acquaintance: about the death of his father and brother and how his mother had reacted to it. I had been feeling increasingly uncomfortable about this recently – there was something about it that did not sit quite right with me. My doubts were multiplied by Crystal's very similar reaction after her own husband's death. The way in which Cipher's mother had passed away had also given me concern. I had always had the impression that his mother was a dreamer, and had felt that this was something to admire about her. And yet it was her reluctance to face reality that had been the probable cause of her death. She could not easily accept that she had limitations and that, I speculated, must have been why she refused to heed the doctor's warning – a warning that could have saved her life.

I saw now the influence that this optimistic dreamer had had on Cipher. She had helped him not be sucked down by the difficult circumstances in which he found himself, but the question is whether there would have been a healthier way forward. I had a niggling feeling that the moment his mother died, the infectious optimism that she had instilled in her son had died too. Suddenly it became clear: the bright spark that had always shone out of Cipher's eyes was his mother's and not his own. I now saw that, after her death, this light must have faded too. Without this light to help him, Cipher must have suddenly had to confront a cold and hard reality. He had never faced it properly before, having buried the feelings caused by the deaths of his family members deep inside himself. All that unprocessed anger and grief, which had lain dormant in the depths of his heart for so many years, must have suddenly erupted. I couldn't possibly imagine what a shock this must have been.

I suddenly realised that his decision to walk out into the road that fateful Monday morning must have been his own way of trying to lessen some of the anger he felt towards the motorist who had killed his father and brother all those years before. As Crystal had told me, the frustrating relationship he had always had with motorists had only caused that anger to fester. But, being an optimist, Cipher must have been desperate to convince himself that the reckless driving that had led to the death of his father and brother was just a one-off – just an aberration and a mistake.

But, despite his best efforts to reach out and connect, he had obviously never found enough evidence to change his belief that all motorists were uncaring, reckless and dangerous. Just one glance or smile in his direction from a passing motorist would have been enough; but, according to Crystal, he had never any seen evidence of true humanity – not even a glimpse – through the glass of a car windscreen. His decision to walk out into the road must have been a final act of desperation – a last bid to prove himself wrong. Perhaps Cipher wanted to force a motorist into an awareness of his presence, optimistically believing that they would slow down and stop. It was a sad irony that this belief must still have been intact at the moment of his death.

As I sat on the sand, I began to think of Abbey and how the same story was repeating itself all over again. Abbey was now ten: roughly the same age Cipher had been when his father and brother died. Crystal wanted to protect her child in the same way Jane had wanted to protect hers; did this mean that in thirty years' time

Abbey would have to handle the same experience of grief? I sincerely hoped that Crystal would be able to allow her daughter to grieve in an honest and healthy way.

But how was all this helping me in my search for Satya? Well, if this was a true reflection of what Cipher had been experiencing after the death of his mother, then it completely challenged the idea that had struck me on that walk in the Blue Mountains. On that walk I had started to believe that the reason I had put on my veil in the first place was in order to conform to society's rules. I believed that if I felt secure and that I belonged, I would be able to develop my self-confidence and fulfil my potential. The conclusion I had come to was that this desire to belong and fear of non-belonging only affected people who went to the best schools and had the best chance of succeeding; I felt somehow that those who had been left behind were immune to it. Why did I think this could possibly be true? I tried to remember why I had assumed this was the case.

I guess, at the time, that I had thought of it as being similar to a fish's experience of water. If all you know is non-belonging – and this is surely the only possibility for those who grow up in a poor environment – then inevitably you must become so immersed in it that there would be no fear of it and no desire to escape. But what Cipher's death had taught me was that the truth was much more complex; indeed, it would be more accurate to say that every fish has a fundamental knowledge built into their DNA that solid earth does exist in this world and, knowing this, they can recognise what water is as well, if only by way of contrast. I was starting to understand that the desire for belonging is not only caused by a child's education and upbringing. I could now see that it was a universal desire built into the very fabric of our species: it was the human condition.

I was reminded of what I had been told on the shores of Lake Lawdi – about how I did not know the purpose and meaning of my existence. I could now see that my feeling of purposelessness was because I had not been assigned a predetermined role in the world; I did not know my place. This is why I had created a veil for myself because this had been the easiest way for me to work out my place in society. All I'd had to do was find a veil that my peers approved of. This was the easy option: I could have tried to assert my own uniqueness, but I had no guarantee that, by doing this, I would be welcomed or accepted by society. No-one had embarked on the journey of being Myrkais Demeritus; no-one had set a valid precedent; no-one had given it the seal of social approval. This must hold true for every human being; I now saw that all people chose to wear veils, different depending on the circumstances they find themselves in, in order to get the social approval they crave from their peers.

But what about Cipher, a man who on the outside had seemed so liberated – someone who would surely never have felt the need to wear a veil? Yet I realised that Cipher had been no different to anyone else: he too had worn a veil, but his was of a different texture. I saw that his was different because it had been given to him by a protective mother whose mere presence in his life had provided him with his own special illusion of security. She had poured so much of her optimistic energy into him after the accident that never again would he feel insecure. She had wanted to help herself and her son to remain in a buoyant, confident state forever, and, nourished with such an abundance of love, Cipher had been able to live his life with real meaning and purpose. But then, of course, with the passing of his mother, his source of love suddenly dried up, and he saw his sense of security evaporate before his eyes. Thinking about it, I felt grateful that at least I had chosen to take my veil away, instead of having it abruptly yanked off by the fateful hands of time.

I lifted my gaze, and looked across the horizon towards the sun – it had now lifted itself high above the waterline. I knew that it was getting late and that if I wanted to make the most of the breakfast included in the price of my stay, I would soon have to head back to the hotel. But, instead, I lingered for a moment longer. I felt full of curiosity about where all these ideas about Cipher had come from. It had almost felt as though he had been right there sitting next to me, casually whispering his innermost secrets. I felt his presence in the atmosphere around me, but the thought that I could no longer see him brought a tear to my eye. So, with a heavy sigh, I stood up and started to move my feet slowly through the soft sand.

After breakfast, I took another long walk along the coastal footpath, but, this time, I went in the opposite direction from the previous day. My mind was quiet and restful, and I felt soothed by the constant coming and going of the gentle waves that lapped the shore. Although my reflections that morning had only complicated the question of what my next steps would be, they had, at least, brought to the surface and soothed the agitation I had been feeling deep inside.

I returned to the hotel after lunch, and, after collecting my belongings from the luggage room, I left again, this time in order to catch the early afternoon bus that would carry me back towards Sarum. My journey home was a swift one, and, by evening, I was back in the comfort of my home. Arriving back, I immediately felt drawn to my notebook and pen. My writing again covered four pages, and, as before, the ends and beginnings followed a flowing pattern, with one page finishing and another immediately beginning.

Chapter Thirteen

Soon after my return from my nourishing, if short, break, I was presented with an unusual solution to my continuing search for meaning. Work had been a lot busier recently, as our team was still a worker short following Cipher's death; but this did at least distract attention away from the joyless atmosphere that now predominated here. But, knowing now that this way of life was not my true path, I was starting to develop itchy feet again, longing to move on and really begin to address the questions that were bothering me so much. Without Cipher around, I just didn't have the same enthusiasm for work; it felt more and more like an unwanted chore. I knew that it was not for this that I had given up my old way of life but still I felt stuck in a state of limbo. I was waiting for something that would put a spark back into my life again. I even felt that maybe the peace, joy and beauty I had experienced during my time away had been intended to tease me – to show me how much more there was to life than shifting boxes across a factory floor.

Eventually, a couple of weeks after my return, our supervisor finally gave in to our complaints about being overstretched, and contacted the employment bureau in order to find a replacement. They offered him a young lad, in his mid to late teens and I felt myself taking a strong dislike to him on his first day working with us. I think this feeling had begun the moment he had walked into the place: there was just something about his manner that irritated me. My initial impression of him did not improve; he arrogantly refused to acknowledge me or the other two guys, immediately getting down to work. He never even told us his name. As the days went by my annoyance became an obsession. This young lad was the complete opposite to Cipher in every way and he was only making Cipher's absence more painful. All this agitation did was accelerate my desire to leave. Cipher would always be smiling, but the young lad would only frown. Cipher would bounce on his heels across the warehouse floor, but the young lad would drag his feet. Cipher would be constantly chirping away to his colleagues, but the young lad would stand with his head bowed, listening to music through a set of earphones. Cipher would shift a dozen boxes effortlessly and at incredible speed, but the young lad would shift them as slowly as he dared. Cipher would be the life and soul of the canteen, but the young lad would be sat outside, quiet and solitary.

Yet, in spite of my frustration, I knew deep down that the problem lay with me, for this teenager was a crystal-clear reflection of myself in the first few days I had spent working there. Now, I could see how arrogant my defensiveness must have made me appear. I knew that, in my shoes, Cipher would have seen beyond this boy's unfriendly behaviour and taken him under his wing. But I was not Cipher and I didn't want to play roles any more. The question facing me now was: how could I deal with this uncommunicative teenager in a free-spirited and spontaneous way? This question bugged me for a number of weeks. My obsession was making me increasingly tense; I could feel it building and building, knowing I had no outlet in which to release it. Whenever I woke up feeling sad, angry or apathetic, I could not stop myself pinning the blame onto this lifeless colleague of mine, even though my emotions were my responsibility alone. It was driving me crazy.

But, at the same time, my mind was consumed by violent images that I felt unable to control. I sensed that these images were linked to the feelings of bitterness that I still held about the way that Cipher had been killed, as well as Crystal's refusal to seek justice. Then, one night, I had a dream in which the grey, nondescript figure of the motorist who had killed Cipher was transformed into a clearly-defined image of the acne-ridden face of my new colleague. I suddenly appeared in the dream and stood behind him, ready to smash a wrench through his thick skull. As I swung the wrench, I recall proclaiming that I was the representative of life, coming to seek justice over the forces of death. At this point I woke up, covered in sweat. But my body was pulsing with adrenaline, and, the next day, I could not help but replay the dream over and over in my head – it gave me a little kick. But my dream world started to blur with the real world, and it was not long before my patience snapped in a bloody explosion.

This happened one particularly tiresome morning, late in the unseasonably hot month of September. I was in a foul mood, feeling tired and irritable because I hadn't slept well the previous night. The day dragged by at an excruciatingly slow pace and it seemed to me as if the speed of the conveyor belt had been turned down a notch. My nemesis had not helped matters by dropping a heavy box onto my foot; he offered not a word of apology for his mistake. Distracted by the music in his ears, he seemed utterly oblivious to the irate glares that I sent in his direction for the rest of the morning. That one incident proved to be my tipping point and, during the lunchtime break, having finished eating, I strode purposely outside. The young man never came to the canteen for lunch; he preferred to sit outdoors in the heat of the summer sun, occupying a space on a small bench close to the perimeter fence. I would sometimes look out and see him there, bathing himself in the sunshine with his eyes closed, and keeping his headphones plugged in all the while. But today he would not be allowed to hide away in isolation; I walked directly towards him.

It took him a few seconds to notice that someone was standing over him. I think it was only my shadow on his face that caused him to open his eyes and look upwards. Startled, he froze like a rabbit caught in headlights. Suddenly, without any warning, I thrust my fist into his jaw, sending him reeling across the metal slats of the bench and down onto the floor. Full of anger, I bent down, grabbed him by the collar and punched his bloody face a couple more times. My frenzied attack was only stopped when someone came running out and pulled me away.

I took a deep breath and walked back inside; the other man

stayed with the teenager and tended to his wounds. As I washed my face in the bathroom, the rush of adrenaline began to subside. Part of me felt foolish and guilty for what I had just done, but another part was tingling: this edgy, dangerous place I had put myself in made me feel intensely alive. Before long, I was called into Mr Dursby's office. I expected to be dismissed on the spot for what I'd done, but he was surprisingly calm about the incident, docking me a day's pay and telling me to go home for the afternoon in order to cool off. He then suggested that I come back to his office the following morning to see how the situation could be resolved.

By the time I reached home, the sensation of being intensely alive had passed, leaving me feeling drained and exhausted. My behaviour had been completely out of character – I had never committed an act of violence before – but I was surprised by the stirring effect that it had had on me. I was filled with guilt, but, unfortunately, had no way of releasing these feelings. I felt so ashamed that I was unsure whether to go into the factory the following day; I didn't know if I could face my supervisor. What would I do if that poor kid turned up at work and showed me the wounds he had suffered?

But in the end, having managed to get a good night's rest, I decided to take my punishment. I almost wanted that kid to be there; I almost wanted him to take a free swing at me – just retribution for my cowardly actions. I walked into the factory, and went straight to Mr Dursby's office. He didn't say much but made it clear, nonetheless, that I would not get another warning about this and that if there was any more trouble from me, I would be straight out of the door. I didn't ask what had happened to my victim or whether he would be coming back to work. As I got up to leave, he added that I was to be moved to a different section, and suggested that I go and take my anger out on some of the heavy boxes that the factory processed.

He led me to the new section where I would be working; it was right at the opposite end of the factory. There was a similar setup to the place I had been working at before, but here boxes were much bulkier and at least three or four times heavier than the ones that I was used to lifting. There were two other men, both in their fifties, I guessed, working off this conveyor belt; they nodded their heads towards me in acknowledgment before turning back to their work. I spent some time observing them that morning. One was short and stocky; he had closely-shaved grey hair which made an awkward fit with his pugnacious, red face. I watched him that morning with admiration: my muscles struggled to handle the extra weight I was lifting, but he moved the boxes effortlessly. The other man was the taller of the two and had a gaunt look to him. He twisted his long, black hair into a ponytail, holding it with an elastic band; he had pinched cheeks that were devoid of colour. Despite his deceptively wiry frame, he was powerfully built, and, indeed, was probably just as strong as his colleague. I guessed both of them must have been shifting boxes for a number of years.

What my muscles lacked in strength, I made up for in endeavour. I followed the advice of my supervisor, putting all of my frustration and aggression into lifting the heavy boxes. Although I had felt drained the night before, today I had found new reserves of energy and was using them to good effect. Yet I was also aware that my colleagues were looking at me with alarm: they seemed unnerved by my moody sullenness and the noisy way I was going about my work. I sensed that they were wary of getting too close and being drawn into my tornado. I also knew that the other workers would have heard – and gossiped – about my behaviour the previous day, and felt that this would add to their wariness, and to the distance that seemed to be growing between us.

It was a surprise, therefore, when lunchtime arrived and the stockier of my two new workmates came over to me. With a few sudden movements, he came up behind me and placed both hands on my shoulders. Although I hadn't invited him to, he started to give them a firm massage. As he did so, I realised just how tight they had become and how much tension had built up inside. When he had finished, I turned to face him. He offered me his hand.

'Hi there. My name's Tommy.'

Still holding his hand out, Tommy looked around for his colleague, but found that he had already left for lunch. Turning back to face me, he continued.

'The other guy's name is Chris. Yours is Myrkais, isn't it?'

I nodded, shaking his hand and thanking him for the impromptu massage.

'You've developed quite a reputation for yourself on the factory floor, Myrkais, after what you did yesterday,' Tommy said to me, mischievously; I blushed.

'It's not something I am proud of, Tommy,' I answered back, a little bluntly.

'No, I can tell that from all the tension you're carrying. Can I give you a little bit of friendly advice, Myrkais? You see, for the best part of 30 years, I have studied the energy flow through the body, exploring ways to maximise the flow and to minimise blockages in order to maximise the amount of life force coming through my body. Do you know what causes energy to become blocked in the body, Myrkais? Well, it's nothing more than too many thoughts and emotions being triggered by the mind that drain the life out of you. I can tell from your reaction to the incident yesterday and from the way you have been pummelling these boxes this morning that you are thinking too much and allowing this to affect your emotions. You need to get out your head, Myrkais. Get right down into your body, and you will find that you have more energy available to you than you knew.'

There it was again. He was the third person to have told me that I needed to get out of my head and to stop thinking too much. I could see what Tommy meant when he said that my life force had drained away from me. The question was how I could better manage my flow of energy. But, continuing, Tommy soon answered this:

'Find something that you are really passionate about and which inspires you, Myrkais. But don't just sit there and think about it; you need to get out there, jump in the river of life, and experiment to find out what really gets your juices flowing.'

126

His message sounded similar to Cipher's, particularly what he had taught me about the importance of finding and following my calling. But when I told Tommy this, he disagreed completely.

'It sounds to me like Cipher was telling you to follow your heart. What I am telling you is to follow your gut. I'm not interested in creating a worthy life that leaves me feeling content and peaceful; I want one that really gives me pleasure, full of things that really put me on edge and that get my adrenaline flowing. This is what it means to live Myrkais. It's about really owning and inhabiting your body. It's about realising that you're only alive once, so you may as well grasp that life with both hands and really seize the moment. Myrkais, I really can't advise you strongly enough that if you allow yourself to spend your time with all these draining thoughts and emotions running through your head and heart, you will end up wasting your life.'

'But what sort of things do you experiment with?' I asked curiously.

He answered by posing another question: 'Why don't you come with me, Chris, and a couple of our friends tonight and find out?'

Having stirred my curiosity I agreed, and Tommy offered to collect me in his car at eight o'clock that evening.

I walked home that afternoon in a contemplative mood, and, as the sun was still bright, I decided to extend my journey by taking a detour. Until today all the things that were causing me pain – the discoveries about Cipher I had made in the summer; my desire to find a lasting antidote for my fear and insecurity; my recent spell of anger and frustration – had been kept, stewing away, in separate compartments of my mind. Yet Tommy's words at lunchtime seemed to suggest that I could integrate the two forces together, and heal myself in doing so. It seemed a new and exciting idea.

For, walking home, I remembered that, fundamentally, I was nothing more than flowing energy. Massaging my left hand with my right, I knew deep down that the appearance of solid flesh and bone was an illusion. I had been taught at school that the more one looks into matter, the emptier it becomes, because, in reality, matter is just energy vibrating at a certain frequency, – like a taut wire being twanged – so that it gives the impression of being more solid than it really is. Why did this realisation bring things together? I think it had helped to draw my attention to a strange paradox. For what Tommy had said was that, because the river of life is fast-flowing, the more I let go of myself and allowed myself to flow with this river, the more vibrant and full of life I would become. The idea of letting go in order to become stronger seemed paradoxical to me; I had always believed that, in order to stay alive, I needed to hold on to the riverbank and protect myself from the river's force. Indeed, this was why I had taken to wearing my veil when growing up for I believed that, in this way, I would have some control over my life. A key aspect of this way of thinking was the belief that I was a solid identity that was separate from life. This appealing illusion obscured the truth from me: the truth that I was nothing more than energy, nothing more than a part of life. I could see now that my mind had concocted this theory to help me feel that I was in some sort of temporary control. But my belief in this idea was only making me weaker; I knew I needed to get my body in sync with the life force itself. Most importantly, I had to let go of any desire to control the flow of life.

Chapter Fourteen

I arrived home and cooked myself dinner, then waited anxiously for the clock to strike eight. It felt strange for me to be socialising again, having spent my evenings alone for the past four or five months. He was late, but, eventually, I heard the sound of a car horn outside. I hurried out, and saw an old rusted banger sat with its headlights on and its engine humming. Tommy, sitting behind the wheel, gestured to the front seat next to him.

Sitting in the back seat was Chris, along with two other figures. Tommy introduced them as Ian and Charles. There was no chance to talk: as soon as I shut the door, Tommy pulled away, turning the music on the stereo right up. We drove at speed, seemingly heading towards the south of the city. My surroundings soon grew unfamiliar. I kept my gaze firmly out of the window, feeling uncomfortable among all these strangers and anxious about where we were going. Doubts were running through my head: I wondered whether it had been wise to trust Tommy so quickly.

I also felt unsettled: this was the first time I'd stepped inside of a car since Cipher had died, and the speed at which Tommy was driving made me think about my old friend's belief that human beings turn into reckless beasts the moment they get behind the wheel of a car. But I tried to remember what I had learnt today about the importance of staying in my body and not allowing thoughts and emotions to drain the life force away from me. I took several deep breaths, trying to stay calm.

Eventually, Tommy pulled onto a side street and parked his car on the corner. I opened the door, stepped out and pulled the seat forward, allowing those in the back seat to step out as well. Walking down the main road that we had just driven along, under the glow of the overhead streetlights, I was able to get a good look at Ian and Charles. Both of them seemed a lot younger than Chris or Tommy, although they were older than me. They were probably around Cipher's age, I thought. Ian was quite short, with a slight build, although the combination of long, thick black hair and narrow shoulders made his head look slightly unbalanced and out of proportion. Charles was also slightly built but, being tall, he looked as if his body had been stretched. His head was shaved, making him look a lot older than he probably was.

Ian, Charles and Chris walked ahead, but I hung back and walked alongside Tommy, hoping I would be able to find out where we were going. He refused to tell me, although, as it happened, it was not much further before I discovered the truth for myself. Ahead of me, the three friends' suddenly turned abruptly and started going down a long set of metal steps sitting in front of one of a long line of shops. We all descended down into the dark abyss, towards what I assumed must be the basement storage area for the shop above. My eyes adjusted to the gloom and I was able to make out a large steel door at the bottom of the steps; Ian proceeded to push it wide open.

Following the others inside, I was caught totally off guard by what I saw before me. The first thing I noticed was the sound of pumping music, but then I laid my eyes on a large open cavern. It was absolutely rammed with people, and all of them were moving to a loud, incessant beat. What on earth was this place, I wondered. Did the people who ran this gathering have permission to do so? I noticed that Tommy was watching my reaction with a sly grin; he walked over and said something barely audible in my left ear. In response, I grinned in a forced kind of way, before walking through and joining the others at a makeshift bar at the back of the cavern.

As my companions queued for drinks, I stood and looked with curiosity at the brick walls around me; the corrugated steel support on the roof gave the place the feel of a bomb shelter, I thought. I could see human perspiration dripping from the walls; the sight of which left me feeling slightly nauseated. Since I had decided that I no longer drank alcohol, Tommy bought me a soft drink, and then the five of us moved out of the main cavern into a maze of passageways that stretched ahead. Walking through the maze, I saw that there were a number of small rooms located off the passageway, with tables and seats to sit at and rest. Chris, who was leading the group, finally found a room that was vacant. He went in to take a seat and we all followed.

In there, I was able to breathe again, for the music was less audible here and it became possible to strike up a conversation. I deliberately sat next to Tommy, and he proceeded to explain how he thought this place could help me to release my tension.

'Have you ever danced sober – without any self consciousness?' he asked.

I shook my head in reply. Although I had visited nightclubs on rare occasions, I had never felt particularly drawn to the idea of dancing, especially not when sober.

'Well, then I guess you've never had the experience of letting the beat of the music flow through your body, and allowing yourself to move freely. What this place offers is not a random selection of music, but an orchestrated programme of rhythms with varying sets of beats, designed to take the body through a cathartic process towards a state of ecstasy and bliss. The whole programme is called a wave. If you can trust and allow yourself to ride this wave of music then I think that, by the time you leave, your body will again be radiating with fresh energy – it will give you a new lease of life.'

I listened intently and decided that I was willing to give it a try. But I still had a few more questions:

'How long does each wave last?' I asked.

'Each programme lasts about an hour; there is always a pause before the next wave begins. There will be seven waves in total, although we rarely stay for the whole experience, especially since we all have to work in the morning. In about ten minutes we will be able to step in and experience the second wave of the evening.'

'How often do you come to these evenings?'

'We usually come twice a week. There are a number of venues throughout the city that hold these sort of events; you can usually find one happening about every other night of the week'.

I had felt surprised that we hadn't had to pay when coming in, and so I asked Tommy why this was – who ran these events, and why didn't they charge?

'The events are usually held in places like this. Often they belong to someone who enjoys the dance and who just happens to have a vacant warehouse or an empty basement to offer. Costs are usually covered by the bar, although this needs to be run discreetly as these places are rarely licensed. However, few people who come here need to drink alcohol and can just let go into the dance. These events are also not publicly advertised, but we are on a membership list, so we hear about where they are going to be held. On rare occasions, the police do get information about a particular event and manage to close it down, but this doesn't happen often. For now, we will continue to dance and to seize the moment.'

I was sure he was getting tired of my probing questions, but there was still one more thing I wanted to ask.

'Is there a specific way you need to dance in order to ride the wave?'

'No, Myrkais. Just follow your instincts and go with the flow. As I said to you earlier you need to ignore your mind – it is just busy trying to imitate the behaviour of others. Create your own path. Believe me, your own body will guide you if you let it!'

Just then, I noticed the moment of pause between one wave and the next. Tommy pulled me to my feet and took me out onto the crowded, sweaty pit that served as a dance floor. I stood there for a few seconds, feeling claustrophobic and uncomfortable, struggling to create space for myself amidst the throngs of people. I felt acutely self-conscious: my target of letting these feelings go and expressing my uniqueness was not going to be a straightforward one, I knew. Tommy was watching my discomfort. I caught his eye and he gave me a warm, encouraging grin. He moved closer and shouted in my ear:

'Remember what I said to you, Myrkais: never stop, don't think, just move!'

I took a deep breath and started to follow their lead. Eyes half-closed, I tried to imagine all the aggression and energy that had built up inside of me over recent weeks. I felt a burst of adrenaline inside me and started to lose myself in the monotonous and head-thumping beat. There were people that started to cram themselves up against me as they pushed their way through to the middle of the hall; but I had begun to let go of my rigidity and my resistance. Strangely, I found that in doing so I could start to flow through the crowd, just as if I was tuned into the rhythm of the collective. Whenever I decided to move in a particular direction it felt as though a space had appeared at that exact spot at just that moment, and when I moved someone immediately moved into the space I left behind. This experience filled me with tremendous energy.

When the music changed to the next rhythm, I was quickly able to shift into the new flow. Not only did each rhythm make me feel a tremendous high, but, as Tommy had promised, the wave also seemed to be taking me on a journey – gradually lifting me into a state of ecstasy and then letting me fall gently back to a peaceful state of bliss. By the end of that first wave I felt so pumped that I decided to stay for the next wave – and the one after that too. Time disappeared as I lost myself in the music, but I didn't feel tired or sleepy at all. I even felt upset when, after the third wave, Tommy came over and told me that it was time for us to leave. I followed him reluctantly through the crowds to the exit.

Woken by my alarm clock the next morning, I realised how bad I felt. I was no longer used to staying out so late, and five or six hours sleep was not enough. Even after getting home, it took me a while longer to relax and drop off to sleep. So I got up with reluc-tance, and, even after showering was still strongly tempted to phone in sick and go back to bed. But after drinking some strong black coffee, and stepping out into the fresh, crisp, autumn morning, I felt a little more stable. That day was a long one for me, and I felt envious seeing Chris and Tommy full of energy; I was curious about how they'd learnt to stay so fresh.

Tommy spent most of that lunchtime deep in conversation with someone else, and so I decided to initiate conversation with Chris. It was the first time we had properly talked to one another. I felt curious to know his story: what had led to him finding this path of ecstasy? Chris thought for a long time before replying.

'I had a lot of anger inside of me from my childhood, and I knew that I needed to find a way to release it. I met Tommy about ten years ago now; it was he who first introduced me to events like the one we attended last night. I think that he saw that I needed some way of finding a cathartic release – just as he knew you did too. I still need to have that experience of release on a regular basis: doing it once is simply not enough.'

'What happened during your childhood to make you so angry, Chris?'

'A lot of it came from my traumatic experiences at school. Tommy mentioned that you grew up in a better-off area, so perhaps you don't understand how bad schools can be in these parts of the city. Teachers simply don't have time to teach: all their time is spent trying to control the class. The few of us who actually believed that an education would help us to make something of our lives quickly realised that this would not be the case. I don't know why you decided to give up your nice life on the other side of the city to come and live here; I've spent my whole life desperately trying to get the hell out of this neighbourhood. But that hope had been completely extinguished by the time I reached adolescence.'

'The disruptive children had their way, then?' I interrupted.

'Unfortunately so. I remember how angry I felt with the two biggest lads in the class. They had worked out the perfect way to manipulate the teacher; eventually, she was broken by the games they were playing with her. The bullying was so bad that I wouldn't be surprised if she still suffered mental scars, even today.'

'What happened then?' I asked.

'It would have been all too easy just to have ignored them; to ignore the fact that most of us were completely wasting our time in that classroom. Even easier would have been to join in their pathetic games – as some others did. But, although I never joined in with the troublemakers, in the end I just gave up trying and left school with no qualifications. I struggled to stick with any work I was offered, so, by the age of 19, my dad refused to support me anymore. He told me to leave the family home and to learn to stand on my own two feet. We get along better now but, at the time, his lack of concern made me feel furious. In fact, I was angry about most things.'

'So, before you met Tommy, how did you deal with that anger?'

Chris fell silent, pondering.

'For a long time I must have just been resigned to it. However, I eventually learnt how important it was to stay busy and active. I realised that as soon as I slow down, as soon as I pull the chain to get off this ride, that is the moment when life stops being of any value. That's the reason why I have never had children, because I never want to settle down. But I found it difficult to find a way that would allow my wishes to come true, and for many years I felt lonely and frustrated. It was then that I met Tommy; he seemed to have the same feelings as me, and he showed me that I really was not alone and that there was a way to achieve cathartic release.'

A silence followed, but then Chris suddenly turned to look at me, wearing a mischievous expression.

'You ask a lot of questions, don't you, Myrkais. Now tell me about your background.'

I blushed, embarrassed that my tendency to ask a lot of questions had been noticed. I had always thought that I must have picked up the habit from my journalist father. Despite these feelings, I was happy to respond to Chris's friendly jibe, and, before the lunch break ended, I was able to tell him a little of my story.

In the following days, I found myself drawn closer to Chris.

Maybe this had something to do with the fact that his childhood sounded like it had been similar to Cipher's, but that, intriguingly, Chris had taken a different path. I also felt frustrated by how difficult it had become to engage Tommy in conversation. He seemed to possess some dark secrets, for he would never respond if I tried to talk to him about his own past; it seemed that, in showing me a way to connect with the pulse of life, he felt he had done his job and so had withdrawn back into himself. But he did at least continue to pick me up in his car on evenings that we had arranged to go out, and I found myself hooked on the active lifestyle he followed. I was even beginning to adjust to a lack of sleep.

A couple of weeks later, with winter fast approaching, something happened to help spice up my life. The five of us had just arrived at an event – one held at the same venue I had visited during my initiation. We took a seat, waiting for the next wave to begin. Before I had had the chance to take a sip of my drink, Chris stood up, and, pulling a pen and paper from his back pocket, made an announcement.

'Gentlemen, I've had an idea. Myrkais has recently joined our group, and as Tommy has told him to begin a phase of experimentation, I thought that, actually, we could all do with a bit of shaking and freshening up. There are ten weeks left until the end of the year; what I would like us to do is to think up ten activities that we could do each weekend in order to help bring some joy and fun to the dark, cold, winter months. Is everyone willing to help with this quest, and to put some money in the pot, if necessary?'

Chris's idea filled me with excitement. We had already missed the beginning of the current wave, so started to brainstorm straight away. Very soon a wide variety of creative ideas were pouring forth. As it had been his idea, we allowed Chris to whittle these down to ten. After he had done so, he stood up and read out the ones he had chosen, as we cheered each of his selections.

'First on the list is surfing; second is snowboarding; third is rock climbing; fourth is sky diving; fifth is bungee jumping; sixth is white water rafting; seventh is motorcar racing; eighth is attending a boxing contest; ninth is cheering on a team at a football match; tenth is joining protest march.'

After we had all cheered the tenth item, we all raised our glasses, and I led the toast to Chris and to our list of activities.

Chris took the list away with him, and, over the following days, had made all the arrangements and collected the money required. I had needed to withdraw a significant amount of money from my savings, but I knew that it would be worth it – and it was. Thanks to Chris's initiative and his organisational skills, I spent those ten weeks with excitement pulsing through my veins. Barely was there time for it to die down before we had moved on to the next item on the list. I felt the primal male instinct that I had lost in my youth return to me. There were not only the activities themselves to look forward to, but also the time we spent together travelling and staying overnight as Chris ensured that all the activities took place outside of Sarum. Also, as plenty of amusing incidents occurred over the course of these weekends, there were always plenty of stories to retell amongst ourselves during the week.

After the last activity had been completed and the old year had ended, I slipped back into our regular routine of dancing ecstatically twice a week. The frustration I had felt over the summer about work seemed to have faded with the new lease of life I had been given. Yet something did occur that momentarily shook my confidence. It happened in the middle of a dancing event; I had taken a pause and sat down to talk with Charles, who was also taking a break. What I was about to find out was that Charles got his kicks from sources other than just ecstatic dance. For it wasn't long before a short, but very mean-looking, gentleman walked towards us and interrupted our conversation. Discreetly, Charles passed across a couple of notes and in return was given two small, dark blue pills. In a swift motion he put them in his mouth, and swallowed. I sat there, left feeling shocked and a little awkward by what I had just witnessed. A wave of fear washed over me; I felt myself becoming drained of confidence and overcome by a sense of exclusion and alienation. Part of me wanted to walk out at that moment: as a child, I had been strongly warned against taking of illegal substances – which was what I assumed these tablets must be. I also started to look at Charles in a less favourable light; I was glad when he stood up alone to go back to the dance floor. But, before he went, Charles turned to me and whispered to let him know if I ever wanted to purchase a couple of pills. I shook my head, feeling truly petrified by the prospect.

Over the following days, I felt troubled by my loss of confidence. But I remembered what Tommy had said about staying out of my head and not allowing my thoughts and emotions to drain my energy. I thought long and hard: were these moral beliefs instinctive ones or had they just been put in my head in order to keep me nice and safe, outside the river of life? Looking at it like this, I felt tempted to try to overcome my prudishness. But then again, no-one apart from Charles had been taking these pills. I decided to talk to Tommy in confidence in order to ask for his views on the matter.

The next day, during our lunch break, I told Tommy about what had been bothering me. He immediately answered:

'I've tried those pills a couple of times, but they have never had any real effect. Personally, I don't think that they add anything to my experience, and so I don't take them. For Charles, it seems that they do.'

'Well, what effects should these pills have then?'

'As far as I know, they don't do much compared to other pills out there, especially considering how much they cost. But Charles swears by them; he says they give him such a feeling of euphoria that he is up in the clouds for hours.'

Tommy chuckled to himself at the image he had conjured up, before asking.

'Are you thinking of joining him up there?'

'Well you keep telling me that I need to let myself go a bit more, so why not give them a try?' I replied.

'Why not indeed, why not indeed!' Tommy replied, patting me

on the shoulder before walking off to the canteen for lunch.

The opportunity presented itself later that week: I saw Charles sitting alone at an ecstatic dance. Discreetly, I asked if he could get any pills for me; he casually nodded his head, and told me how much they would cost. I took some money from my wallet and, after taking it, Charles told me to wait whilst he went to find his supplier. I sat there, feeling distinctly edgy, and was relieved when Charles returned. Taking the pills from him, I forced them to the back of my throat before taking a swig of water to help me swallow them. For some time things seemed no different. Only when the others came back and dragged us to our feet did things start to become a little blurry at the edges. Taking to the dance floor, I noticed that my mood was rapidly improving, and I felt myself floating along with the beat. The rest of the evening was a magical sensory experience.

The memory of this experience stayed with me for some time; it was almost unbelievable that I had let go of myself and stepped into this transcendent state of consciousness. I felt that I needed to carry on experimenting with these pills. However, it was not only my use of illegal substances that was changing my moral boundaries. There were other elements of this experience of ecstatic dance, including interaction with members of the opposite sex. It was a rare indeed for all five of us to leave these events together; I even sometimes had to catch a taxi home if Tommy had found himself a companion for the night. Although I knew that exploring my sexuality would give a tremendous boost to my levels of energy, I was very shy and hesitant about experimenting in this field. My only previous sexual experiences had been with Jen; before that I had never dated women long enough for more intimate relationships to develop. I was unsure as to whether my sexual impulses could be used to deepen my connection with my body and with life. Sex had never before taken me fully out of my own head and away from my thoughts. I felt awkward about the idea of being physically intimate with women I had picked up.

Yet I knew that this was an avenue to be explored and Chris

soon broached the subject with me, as though he was a father nurturing his young son. As we sat together in the canteen one day, he asked me directly, if a little awkwardly, whether I ever felt lonely. Understanding what he meant by the question, I replied honestly.

'I guess I have been missing female companionship; I left my last partner more than two years ago now.'

'Do you mind me asking why the relationship broke down, Myrkais?'

I told him I didn't mind and proceeded to tell him about Jen, our relationship and why I had decided to end it. While talking, I noticed that my emotions were still a little raw; I thought that Chris picked up on this as well.

'It sounds like you are still getting over her, Myrkais. Is that why you are hesitant to move on and find a new companion?'

'No, I don't think that's the case. I guess I'm still coming to terms with accepting who I am. Until I do that, I don't think I'm ready for a new relationship. Anyway, I'm enjoying my new lease of life so much, I'm not even sure that I want to be tied down.'

After my response, there was a long silence before Chris spoke; it seemed as if my words had touched a nerve.

'I've told you before that I never want to settle down either. But surely when we are out and about you must have desires; you must long for, shall we say, at least a brief encounter?'

'Not really, Chris. Where I grew up this sort of behaviour was considered rarely acceptable, and certainly not civilised. I still feel that it is inappropriate to let loose that part of me.'

I knew what Chris would say next.

'How many times have Tommy and I talked to you about this, Myrkais? We keep telling you that you have to learn to let go of your self-control, embrace your fantasies and desires, and stop your worrying!'

'I know you keep saying this, but I can't just overcome a lifetime's worth of conditioning overnight, can I?'

Chris ignored my pleas:

'You know what I think we should do tonight? Give those pills a break and we'll drink as much alcohol as our bodies can take. Let's see if that helps you to loosen those inhibitions of yours.'

'But you know I've given up alcohol, Chris. I don't think I want to go down that road again.'

'Just do it for one night, Myrkais. As I always say, this is a time for experimentation. All I ask is for you to try this once – if it doesn't work you can forget about it.'

'OK Chris, just this once.'

I shook his outstretched right hand, although I was still not completely convinced by his plan.

That evening, the two of us went and sat at the bar together; the others left us to it. I started to knock back shots of vodka; Chris had promised me these would be the best things for the job. After two years of abstinence, I was no longer used to alcohol, and soon my head was spinning. But Chris was unrelenting; after I had knocked back a shot, hardly a moment would pass before he would call over the barman and order another round of drinks. When he felt that I'd had enough he pulled me to my feet, led me into the main dance hall and tried to move me close to a group of young women – in their early twenties, I thought – who he had spied from the bar. But I had drunk so much that I just stood there in a stupor, barely able to stand up. Chris tried unsuccessfully to get me closer. Then I saw one of the women give me a look of pitying disgust. I immediately pulled myself out of Chris's clutches and stumbled back to the bar.

Chris seemed frustrated that his plan was failing; he would not leave me alone, and, at the end of the night, he decided to take me with him. I was still in a drunken stupor – in no state to put up any resistance. As we walked home, the cold January air helped to sober me up a bit, although Chris still had to hold me up at points. He led me to a dark place, notorious for prostitutes; I could see several standing in the shadows, waiting for clients to drive past. Chris walked purposefully and, from the way he quickly navigated the dimly-lit passageways, I guessed that he must have been here before. Finally, we arrived at a large building that stood alone, some way off the main road.

We were met by an ominous sight: a large burly man in a thick puffer jacket stood in the doorway, holding a cigarette between his fingers. Chris walked confidently up to him, thrust a few notes into his hand and walked inside; I followed him up the steps. I was unsteady on my feet, but had just enough poise not to make the pimp suspicious. It was only when we were inside, walking down a long corridor, that the reality of where I was started to dawn on me. But Chris did not give me the chance to stop and think, pushing open a door on the right of the corridor and sending me tumbling inside alone.

Once inside, I could barely see. There was a faint light from a couple of flickering candles that were almost burnt down to their wick, and, through the gloom, I was just able to make out a figure, sat upright in a bed. There was no other furniture in the room, other than an electric heater in the corner, which emitted a red glow. Nervously, I walked towards the figure on the bed and was able to see her face more clearly. She looked extremely young, probably only in her late teens, I thought. But as her face was slathered thickly with make-up it was hard to be sure. Standing in silence, I felt awkward, but, before long, she revealed her naked body to me and I was overcome with feelings of sexual desire. Clumsily, I pulled off my own clothes, and forced myself into her. Like an untamed animal, I thrust my pelvis rapidly, quickly coming to a manic climax. She had shown no emotion or sign of life, but, at that moment, as I held her body tightly against mine, I did not care. Finally, she pulled herself away from me and told me forcefully that my time was up.

I dressed hurriedly and stumbled out into the cool night air, without waiting for Chris to join me. I eventually found myself on a street that was vaguely familiar and, unsteadily, started to make the long journey home. Even though there were taxis passing, I stubbornly resisted the temptation to hail one: the walk would help me to sober up, I thought. It was after two o'clock in the morning when I finally made it home. I went upstairs and collapsed into bed.

Chapter Fifteen

The experience with the prostitute haunted me for days. The alcohol had given me a terrible hangover and, since my immune system was low, I developed a viral infection that kept me in bed for a week. Forced to take time off from the factory, I had the space to think about my horrible behaviour that evening. I felt disgusted by my actions with the prostitute, but was especially haunted by the look that the young lady on the dance floor had given me. What had become of me, I wondered? During this period, I saw that the more involved I became in this lifestyle, the more I would need to push back the boundaries, because my body and mind would always need something fresh and new to stimulate it. I could see that I was becoming addicted to adrenaline rushes, and that, one day, this would destroy me. Was pleasure really all there was to life?

My thoughts turned back to that first conversation I'd had with Tommy – when we had talked about jumping straight into the river of life instead of wasting time and energy trying to control things from the water's edge. Yet I now realised that I had principles too, and that my sexual encounter with that poor, lifeless girl had contradicted what I stood for. Her obvious fear should have made me stop; I shouldn't have allowed myself to get carried away by the moment. I now had doubts about my other recent experiments too. What I began to realise was that the impulses of the body cannot always be trusted; after all, only the brain is aware of the consequences. Somehow I needed to find some way of balancing all these different aspects of myself.

Now that I had stepped off the pleasure train, however briefly, I was unable to overcome my doubts and step back on. After my return to full health, I did try to continue going to ecstatic dances, because they helped me to release tension and gave me a break from thinking. But I was starting to deliberately put some distance between myself and my four friends. I did this discreetly, for I was not ready to make a clean break yet, but after a couple of weeks of this behaviour, Chris seemed to realise that something was amiss, and, one day while I was sat eating my lunch in the canteen, he came over for a quiet word.

'You've been very quiet recently, Myrkais. Is everything okay?'

'I'm still getting over this viral infection, Chris. It really has hit me quite hard,' I responded.

'Is there nothing more to it than that? I can see something is eating away at your mind, and has been distracting your attention. I am here if you want to talk,' he said, kindly.

I appreciated his offer, and started to feel a little more relaxed about sharing my concerns.

'Thanks, Chris. I guess part of it comes back to that night when you took me to the brothel. The experience hit me quite hard. We haven't talked about it since but you should know that that particular experiment didn't work for me. It is actually causing me to question the wisdom of this way of life.'

Chris interrupted my flow and stated, rather bluntly.

'Myrkais, stop worrying. If the experiment didn't work, just move on to the next one. It's that simple. Why are you still stuck in your head trying to complicate things? Live in the moment. Seize it with both hands rather than thinking of the past or the future. Don't let these negative thoughts drain your energy, Myrkais; just drop them.'

I understood what Chris was saying, but, at the same time, I knew that this was not the true path for me – something was missing. But I did not know what it was that was missing from this life, and so could think of nothing to challenge his view. At that moment I was reminded of my last conversation with Jen; I remembered how I had been in a similar situation then. I answered Chris by shrugging my shoulders; a silence descended. Chris appeared frustrated but seemed to be trying to accept that the two of us were now on different wavelengths. But then suddenly, he changed tack.

'If you're not comfortable trusting your gut, then there still might be another way for you. Someone gave me a book a while ago: it put a lot of emphasis on working with the mind rather than bypassing it altogether. I couldn't really connect with it, but it sounds like it might be what you need.'

My ears perked up, and I asked Chris if I could borrow it. Chris said that, since he didn't want it, I could have it; he promised to bring it in the following day.

Over the next few days, I read through this weighty book. It was an interesting read, written in a logical way that appealed to me; as Chris had said, it talked about working with the mind and changing one's thoughts and beliefs, so that, rather than allowing negative thoughts to drain your energy, you learn to think positively, meaning you attract energy. The author wrote at length about the impact that a person's thoughts have on their environment and provided evidence from scientific research to show the truth of this theory. The author wrote that all his readers had to do in order to change their lives for the better – whether they wanted more money, a successful career or a fulfilling relationship – was to visualise these things in their minds; in time, he said, these changes would manifest themselves. Although the author used many personal anecdotes to help prove his point he also incorporated the latest scientific research into quantum physics to try to show the influence that our thinking has on the environment. Even though his ideas seemed simple, they were highly intoxicating nonetheless.

I could see why Chris had given me the book. While he and the other three men believed that to increase their flow of life force they needed to use their physical bodies, this book suggested that it was equally possible to achieve the same thing using the mind. However, to me, the crucial distinction was that the mind was not limited – it could go anywhere. This argument suggested that, at least in theory, I was more likely to find a suitable sexual partner by using my mind to visualise one, than by using my body to scour the streets. I could also see that the law of attraction allowed for a discerning approach towards the visualisation process. Maybe acting on the author's advice would help me to resolve the battle for control going on within me?

Yet at the same time I did not feel completely convinced by this message. This left me feeling impatient and a little frustrated. I suddenly felt drawn back to the little notebook under the bed. Picking it up, I wrote four pages, experiencing the usual rhythm of ending and beginning at the bottom of one page and the top of another. Doing this helped me release some energy; I also felt a sudden sense of clarity, realising I needed to take time to take stock before I jumped into the next initiative. I also felt that in order to move on to the next phase in my life I needed to work out exactly why I felt unconvinced by this book. It was also time for me to get away from the company of other people for a while and to perhaps take a break from the city again.

It seemed appropriate that the moment I had to show my hand and announce my decision to leave was a moment designed perfectly by fate. It was the end of February and a week before I had told my landlord that I would be leaving my flat in a month's time. Even though the weekends of adventure at the end of the previous year had cost me a lot of money, I still had enough saved from my two years working at the factory to afford some time away. Difficult questions now facing me were how I could best bring my time here to a close and how I should tell my friends at the factory about my decision. Yet in the end, despite my best intentions, these problems were resolved in an unexpected and surprising way.

It happened on a cold Friday afternoon. My friends and I had been to an ecstatic dance event the previous evening. The factory floor was chilly, and I could feel the cold right down to my bones. So when Tommy suggested to Chris and I that we get a hot drink in a bar before going home, we both happily agreed. We walked around to the bar which I had been to a couple of years before with Cipher. I hadn't been back here since then but the bar reminded me of the bold way I had decided to bring him there and share my story. Thinking of Cipher reminded me that he was no longer around, triggering again strong feelings of sadness. While the others were finding a table, I walked to the bar and ordered three mugs of hot chocolate, asking for two of them to be laced with a shot of rum. I easily resisted the temptation to get a shot for myself as well, remembering my experience of the previous month. Tommy came over to join me and helped me bring our drinks over to the corner of the room where Chris was sitting. The three of us soon became engrossed in conversation.

Only when the two of them left me to get themselves a refill did I look properly around the room. Glancing to the right, I froze as I made eye contact with someone I had managed to avoid for the past five months. It was the young lad that I'd mauled outside the factory. Looking at the scars that now marked his face, a result of my momentary loss of control the previous September, I felt a deep sense of regret and shame. Although I knew that my actions had been neither brave nor strong, I had never summoned up the courage to seek him out and apologise. But now I suddenly felt very nervous and vulnerable: I could see the glint of anger in the boy's eyes. I knew instantly that he hadn't been able to put the violence of that day behind him – I would have been surprised if he had. I glanced over to see if my colleagues were returning but they were still standing at the bar, oblivious to the furtive and pleading glances I was sending in their direction. Looking back, I saw my wounded victim rising slowly and purposefully to his feet. He walked over, eyes fixed firmly on mine. Judging from the way he moved, he was full of alcohol and lacking inhibition.

He came and stood over me, the same way that I had stood over him; he was snarling fiercely, filled with intense anger. A swift, sudden movement of his hands sent the small glass table flying forwards, the remains of my unfinished drink toppling over and spilling warm liquid down my shirt. The table crashed down loudly onto the wooden floor. The room suddenly fell silent, and I saw the eyes of everyone in the room turn towards us. Time stood still for a few seconds. Both of us had friends who were ready to step in if necessary, and it felt as though everyone was watching, just waiting for me to explode so that they could all pile in. Even my aggressor was breathing heavily, obviously expecting me to respond to his provocation by lashing out. The time had come for me to make my decision; I needed to show my hand. My body may have wanted to react forcefully, but my conscience told me that I shouldn't cause this young man any more pain. I could not keep playing this game with Tommy and Chris any longer, and it felt appropriate that the closure I needed would come from the victim of my own aggression. So, with a wry shake of the head, I got to my feet and brushed myself down. Looking the frightened boy straight in the eye, I told him that I was sorry for what I had done and walked off towards the exit. I walked past Chris and Tommy, who were standing at the bar, but didn't dare look them in the eye.

I spent the weekend alone; it passed quietly without contact from my friends. It was during this time that I decided that the incident in the bar gave me the opportunity to make a clean break with my past; it was clear to me that I would not be returning to work at the factory. The timing was perfect: we were always paid on the last Friday of the month, so I wasn't owed any money by my employers. But the prospect of ringing them and explaining my decision to leave was an intimidating one: I knew that they would try and insist that I work my four-week notice period. Reminding myself of Tommy's words, I decided that I didn't want anything from the past pulling me back and draining my energy. It was not only my employers who would try to drain my reserves of energy; I knew my four friends would not let me go quietly either.

Having ignored a few phone calls from both my supervisor and Tommy at the beginning of the week, on Tuesday I heard the distinctive sound of Tommy's car pulling up on the street below. Fortunately, I had time to turn the lights off and draw the blinds before he knocked on my door. He soon walked away.

Eventually, on Wednesday evening, I decided that I would write him a short note asking him to please leave me alone. I walked around to his house on the Thursday morning so I could post it while he was at work. After that, I was given the peace and silence I craved and my mind began to consider the future. I only had two weeks in which to arrange alternative accommodation, so, on the Saturday morning, I walked to the library in the centre of Sarum that I had visited during my earlier search for accommodation. Inside, I found a map that showed the whole of Arasmas and felt my attention being drawn a region south of Sarum. I knew that only a couple of hours drive out of the city there was a large area of ancient woodland. It been preserved over the years from deforestation and new development, and, as I was suddenly feeling a need to be around trees and nature, I felt drawn to this area. Dotted in between the more heavily wooded areas lay a few small settlements. I scanned through looking for one that could be reached by rail. There was only really one suitable place, and that was the small town of Pugnillay. Impulsively, I decided to immediately head to the train station and travel there that very afternoon.

The journey took just under two hours and I arrived into the town at two o'clock. It was an unseasonably warm, early spring day, and the place seemed busy with both tourists and locals. The town was very picturesque, located on a river that wound through the forested valley. Just the experience of being in such a pleasant environment lifted my mood. But it did look very exclusive; an impression confirmed by the property prices I saw in the window of a real estate agent on the high street. I started to question whether I could really afford to stay in such a place.

Trying not to let these thoughts deter me, I walked into a newsagents' to pick up a copy of the local newspaper, intending to investigate whether there was anything to rent over a coffee in the neighbouring café. I went in, bought myself a drink, and took a seat. As I turned to the right section of the paper, something immediately jumped out at me: I saw an advert for a small chalet situated in the middle of a large woodland estate outside of the town. The chalet was available for rent through an agency which was based on the high street, and so, without further thought, I quickly finished my drink and walked straight there.

They were still open for business, so I confidently went through the door and up to the lady sitting at the reception desk. She told me that the chalet was still available and explained how far out of town it was; I calculated in my head that to reach it would be about a two-hour walk. That seemed close enough that I would not feel too isolated, I thought. She continued, telling me was that the chalet was part of a complex of six but that the owners had decided to rent these out to long-term tenants, rather than using them as short-term holiday homes. However, she told me that, because of legal restrictions, they could only offer leases for periods of three months, rather than the standard six or twelve. Far from being a problem, this seemed a perfect amount of time to allow me to re-evaluate and begin afresh. I also liked the idea of living in a place that was remote and surrounded by nature. I asked the receptionist if it would be possible to view the property today, but she told me that she could not arrange a viewing at such short notice, so we pencilled in a time for the following week instead.

But after I had left and begun to walk back to the train station, I felt an urge to stop and take a seat for a moment in the nearby cemetery. The next train back into Sarum was not due for another hour and a half, and I felt there was something I had to do in the meantime. Looking up, I saw a couple of taxis lined up outside the station, waiting for passengers from an incoming train, and, impulsively, I decided to take a cab out to the property, just to get a feel for the area.

I followed my impulse, but when we arrived at the address I was dismayed to see that my entrance was blocked by a boom gate, which required a card to open it. Telling the driver to wait for me, I got out and walked around the barrier, trying to see where the six chalets were located. The place was beautifully landscaped, and, as I walked cautiously down the driveway, I could see that each chalet was secluded, having been screened off so that it was hidden from the rest of the complex. They all looked modern and well-built; I was also struck by the quietness and tranquillity of the

151

surroundings. It seemed perfect. I left without being seen and decided to ask my driver to drop me back at the agency in town. I boldly walked inside; the receptionist seemed surprised to see me back so soon. It was not long before closing time, and even though I was bringing new business, she seemed a little put out by my insistence that I go ahead immediately with an application to rent the property.

After successfully persuading her to go along with my wishes, I made it back to the station just in time to meet the train heading towards Sarum. On the following Monday I received a phone call confirming that my application had gone through, and I made arrangements to move in on Friday March 17th, my preferred date, as this was the same day that the lease expired on my flat in Sarum.

Chapter Sixteen

Thursday, 20th April 2028

I had been settling well into my new home and time had flown since my move the previous month. The chalet was as welcoming inside as it had seemed from the outside. There was a lovely patio just outside the front door, and it was there that I would sit eating my breakfast, watching the birds come and go. The property was well-furnished, and so I had only needed to bring a few personal possessions with me. It had been satisfying to clear out even more of my belongings; I'd thrown away my two suitcases so that I would be able to fit everything into the rucksack that I had bought the previous summer. Spending time in this environment left me feeling healthy and energised and, in my free time, I had regained my enthusiasm for cooking. Since arriving, I had kept myself to myself, choosing to spend my time reflecting quietly, rather than interacting with the neighbours. Enjoying my solitary life, I spent a lot of time walking in the forest. Occasionally, however, my feet would take me into Pugnillay, for groceries or a change of scenery.

Whilst walking, I thought about all that had changed since those minutes when I had sat, blissfully happy, above the clouds, in the mountains next to Lake Lawdi. So much had happened over the past two and a half years and I had learnt so much. But as I had deliberately silenced my mind for the past six months, it seemed that I needed some time for reflection, both to digest all that had happened before and to work out where I was going on this journey of discovery. Chris had been right when he had told me that I was not yet ready to fully let go and trust that my life would still go in the right direction. I knew that relaxing control was still a challenge for me and accepted that part of the reason that I needed so much time for reflection was that it helped me regain a feeling of security. Yet even though I knew that by needing to make sense of everything I was just repeating a pattern. It was a pattern I felt unable to stop or slow.

But, eventually, I moved on from this period of reflection, and new, more exciting insights started to enter my consciousness. I learnt to ignore my own inner dialogue and begin observing the outer world. Doing so, I learnt new lessons. For, feeling calm and grounded in nature, I would spend hours every day watching the seasons gradually change, watching plants begin to flower and new leaves shoot from the trees growing in a dense canopy over the forest. Life seemed to be unfolding right before my eyes; there seemed to be a much gentler rhythm to it than to the life of a human being. Surrounded by this vast space and stillness, I started to question how nature's teaching differed from Tommy's. I knew that Tommy had taught me a powerful lesson when he advised me to let go of the thoughts and emotions that were draining my energy and jump into the river of life. I saw that this teaching applied here in nature too: the natural world didn't need to think and plan in order to live, for life is something that just seems to happen of its own accord, without any need for control. Tommy had been right to point out that, as we are part of nature, life becomes easier when we allow ourselves to flow with its rhythm rather than trying to separate ourselves from it and living up in our heads with all our thoughts and dreams.

But Tommy also understood that we are not merely passive actors in the story of life; we have developed the capacity to take a more active role and to make choices; we have the power of free will. Yet I saw now that the choices he took – the same choices that he had inspired me to take – were in violation of the laws of nature. Tommy had chosen to live only with the seasons of spring and summer and to ignore the seasons of autumn and winter. As I reflected,

I could now see that, in the long term, this was not a wise choice to make, being fundamentally unsustainable and, paradoxically, going against the real flow of the river of life. Not only the flow of the seasons, but everything in nature arises from the contrast between two opposites – and one could not exist without the other.

I saw now why Tommy's views had attracted me so much: I was recovering from the shock of Cipher's death and was longing for a new lease of life. But now, after a few months of ceaseless activity, I was longing for rest; my body was moving into autumn as the rest of the world moved into spring. I also realised that by putting myself in direct opposition to the nature of the season last autumn, I had only added to my exhaustion. Instead of winding down into hibernation I had been starting to sow the seeds of spring. My decision to retreat to this rural setting had been a bid to try to balance the scales. I felt humbled by the constant reminders all around me that rest was a necessary part of the cycle of life. For without the fallow winter months, there could be no spring.

Eventually, my attention turned to the book about the power of positive thinking and the law of attraction that Chris had given me. Now I was able to explain why it had left me feeling so uneasy. For it was a book that was, like Tommy's teaching, calling on me to expand, and I had read it at a time when my body and mind needed to contract and rest.

I decided to go for a walk to further reflect on the book. As I walked, I felt myself coming to a deeper understanding: I realised that the author's theory about the law of attraction was a true one but that it needed to be used responsibly. Basically, to work successfully, it required the individual to know what it was they needed in their life at that particular moment. This was what had really troubled me because, in thinking about the complex and subtle forces that moved the natural world, I realised that it was way beyond the capacity of any individual to even begin to understand or formulate what it was that they really needed in their life. I was finally beginning to understand, in a more profound sense than ever before, that the human mind could not appreciate the working of these complex forces. For I realised that the mind is inherently optimistic, seeking to attract only those things that would keep it in the seasons of spring and summer. But change was an inevitable part of life. Accepting this, I began to see that sometimes challenges are needed in life in order to grow; that sometimes pain is needed; that sometimes rest is needed; and that sometimes patience is needed. Certainly, I'd read in the newspapers of many people who had said that, in hindsight, their most difficult challenges were their greatest gifts. But would anyone, even someone who was totally focused on positive thinking, really seek to bring cancer into their life? Of course not, but then again, maybe the cancer was just nature's way of helping the individual to further develop and grow. It was a terrible thought, but perhaps it was true.

Not only this, but, by deciding to meddle with these natural laws, the individual was altering destiny's script. The example that came to mind was a sporting contest. Perhaps, in the script, one contestant had been intended to take the top prize, but a competitor was able to use the power of positive thought to gain an unfair advantage, to rewrite the script, and claim the victory. Looked at like this, it seemed a pretty hollow path to take; I knew in my heart it was not one that I wished to follow.

Even though I had no real answers to the questions that were bothering me, I enjoyed resting in my place of retreat. The peace and tranquillity helped keep me in a place of stillness, and, when conditions were right, I loved lying out on the grass in the evening, looking up at the starry skies. It had been many years since I'd had an experience like this: when I was living in the city, the stars were always dimmed by light pollution. The vastness of the universe was just too much for my whirring mind to comprehend and it helped me to stop thinking for a while. I was also reading a fascinating new book, one I had stumbled upon in a bookshop on a visit into Pugnillay. It was a book on meditation. What this book described to me, in unerringly similar terms, was what I'd learnt from my obser-vations of nature. This suggested to me that I could use meditation as a tool to help me overcome my limited way of thinking and tune in to the vast web of life of which I was a part. The author used two powerful metaphors to explain the concept of meditation. First, she conjured up an image of passing clouds, intended to represent the distracting thoughts of the mind, explaining that the blue sky behind the clouds represented the vast truth with which we need to connect. The second metaphor was the image of the moon reflecting on a pond; the author explained that it is only when the water is perfectly clear and still that we get an accurate reflection; she said that our distracting thoughts are like pebbles tossed into the water, distorting the reflection.

I immediately took these images to heart, realising that only when I was in a state where the water was calm, and where I was connected to the blue sky beyond the clouds, could I begin to find my true calling. Significantly, the author suggested that any impulse to take action would then come from a different place than where decisions were usually made.

As I completed the book, I was struck by an important realisation as I recalled my walk home last September after my initial conversation with Tommy. Yes, it was true that I needed to let go and jump into the river of life, but my mistake was that I had believed that the reason I needed to do this was in order to increase the vibration of my energy field and to make myself more prominent. However, I was learning from this book that this view was wrong. Meditation, as a tool, was designed to lower the vibration of my energy field and to help me transcend the self completely by making it less prominent. It was only by doing this that I could truly begin to connect with the river of life. Reading these opinions also helped to confirm my feelings about the book about positive thinking: that author's mistake had been focusing entirely on changing what the clouds looked like or on changing the size of the pebble that you throw into the pond, rather than focusing attention on the deeper truth that lies beyond it. Reading about meditation in that particular place and at that particular time was a very poignant experience. I took it to heart and focused my energy on meditating for the remainder of my time there.

So absorbed was I by my meditation practice and my struggles to reach a place of absolute stillness that I didn't want to leave. So when spring turned to summer and my three months ran out, I made the bold decision to try to renew the lease for an additional three months, which would take me up to September. I was concerned about the money that was draining rapidly from my bank account but I had not yet achieved the sense of clarity I was searching for. Despite these concerns, and occasional feelings of restlessness, my belief that this new way of being was the right one for me was slowly deepening.

That is not to say that when these clouds of restlessness floated in the sky of my consciousness, I could always return easily to my state of peacefulness. Most of the time they still caught me off guard: the need to always be busy and on the move had been so strongly ingrained into my psyche by my upbringing that breaking the habit was difficult. I remember writing a letter to my parents, and how difficult it had been to try to explain to them that by patiently doing nothing, I was actually doing something profoundly important.

At these moments life became difficult, and it seemed as though I was throwing bigger and bigger stones into my pond, distorting the reflection of the moon more and more. Most of the restless thoughts were concerned with the subject of my need to act as a responsible citizen, influenced by the beliefs I still held about needing to wear a veil that earned the respect of others. The life I now led, hanging out in a holiday chalet and not earning money, was certainly not the sort of existence that I had been brought up to value. Nor was it considered socially responsible. But again and again, as I had been taught, I needed to let these thoughts go and focus my attention back on the stillness that lay beyond them.

One morning when these stories were noticeably strong, I felt the urge to get out my notebook and fountain pen, and to sit down and do some writing again. This time my writing extended over five pages, but, as before, it proceeded in the same flowing way, beginning and ending at the top and bottom of each page. As I let the pen move freely across the page, the restless thoughts in my head stopped, but I knew that was only a brief pause and that they would not be gone for good.

Chapter Seventeen

Having practiced meditating and deepening my patience all through the summer months, I was ready to learn what I would be called to do next. The process of finding out began about three weeks before my lease was up; I woke one day with a strong feeling that it was now the right time for me to leave this place and I should not seek to renew my lease. I was beginning the slow process of learning to discern the difference between what my mind wanted to do and what life was calling me to do. I reflected on this, thinking how interesting it was that most of the big decisions I had taken since walking out of my office three years before had come from a place beyond my own thoughts. I felt almost certain of the truth of this and so with some relief, I began to consider the idea that maybe the choices I'd taken had not been wrong, but necessary. I realised that if I had allowed myself to follow the logic of my rational mind, I would surely now be married to Jen and stuck miserably in my old way of life. This reassured me greatly.

However, while I had experienced a great deal of joy and peace during my time at the chalet, I still felt as if there was a piece missing from the jigsaw; I felt that dwelling alone in this state was not quite enough for me. Also, I was tired of this long process of discovering all the things that I didn't want to do with my life; I was desperate to find my true calling. Strangely, at this time my parents were appearing more and more frequently into my consciousness; maybe, I thought, this meant I could learn something useful from their own values and beliefs. Starting to reflect on this, the first thing that struck me was how much I had grown into the mould of my father and not my mother.

I knew that my father's journey in life had often been a struggle: he had fought valiantly to make something of his life after experiencing a very difficult upbringing. Until his move to the coast, he had lived all of his life in Monkscaph as one of five siblings. His father had walked out on his mother when he was just nine, leaving her to try to raise the family on her own. Three of his siblings were younger than him, the youngest being barely two years old, and so it was not surprising that very little of his mother's limited supply of love came his way and so he had to grow up fast. Because his mother was short of money he was forced into leaving school at 16, going out to find work in order to support the family. I knew that my father hated the obligation to put the family's needs before his own because, as an intelligent man, he would have dearly loved to go on and further his education. I was sure it was this sacrifice that explained his determination that his only son should be an academic success. My father had lived at the family home until his mid-twenties, only moving out on marrying my mother. They had made exciting plans to set up a marital home together and had been able to afford the mortgage because, through sheer hard work, my father had found a respectable job working a journalist – this was to remain his profession for the rest of his working life. I knew that my insatiable curiosity – the very reason I was engaged in this quest for meaning – was a trait that I had inherited from my father; this was what motivated him when searching for stories or crafting his copy.

I knew my restless desire for self-improvement had come from my father, but the values and beliefs that my mother held had, to me, always seemed of only secondary importance. While my father was assertive, concerned largely with developing his own personality, my mother was a more passive person, who was more focused on serving others. Like my father, she had grown up in Monkscaph but, because she was a couple of years younger, their paths had not crossed until she was 20. Caring for her family had always been an essential part of her life and marriage to my father had given her the opportunity to extend that care to children of her own. I knew,

161

though, that she had been disappointed by their inability to conceive siblings for me. She was generous not only to her family, but to the local community as well. When I was a child she was employed at a small shop in town. It was a simple job but she relished her interactions with customers, becoming known and liked throughout the town for her warm and generous heart. The similarities between my mother and Cipher at that moment were striking.

Yet even though my mother's path through life was a noble one, my father was the one who had always had more of an influence on me. It suddenly struck me that the reason I had been reflecting on this theme was because there was something about my mother's life that I could learn from – something that could help me achieve a greater sense of balance. I realised how much time I had spent preoccupied only with myself and my own personal journey; I knew that now it was time for me to step out of myself and think of others. What my mother's life had taught me was that it was not necessary to abandon the calm, meditative state I had reached in order to do so: even doing something very small was sufficient. I had also learnt from her that I didn't necessarily need to engage in the process of self development and expansion too much either: a warm smile and a friendly word to a passing stranger might be all that was required.

My mother was still on my mind when I took a walk down to Pugnillay later that afternoon. I had no special reason for going; it was almost as though something was deliberately trying to push me back into contact with other people, aiming to lift me out of my isolation and self-absorption. The experience helped me to discover a sense of perspective; I began to see that I was not the only person ever to deal with serious matters of the heart. I knew that many people kept their suffering hidden, but, perhaps because I had spent so much time thinking about my mother and her caring nature, that afternoon I felt somehow able to sense all that was amiss in the hearts of those who crossed my path. For what was quite probably the first time, I looked into the eyes of my fellow human beings with a sense of curiosity about what they were feeling. Of course I had always felt this concern for my close friends and family, but for me to feel the same way about strangers was definitely a new phenomenon.

I decided to investigate this a little further, and, taking a seat in a coffee shop, I began to observe the people surrounding me, as well as those walking by the window. As I did this, I felt my heart urging me to reach out and connect. I saw that if I could adopt my mother's spirit of generosity and start to care about the happiness of others, this would nourish my body and soul, making my life more meaningful in the process. The only question remaining was how I could express this spirit of generosity. Surprisingly, I only had to wait a few minutes for an answer.

Finishing my drink, I continued my walk down the high street, eventually coming to the town's main bookshop – the place I had stumbled upon the book about meditation. This time I didn't go in immediately because the owner had put a long wooden table outside the shop; it contained a whole array of second hand books, which were available at very low prices. The table was blocking half the pavement and, as there was a lady pushing a pram coming the other way, I had to stop and wait for her to pass. Standing there, I noticed a small paper sign stuck on the window next to the door, only just visible above the books stacked in front of it. I don't know why it caught my attention, but I moved closer to take a look and saw that on it there were just three words; Shop Assistant Required.

The sign made me instantly think of my mother and the way she had seen her role as a shop assistant as an opportunity to be generous. I took this as a promising sign and, without further delay, walked inside. I assumed that the teenage girl behind the counter would not be the best person to speak to regarding this, and so I asked her if she could fetch the owner for me. She went to a door at the back of the shop and knocked timidly against the wooden panel. The door opened in a sharp, sudden movement and a stern and spindly man was revealed, wearing a pair of thick-rimmed spectacles perched on the end of his nose. The young girl spoke to him in a tone so timid and quiet that I could not make out the words; the man nodded before looking up in my direction, wearing a quizzical expression. The girl returned to her stool behind the counter, and the owner walked across to greet me politely enough. However, when I asked him about the sign in the window, he looked startled by the question.

'What interest is it to you?' was his blunt response.

'I am looking for work,' was my equally blunt reply.

My presence here seemed to make him suspicious; it appeared that he had expected interest from teenagers – perhaps the elderly as well – but not from people of my age. But after trying unsuccessfully to put me off the idea, he eventually told me, with a sigh, that, as no-one else seemed interested in the job, he would be willing to give me a trial shift to see how I got on. The wages he offered seemed desperately low, though – it was then that I understood why he had been taken aback that someone of my age had been interested in the position. But after briefly considering, I decided that the job would probably earn me just about enough to support myself, especially considering my new simplified lifestyle. I agreed to start the following week.

Although I had found something that would keep me in the area for the foreseeable future, I still felt that I needed to leave my holiday chalet and move somewhere closer to town. I needed a clean break, and was also worried about the feasibility of travelling to and from work each day. Instead of returning home, I decided to act immediately and seek out places that were currently available to rent in the town. I bought a copy of local newspaper, but this only listed one available option: a room in a house just off the main high street. I called the number to check the details and had a pleasant conversation with the owner of the house. He told me that during the week he stayed in a flat in the centre of Sarum, where he worked, and spent only his weekends in Pugnillay. He told me that the room advertised was a self-contained studio flat in the upstairs part of the house. The price he was asking seemed reasonable, so I arranged to meet him the following weekend.

As agreed, I viewed the property and liked it, eventually agreeing a six-month contract. With new accommodation now arranged, my time in the chalet came to an abrupt end. I made the two-hour walk from the chalet into Pugnillay for just one week before moving out. Taking one last walk around the woods before leaving, I felt sad at the prospect of leaving the surroundings that had nourished and served me. But I knew that what I had learnt here would stay in my heart – and at least I wasn't moving too far away.

I settled in quickly. I continued practising meditation in the morning, but the rest of my day became filled with new activities. I fell in love with my new job at the bookshop straight away and soon learnt the owner's particular way of sorting the books. I felt reassured by the proof that my long period of solitude had not adversely affected my social skills and soon built up a good relationship with the owner. It wasn't long before he told me that my trial period was over and that he wanted to offer me the job on a permanent basis. I enjoyed interacting with the customers who came into the shop, and, for the first few weeks, I had no problems putting myself in my mother's shoes and using her style of working as my guidance.

It was not only during the day that I was busy as in the evenings I also sought out different ways to connect with the community and to make myself known in the area. I remembered that my mother had once been a member of a rotary club that had organised community activities and fundraising events; I managed to find a contact for the club in Pugnillay and started attending their weekly meetings. They were running a number of events, for which people could sign up: the first of these was to be a litter pick the following Saturday in the nearby woods. I also discovered that Pugnillay had its own walking group; they met up during the week and would arrange a walk somewhere in the area every Sunday. I also made contact with the local scout group, offering to help out on one of the evenings that they met. Finally, after visiting the local community centre, I signed up for a weekly evening badminton session.

Having filled my diary with all these activities, I now had little time to myself. All these arrangements reminded me a little of the busy time I'd had at the end of the previous year, and I was wary of burning myself out again. However, this schedule did feel a lot lighter. Although I missed the tranquillity and the sense of open-ness that I had enjoyed at the chalet, I did like my new home, especially its big windows which looked out over a small park to-wards woodland. It was nice that the owner was away in Sarum during the week, although our paths rarely crossed even when he was here. Not that he was unpleasant – whenever we did meet our conversations were always warm and friendly.

This new pace of life continued right through October. Despite being so busy, I felt comfortable with the ebb and flow, and my meditation was helping me stay focused and calm. At the same time, directing a lot of my attention outwards gave me a wholesome and nourishing feeling. But alas it was not long before I noticed that something was amiss. For whilst I enjoyed meeting and socialising with a lot of different people during the week, it was proving difficult to establish deep connections and friendships, as most of my interactions were brief and fleeting ones.

Walking alone one Saturday towards the end of November, I started to reflect on why establishing true friendships was proving to be such a challenge. I realised that most of the people I had been coming into contact with in Pugnillay had fairly settled lives. In my head, I thought of them as being like planets on set paths orbiting the sun. While there were moments that I crossed their orbits, I knew it would be hard to build lasting friendships unless I was willing to be pulled into their orbits completely. There seemed no possibility of another person meeting me on my own orbit or of anything spontaneous occurring.

Following this insight, I started to feel a lot more resistance to the idea of making an effort to connect with someone else: it had begun to feel as if it was always down to me to take the initiative. It was not in my nature to always be on the front foot, and it was becoming tiresome to do so. Before long I had begun making excuses to myself so that I wouldn't have to go out after work. The cold, dark nights seemed to encourage this step back. It was hard to regain my sense of initiative and I started, once again, to become entrenched in my isolation. I did, however, continue my work at the bookshop, and, as there were a number of events I had signed up for, I also carried on attending the rotary club. If nothing else, both of these gave me the chance to continue exploring my mother's character and style.

However, we were now coming towards the end of the year, and I knew that there was one event that would really test the limits of my compassion. The biggest event that the rotary club organised was the temporary opening of a soup kitchen to provide for those living on the margins of society. I was willing to help out at this event, and, with perfect timing, just as it was about to start, the bookshop owner closed his shop in order to go away and see his family. The knowledge that I was involved in charitable work at least helped console my mother, who had been upset that her son would be absent from the family gathering for the fourth consecutive year. So, the weekend before the official opening, I helped to set up the temporary kitchen in its usual place in the school hall. I enjoyed being part of a small team and being entrusted with the responsibility for installing the equipment.

Nevertheless, the confidence that had grown while we were setting up completely evaporated the Monday morning we opened. The day started well: I came in early and helped to make a hearty soup by chopping up vegetables. We were expecting a hundred or so people to visit that lunchtime, so there had to be a lot of food. But when the bell had been rung and hordes of people piled into the temporary dining area that we had set up, I immediately felt my energy levels decreasing. I stood behind the serving table, watching anxiously. Many of the people were pushing and shoving to get to the front of the queue. This seemed to trigger old prejudices; I looked furtively, pityingly at the misfits, as society had labelled them. I was unable to give the same friendly polite service that I would normally give to my customers at the bookshop, and this made me feel awful. Whenever I saw someone reaching out to me, their eyes longing to make contact, I would feel uncomfortable and look down at the ladle in my hand. My confidence was shot and, after the queues had died down, I left as quickly as I could, without drawing attention to myself.

The week continued in much the same way; despite my best efforts I was not able to open my heart. One lady in particular both fascinated and troubled me. She came in every day and would always sit in the same seat, away from the others. She always looked lonely and vulnerable, huddling over her bowl of food as though she was trying to get its warmth right into her bones. I thought she was probably not as old as she looked, and she had a ghostly white complexion and dilated pupils, suggesting, to me, that she probably was a drug user. Her deathly pallor was haunting: this was true for me in particular, as it brought back memories of the frozen white body of the prostitute upon whom I had forced myself. That was a memory that still carried a lot of painful emotion with it. However, I was curious as to what could have caused this poor woman to sink so low, but my fear held me back from really engaging with her suffering, even from this safe distance.

But one bright light shone during these dark and gloomy days. The light came in the form of an elderly lady; she was a member of the club and was normally very quiet and unassuming. But, that week, this lady suddenly opened up, revealing a powerful, compassionate heart. She was the one who showed no signs of anxiety or of coldness towards those she met. The way she could transform the atmosphere of a room reminded me of Cipher; like him, she could put people at ease with her lightness of touch. I remember one touching moment in particular: she was sitting with a young man who had seemed sullen and agitated when I had served him, just ten minutes before. Yet now I saw this boy wearing a calm, soft expression, tears streaming down his cheeks; the lady was holding both of his hands in hers and looking into his eyes. This poignant moment was a reminder of the power that compassion could have; I only wished that I could find it in my heart as well.

Intrigued, I wanted to know why this old lady was treating this young man with such love and care. Taking her to one side, I asked her this question. What she told me was surprising: she said that she was drawing on her faith, which helped her to overcome her fears. Registering my interest, she spoke gushingly about the power of prayer; she said that it was this that she relied on for the strength and support she needed to get through each day. This reminded me of the prayers I had made to help me through my first year at Studley, but I still felt surprised at coming across a fully grown adult who believed in their power. Back then, I had not known to whom I was praying; I wondered whether this was the case for her too. The answer I got in return surprised me though: she told me that she was praying to Pantheon.

Chapter Eighteen

Her answer had knocked me a little off balance but, nonetheless, I took a little while to consider whether there could be any truth in the beliefs of this elderly lady and what, if anything, she had to teach me. I had been knocked off balance as I had never before met anyone who spoke about Pantheon as though she was a living entity. But I knew that this woman had been deadly serious in what she said, and that her faith and beliefs were sincere. Feeling that I had stumbled onto sacred territory, I hesitated and refrained from questioning her further. While I pretended to respect her faith, actually I wanted to laugh at her for being so foolish at to believe in an old fairy story. The story in question told the tale of a female deity called Pantheon, who was said to have created the world and ruled over the human kingdom. This story was an important part of the folklore of the ancient civilisation of Arasmas, as I had been taught early on at school, but most people now believed that scientific reasoning had disproved it completely. Pantheon had never again been mentioned by name after I'd reached the age of seven or eight.

Yet, on reflection, I knew without a doubt that this lady's faith was helping her to stretch herself beyond her natural limits; I also knew that I no longer believed in everything I had been taught at school. So if I could not rely on what my teachers had taught me, the only option was to go and explore the stories of my ancestors myself. When the bookshop reopened the following week, I asked the owner whether I could borrow his books if I always returned them the following morning, thus ensuring they remained available to sell. He reluctantly agreed, and I began to search through the relevant section of the store, making a list of all the books I found on the subject of these ancient myths and legends.

But no matter how much I tried to accept possibility that these legends might have some truth to them, I could not fully let go of the rigorous, intellectual worldview that was the legacy of my education: I needed hard evidence, not just fanciful stories. One day, as I was reading, I felt inspired to take a look at one supposed piece of evidence, and so, on the spur of the moment, I decided to take a day away from the town in order to visit Sarum's old centre of worship. I was drawn to this place in particular because I knew that it was one of the few remaining centres of worship that hadn't been abandoned and neglected and that was still open to the public. Maybe it was there that I would find the evidence that I needed.

By now, it was getting towards the end of January, and, arriving in the city after a long, slow train journey, I headed straight in the direction of the ancient building. There was a cold wind blowing outside, and, inside, the old stone building was draughty. I took a seat in one of the pews and tried to connect to the peaceful energy that I knew must exist in a place that had been a centre of worship for hundreds of years, even if it was not currently one. But, although it'd been neglected for three hundred years, it seemed to me as if the walls still carried distant echoes of prayers within them; it was an easy place for me to slip into a state of calm meditation. I looked around me and, while doing so, noticed and marvelled at the incredible intricacies and hidden details of this vast and incredible building. If I had needed any evidence of what faith in Pantheon could achieve, I found it here.

Before my eyes was a building that had taken nearly one hundred years to build. I thought about the huge number of people who must have been involved creating a piece of architecture like this and realised that these people must have had a very deep sense of faith to carry out this great act of service, especially considering that many of those involved knew they would not live to see its completion. I felt profoundly sad that this magnificent building was these days dismissed as the work of a backward civilisation and that all the love and devotional care that went into its creation had not been enough to inspire our generation to maintain the building as a house of prayer.

Sitting there in this moment, I felt deeply embarrassed of our modern ways and our impatient desire to do things instantaneously. Who in our time would conceive such a project and who in our time would be willing to put vast sums of money into a building that had no functional purpose and would offer no financial return? Most importantly of all, who would be willing to sacrifice their whole career to work on a project that would not be completed? This was a labour of love, a demonstration of a spirit of generous service. I felt angry and frustrated that my education had denied me access to something that would have given me strength and patience, would have enabled me to devote myself to the callings of my heart rather than my head.

I felt a strong desire to put my faith in Pantheon, wanting to be inflamed with burning passion, but knew that it would be a fruitless exercise even to consider. For, as I travelled back to Pugnillay, I sensed ominous doubts surfacing from the recesses of my mind. These doubts principally concerned themselves with Cipher and his relationship with his mother. Was Pantheon just another rock, something for people to depend upon and to blindly follow in the same way that Cipher had done with his mother?

I did notice one key distinction, however: namely, that Cipher's mother was merely mortal whereas Pantheon was considered to be immortal. This meant that, by believing in Pantheon, it was possible to go through a whole lifetime without having to endure any of the sort of pain that Cipher had suffered when his own mother had passed away. Perhaps the belief that an omnipresent, loving entity was here supporting them was what had given these older civilisations solace – after all death and illness had been much more a part of life in those days. I sensed that the need to believe in the old stories and have faith in Pantheon had become redundant as mankind gradually discovered that they could control and overcome nature's rhythms and found ways to put the human kingdom at the very centre of the universe.

All these reflections led me to think about my mother again; I wondered where she had drawn the strength to enable her to be so generous. Only when I arrived home did I receive an answer. For what I realised was that the spirit of generosity was not something she had acquired through faith; quite the opposite, in fact: she had acquired it through reason alone. Like my father she had grown up in a large family, one of seven siblings; but, intriguingly, her reaction to the situation in which she found herself had been very different. Whereas my father felt that, in order to have his needs met, he needed to become independent, my mother learnt that generosity was a more effective way of achieving fulfilment, because it brought her the love and appreciation of those who received her gifts. I was certain that, because this had been so successful in her childhood, she had continued to employ it right through her adult life – and was still doing so.

This sudden realisation hit me hard: the implication was that her generosity was just a veil she had worn in order to belong, and so wasn't an authentic generosity of spirit, as I had hoped it was.

The startling truth was that, in order for this strategy to succeed, she was dependent on the other person taking the role of the willing receiver. It was no wonder that she had found it hard to let go when I left for university, and still finds it hard to let go of me even today: it was because after I discovered my independence, I was no longer willing to play this role of willing receiver. It was unnerving to think how her strength and confidence must have diminished the day I had relinquished this role in her life.

So where did all this leave me? In truth, what I had learnt today left me feeling shattered and exhausted. I had seen that faith and a generous spirit could be a powerful force for good in the world but also that these forces could be used by weak-minded people merely wishing to reduce their own feelings of insecurity. Whether this took the form of Cipher, whose faith came from a deludingly optimistic mother; or those people who carried out a labour of love on behalf of an illusion; or my mother, whose apparent generosity stemmed from the roots of a cold-blooded strategy; it made no difference.

This was a depressing conclusion to have reached; the clear perception I had enjoyed during my time living in the forest suddenly seemed a long way away. Disillusionment set in as February began; I retreated more and more into a quiet inner space, having completely lost any remaining desire to join in with any of the   activities in which I had been interested during the previous autumn. I even stopped signing up for events at the rotary club, and my enthusiasm for working in the bookshop began to wane as well.

Not only was I feeling disillusioned, but I also sensed that I was entering a spell of transition. Well aware that I only had just over a month left on my lease, I felt that my time in Pugnillay was coming to a close. But I had no new ideas about what to do next, and my new found-cynicism was filling all my thoughts with negativity and gloom. I could not hear the call of my heart, and I seemed to be losing my faith that I would be able to piece together this puzzle together and create a stable, meaningful life for myself. There was still a part of me that just wanted to give up and return back to a life of ignorance, where I wouldn't have to grapple with all these big, and often confusing, questions that had no clear and fixed answers to them. The pieces of the puzzle just didn't together into a coherent picture.

As I pondered this gloomy thought, I remembered what the wise old man on the shore of Lake Lawdi had said: how I wasn't strong enough to get out of my head and take the leap of faith that would help me to discover why it was I was a human being, not just another pebble on the shore. I had taken his stinging words to heart and had sought out this gift of Satya that he had spoken of, but felt that I had got no closer to understanding exactly what was involved. Maybe he had been right to tell me that I wasn't strong enough to embark upon this journey: I failed to see that what I had now was any better than what I had had before.

<u>**Part III**</u>

Chapter Nineteen

I had only three weeks to go before my lease ran out, but I was no closer to figuring out what my next steps would be. But yet again, with perfect timing, something emerged to get me out of the rut in which I was stuck. It happened on the Friday, at the end of a long afternoon of work. I had been restless and bored all day, trade had been slow and I was eager to get out and enjoy my two days of freedom. It had been like this for a while: by Friday afternoon I would be longing to finish and then on Sunday evening I would be dreading work the next day. Looking up at the clock, I realised that it had been almost half an hour since anyone had come into the shop and that there was still more than an hour to go until closing time. To help pass the time I decided to take some of the new books, which we had received that morning, out of their boxes and to arrange them like a pyramid on the display table.

Not long afterwards a young boy walked in. He was barely into adolescence, and I could not help looking at him with suspicion. The mischievous look in his eyes made me feel wary; it was strange also that, after entering, he did nothing apart from staring at a row of books, his hands in his pockets. After a while, he walked over to the display table, as though it had suddenly grabbed his attention. For a while, he just stood there motionless, surveying the arrangement. At last, he leaned forwards – to pick up a title, I assumed – but instead of reaching for one of the books at the summit of the display, he reached for one at the base. Grabbing at it violently, he sent the rest of the books tumbling across the table; a couple fell down onto the floor. Before I could react, he had taken a brief look at the back cover and calmly put it back on the table. Without flinching, he turned swiftly on his heels and walked out of the shop, ignoring the evil glare that I sent in his direction. My patience had finally run out, and, as I went over to pick up the books off the floor, I muttered to myself about how demeaning and meaningless my life had become.

I arrived home that evening still consumed with feelings of helplessness and frustration. I felt compelled to leave the flat in order to visit one of the local bars. Having spent too much time with only my morbid thoughts for company, I was desperate for a change of scenery. When I arrived at the town's most upmarket bar, I resisted the temptation to buy something alcoholic and, instead, asked the barmaid for a coffee. I could see that she was a little surprised by my request, for it was Friday evening – a time when a lot of young people were out socialising and partying. It was hardly the best time to go for a quiet drink alone, although, as it happened, at such an early time of the evening the bar was relatively empty and there were plenty of spare seats.

While waiting for my drink to be brought over, I was distracted by the sound of a stool scraping on the stone floor. Suddenly, I realised that two people had stood either side of me. Puzzled, I looked around, seeing a man to the left of me and another man on my right, both with their gazes fixed towards the bar. I didn't recognise either man, and, somehow, they didn't fit in with the surroundings. My coffee arrived and I turned to walk away from the bar area, looking for a quiet place to sit. It was then that the man on my left spoke, in a quiet, almost inaudible tone.

'We know what it is that you are going through.'

I turned back around, facing the man squarely, but, puzzlingly, his gaze was still directed away into the distance, and it seemed like he hadn't been speaking to me at all. But, just as I was about to say something, he repeated himself, as though to make what he had said absolutely clear.

Still unsure whether he was talking to me or not, I hesitated just long enough for the man on my right to collect his change from the barmaid. When he had done this, he turned and asked me to join them both for a drink. Dazed, but curious, I nodded my head and followed them over to a vacant table by the window. Both men had long black coats that fell past their knees and gave them a sinister look that was quite out of keeping with their surroundings. They sat next to one another, backs to the window, and gestured for me to sit opposite. It was only then that I was able to look them in the eyes. I saw that although both men were coming to the end of middle age, they were neat and well-groomed. The man who had spoken to me had thick black hair which was slicked backwards behind his ears; he wore a pair of spectacles, which were perched at the end of his nose. His head was tilted, and he was staring at me, with an inquisitive air. The second man had long flowing grey locks that fell back past the nape of his neck, a high forehead and a long, drawn face; his wrinkled skin already showed some of the blemishes of age.

As both men drank there was a long, drawn-out silence, which only made the atmosphere more tense. My drink was too hot for me to able to copy them, and I felt that I was being kept waiting on purpose. This only intensified the feelings of frustration that had been bothering me since finishing work. Eventually, the second man slowly leant forwards and started speaking, in a manner that did not seem especially welcoming.

'Good evening, Myrkais. Can I begin by congratulating you for the courage you have shown so far. It is this that has proven to us that you are worthy to hear what it is we have to say.'

Feeling incredulous, I was unable to restrain myself from blurting out a shocked, hostile and not too pleasant retort.

'How on earth do you know my name, let alone anything about the nature of my character?'

With a smile that revealed badly stained teeth, he responded.

'Please excuse my abruptness; I didn't intend to alarm you. We've been watching you for some time now and we believe that you are ready to hear what we have to tell you. It is clear to me that you are feeling a sense of frustration with the world in which you find yourself. You are not alone, Myrkais. Many are suffering, but there are also many who are taking that frustration and energy and using it to end the struggle of mankind, once and for all. We feel that it is time for you to join them in this work; but only you can decide whether or not you are prepared to take this one final step of your journey.'

His words made me feel extremely agitated: I was tired of people talking to me in vague riddles laced with false promises and false hope.

'I am not interested,' I said abruptly, before taking a sip of my drink.

Both men looked surprised, as if they had never encountered such hostility and resistance before. The first man simply ignored me, sticking to his pre-prepared speech.

I surprised myself with my assertiveness, interrupting him as he was in full flow and speaking firmly.

'Look, I don't wish to be rude, but I just want to have a quiet drink by myself. I really don't want to have to deal with this. I don't know why you have taken the trouble to stalk me, but please just go.'

Finally they seemed to understand, and, seeing that they were not being listened to, they both got up to leave. However, before leaving, the first man reached into his coat pocket, pulled out a tiny black leather-bound book and dropped it onto the table, saying:

'Can we at least leave you this to read? We truly think that you will find it useful. We'll give you time to digest the contents and have a think before coming back to collect it.'

I did not answer, and they left. But when I had finished my drink, I found that my temper had cooled a little. Softening, I picked up the book they had left and looked at the front cover. 'The Modern World: By Joseph Krugman' was spelled out in small gold letters, badly faded. Although I felt no urge to read it at that moment, I didn't see what harm could come from keeping it, and put it in my pocket. The bar was now filling up with Friday evening crowds; I took this as my cue to leave. When I got home, I dropped the book down onto the sideboard and decided to ignore it completely.

It took until Sunday lunchtime for my mood to lift enough for me to realise that no harm could come from reading a few words. So, putting the book in my pocket, I took a long walk through the woods, enjoying the pleasant, warm, early spring weather. There was a picnic area that I often went to, and, when I arrived there, I sat down in a bench bathed with sunlight. I started leafing through this little book, the poison of cynicism still flowing through my veins.

Eventually, taking a deep breath, I started to become aware of the sights and smells of nature that were all around me; this helped me to finally settle down and to concentrate on reading. The book was very short – barely fifty pages – and did not take me long to finish. It was split into three chapters. The first was the shortest: it gave details about the eighteenth century, the turning point in Arasmas' history. Krugman described this as the point where Arasmas changed from being a society built on faith to one built on reason. I had no problems understanding this, as it was closely related to much of my recent reading matter.

I had more difficulty grasping the second and third chapters, and, in the end, was forced to read most of the text for a second time. The second chapter focused on how daily life in Arasmas over the following two or three hundred years had been impacted by these gradual changes, placing particular emphasis on changes in the political and economic structures; while the third chapter described some of the negative consequences that Krugman believed had resulted from these changes. He had some particularly cutting things to say about our modern education system.

Feeling I had grasped the meaning of Krugman's book, I decided to leave my quiet spot in the sunshine and begin walking again. The natural rhythm of walking helped me to gradually absorb the nuances of this book. Some of Krugman's opinions kept revolving through my mind. What I was struck by the most was the idea that the inner conflict I had been experiencing over the past few years was fundamentally of the same type as the outer conflicts that marred daily life in our modern world. Hearing this did reassure me that the issues I was grappling with were not restricted to me alone, but were inherent parts of the modern collective consciousness.

It also boosted my confidence to read that the difficult journey of self-discovery on which I had embarked was a journey which all human beings would have to make at some point in their lives. Krugman firmly believed that this was the only way to resolve the pressing issues that were affecting our lives. But Krugman said that the reason that most people were afraid to take this journey was because our education system actively discouraged it. He lamented the spiritual desert that is the modern world, and how the only things that were valued these days were cheap, quick and practical; people now had neither the time nor the patience to savour the things that give life real meaning and joy, he observed. This lament seemed to be at the heart of his message.

Reading his points of view did help to shift my perspective a little. Up to that point, I had genuinely believed that I was the only person in the world who was plagued by this anxiety about the direction of their life. Although I had learnt that everyone I knew was wearing a veil of some kind, I had never before considered that all of us had to find a way to rip it off and to find a purpose beyond the human instinct to fit in and belong. Even someone like Jen, who seemed so comfortable with her life, needed to give it all up and undertake a journey of self-discovery. I felt angry when I thought about Krugman's belief that our world was deliberately designed to make this journey as difficult as possible to undertake.

The more I pondered, the more Krugman's words seemed to make sense. The method he used to explain his ideas also helped me to understand: he did so by making a clear distinction between the right and left hemisphere of the brain. His research had shown that people, both individuals and society as a whole, need to find not a healthy balance between the two hemispheres, but a healthy relationship in which the left hemisphere is the servant and the right its master. In the second chapter he had explained that our modern world was created out of the left hemisphere alone. This meant that we were able to create a very functional and highly efficient world for ourselves but, in doing so, we neglected the part of the brain that allows us to reach a deeper understanding and wisdom of who we are and what we are doing.

This was why he thought the education system should be reformed: at the moment children's education was purely left-hemisphere based. They were being trained to be nothing more than functional machines. Reading his angry observations about how large parts of this training simply involved memorising reams and reams of useless information that were to be regurgitated in examinations so that children could prove how meek and dutiful they were, I sensed that Krugman felt a lot of anger about his own education. I also picked up a hint of sadness and regret when he wrote that he felt that, nowadays, a school was not there to help a child to grow or develop the right hemisphere of the brain at all. Laconically, he wrote about the ways in which modern world dismissed pursuits of the right hemisphere such as art, poetry, religion; also belittling the value of the noble qualities of wisdom, love, compassion, tolerance and understanding. Turning all this over in my mind, it suddenly struck me that meditation had been a way for me to reconnect with and develop my own right hemisphere so that I could live a fuller and more meaningful life.

I continued with my walk and the more these thoughts sank in, the more I regained my confidence that my decision to leave my old life behind had been the right one. I don't know why the lucid words of this complete stranger had been so helpful, but I was grateful for them. However, the book did not conclude on this positive note; the third chapter ended in what I felt was very dark territory. For, having explained that we are preoccupied with solving our problems using only the left hemisphere, he then went on to explain that when we approach life in this way the set of problems increase to infinity. Krugman said that the reason for this was that most of the big problems we face as human beings can never be solved by the left hemisphere alone, and that trying to do so only makes the situation worse. He claimed that for each problem that the left hemisphere solves, it creates a dozen more. Instead of the modern age making our lives simpler, Krugman argued that it had in fact done completely the opposite - our lives now were far more complex than those of our ancestors.

These words of warning had haunted me, and recalling them now sent a shiver down my spine. For Krugman had lamented that this complexity had not arisen by accident; indeed, he believed that the human race was now diseased because we spend our lives in this fragmented and meaningless world full of dysfunction and disorder. We had become a cancer that was killing the world that supported us; he had concluded that this was the price we paid for emphasising the importance of one part of the brain and ignoring the other.

However, while I found the book stimulating and thought-provoking, there was something about this last conclusion that made me feel uneasy. For, by the time I got home, the negative ideas with which the book finished were making me feel depressed. I needed to find some release and was immediately drawn to my little black notebook. I now kept it in the side pocket of my rucksack, which I kept under my bed. This time my writing covered six pages and, once again, it flowed, ending and beginning again with each new page.

Afterwards, I felt a little clearer but still didn't know exactly what to think. I was left with an uncomfortable feeling about Krugman's message and also about the two men who had given me the book. I guessed that my feelings of discomfort were partly down to their air of secrecy and partly my suspicion that there was something very sinister about this mysterious mission.

It wasn't only the secrecy that bothered me: a lot of my discomfort was due to the absence of any solutions in Krugman's book. True, he may have accurately described the state of the world, but he offered no suggestions as to what I could do to improve this grim picture he'd painted. I could not yet trust these two men, although I did still wonder about what exactly it was they were proposing. Essentially, I was feeling sceptical of these new, apparently appealing, avenues; I felt that, as had happened before, they would turn out to be deceptive and false. I needed to be reassured that this mission was the right thing for me to do.

Taking a deep breath, I allowed some of my feelings of pessimism to fade. While doing so, I realised that there was a tiny part of me that was still struck by the co-incidence that this book had fallen into my lap at just the moment when all avenues seemed closed to me. Despite my feelings of cynicism and overwhelming sense of hopelessness, there was still a fire of curiosity burning inside of me, and the willingness to discover, albeit slightly reluctantly, exactly what it was that these men had to offer.

Chapter Twenty

I spent much of the following morning at home sitting on my couch watching the drizzle outside. The weather seemed to reflect my mood: I experienced many grey Monday mornings of the soul recently, and it had been a struggle to rouse myself to walk even the short distance to work. Eventually I heard the front doorbell ring, and, as I was sure that the owner had already left, I went to answer it. I walked quickly downstairs to the side door that was my own private entrance into the house and went around the front to see who was there. Standing there was a petite young woman with bright blue eyes and short blonde hair. Before I had the chance to tell her that the owner had gone away for the week, she told me that she had come to collect the book I had been given. I noticed that parked in front of the house was a car – an expensive four-wheel drive – with its engine running. I hurried back upstairs to collect the book; she followed as far as the side door and stood there waiting.

On my return, I immediately handed the book to her. She asked whether reading the book had softened my resistance, then invited me to join her in the waiting car. It was clearly time for me to decide. I had been caught slightly off guard: I was not expecting to be pushed for an answer quite so soon. She must have seen how taken aback I was because she went on to tell me, in a more gentle tone, that I didn't have to make any commitments at that moment. She just wanted to know if I was open to learning more about the mission. Feeling reassured, I decided that satisfying my curiosity would be worthwhile so went back in to get my keys. Only when I was back in my flat did I remember about work. Struck by this thought, I took my phone with me as I went back outside and asked the lady how long I would be away, so that I could inform my boss of this. "A few days" was the surprising answer.

She got in the car, and I reluctantly made the call. The only excuse I was able to come up with was that my mother had been taken sick over the weekend and that, because of this, I needed to go to see her for a few days. I knew that for my boss family always came first so I thought that he would be sympathetic and unlikely to question me about it too much. My excuse seemed to convince him; the call was a short one. I walked back to the car and took a seat in the back. As I was getting into the car I noticed that the windows were tinted, preventing me from looking inside. This only strengthened my impression of the mission as being a mysterious and sinister one. I was surprised to find that the two men I had met in the bar the previous Friday were not in the car. Alongside me in the back sat a man and a woman, neither of whom I had ever seen before. Neither paid me any attention; it seemed that their thoughts were elsewhere.

In silence we travelled northwards along the main highway that connected Pugnillay with Sarum. It was the tail end of the rush hour so the roads were fairly quiet and we made good progress. But before we got to Sarum, we turned off the highway and drove into a town I was unfamiliar with. It sat near the southern edge of Sarum, near the city boundary, but, surprisingly, was very different from the new dormitory settlements full of commuters and their families. Driving through an old disused industrial estate, I realised that this place belonged to the old world instead. We passed down a wide, empty road; a complex of large, imposing brick factory buildings stood on one side of the road, perhaps an old printing works. I started to wonder where exactly we were going, and I felt slightly anxious when we slowed down and stopped outside a rusty iron door, set into the brickwork of one of the buildings. Turning around, the driver told us to get out and wait. Someone would come and meet us, she said.

I was the first one out of the door; the other two followed, and I shut the door behind us. The car immediately made a sharp U-turn and drove away at speed, leaving me wondering what would happen next. In silence we all gazed at the locked iron door, waiting for it to open. It wasn't long before it did just that, and, facing us on the other side, we saw a tall, blonde-haired lady wearing a short skirt and high heels. She gestured for us to follow her inside.

We followed her down a narrow corridor and through a complex maze of passageways. It seemed that we were being taken to the very core of the old warehouse. We kept up a brief pace; only halting when we came to a large, imposing oval door. With an air of confidence, our guide stepped forward and rapped sharply on the steel panel. Then, without waiting for a reply, she opened it in a swift motion and let the three of us walk through before gently closing it behind us. We now stood in a cavernous room; its ceiling must have been over 30 foot high. For a moment, the three of us stood clustered together, struck by the contrast with the cramped, claustrophobic passages we had been walking along just before.

Eventually my eyes came to rest upon a woman sitting expectantly behind a grand white marbled desk on the other side of the room. We walked forward in unison, but in a tentative and apprehensive way and acutely unsure of what was expected from us. She smiled warmly, obviously trying to put us at ease, although her booming voice had the opposite jarring effect.

'I hope you are all having a very good morning,' she bellowed, arms gesturing towards three chairs before her. 'Would you care for some tea?'

I immediately responded in the affirmative and stepped forward to take a seat. The other two followed my lead, and, with a nod of her head, our host pressed a buzzer on the corner of the desk, bringing a nervous assistant scampering into the room. She ordered him to make us a pot of tea. As we awaited his return, our host led us over to the corner of the room, where there was a tank of tropical fish. We watched the fish and she tried to engage us in idle talk, obviously trying to get us to relax. But, having spent the journey here in complete silence, none of us seemed ready to talk much. So after her assistant had returned and poured out four mugs of tea, we walked back to our seats, and, without a moment's hesitation, she plunged straight into the topic which was on all of our minds.

'I can tell that you're nervous, but I wish to reassure you that I am not here to test you. Our spotters have already confirmed that you are fit to hear about our mission. My name is Drayton; I've been working in this warehouse for the past five years; my role is to act as gatekeeper. I will ensure that you will pass safely through to our court and our teachers, if this is what you wish.

'I trust that the three of you have read Krugman's book, which sets out the terms of reference for our mission. I am aware, however, that the book is difficult to understand at points and that you will want to ask some questions before making a decision about whether or not you will continue this journey. I will try to answer any questions that you have.'

The first question came from the lady sitting next to me.

'I found the book fascinating; I'd like to know more about when it was written and about the author.'

Drayton nodded her head approvingly, sipped her tea, and immediately responded.

'I was not fortunate enough to meet Joseph Krugman myself but have talked to a lot of people who were. Joseph was a very intelligent man, and received a good education. But he was an outsider, and, as such, was someone who was prepared to ask some searching questions of the society of the time. The more he delved into the past, the more different events seemed from how he had been taught to see them. During the 1960s he channelled his rebellious energy into writing this little book.

'Unfortunately, Joseph was also extremely naïve – the caution and secrecy with which we operate is due to the lessons we learnt from his experiences. For, initially, Joseph thought that it would be possible to publish and sell the book, but events seemed to conspire against him. To start with, things looked promising: he found a publisher who was willing to print his work. But halfway through the printing process, the publishing company suddenly went bankrupt. The books that had already been printed were being taken to Joseph by a delivery truck when the vehicle somehow came off the road and burst into flames, killing the driver and burning all the remaining copies to a cinder. Fortunately, Joseph had kept a few copies of the book before sending it to be printed, but these two incidents made him wary of contacting another publisher. Instead, he simply disappeared without a trace, along with his meagre possessions. It was a blessing that, before going, he had decided to leave a couple of copies of his work with a trusted friend. Thanks to her endeavours, his message slowly spread, and a community of followers blossomed. We are members of that rapidly expanding community.'

I had been listening intently, but was suddenly struck by the realisation that Drayton had stopped abruptly and appeared reluctant to say something about what exactly the community wanted to achieve. Was it this lack of information that was the cause of my doubts, I wondered. Was this community of followers only dedicated to publicising Krugman's warnings or was there something bigger? But something was stopping me from asking Drayton this obvious question. The other man filled the silence by asking the next question:

'If you are implying that Krugman was killed for trying to tell people about his discovery, then isn't it suicidal to follow in his footsteps?'

'That is possibly so,' Drayton replied. 'I can offer no guarantees that this it will not be risky. But, as you will already appreciate, we now operate with greater caution and we also now have greater strength in numbers, so you would be more protected. But I cannot lie to you by saying that there isn't significant risk involved. What you have to ask yourself is whether you really want to go back and follow one of the other two paths that are available; either accepting a false reality and living in ignorance, or rejecting it and struggling on the fringes of society. Are those two choices really viable for you now? Can you embrace the third option – being part of a revolution that is trying to change things completely? But, at the end of the day, it is your decision; if you choose to walk away we will not hold it against you. Perhaps it would be best for me to leave you to think about this,'

The gentleman who had just spoken said confidently that he didn't need any more time to decide and Drayton nodded her head respectfully. The woman also put herself forward without hesitation. However I did not wilt under the pressure to conform and insisted on being given more time to decide.

'Very well, Myrkais, I will give you more time to decide; you can stay here for a while. Just press the buzzer when you are ready to leave. If you're still not sure you can always stay here for a few days while you come to a decision; we will not be moving from here until Friday.'

'Where are you taking us on Friday?' I asked, feeling curious.

'To an induction gathering. We hold one when we have enough new recruits. This will give you a better idea of how we are trying to spread Krugman's message. Even during the gathering you will still be able to leave freely, so do not feel that you have to make a final decision now. All I need is for you to commit to join us for this event.'

With that, Drayton rose. She and the other two left the room, leaving me alone. I got to my feet and walked across to the fish tank that stood in a corner of the room. Staring into the tank, I felt envious of the fish and couldn't help but wish that I had a similarly limited memory. Their life in this glass cage seemed no different from mine apart from the fact that I was fully conscious of my nightmare. I still had plenty of unanswered questions, but there was something about the gatekeeper that I didn't trust and so I didn't want to seek more information from her. The whole introduction had been far too brief for my liking and she hadn't seemed very forthcoming. But, at the same time, I was intrigued to find out whether this gathering might answer some of my questions. Anyway, if it turned out to be just another false dawn, then I would surely be able to walk away, I thought.

One thing that she said had affected me though: her comment that I could no longer fight alone against the world. She was right, of course; the idea of fighting for revolution as part of a community was an attractive one. I needed a new cause to fight for, and maybe the motivation for me to act could be provided by the anger that Krugman's words had stirred. But, despite this, I still felt a need to be reassured. Was this truly a just cause? It seemed that, at the moment at least, I had no choice but to dive in and see where the journey would lead me.

Feeling my resistance melt, I breathed a heavy sigh, looked up to the high ceiling and scratched my chin. I took one last look back down into the clear glass bowl before walking back to the desk and pressing the buzzer. The assistant I had seen earlier promptly appeared, and I informed him briskly that I wished to stay. He nodded once and then led me along the corridor and up two flights of rusty iron stairs. I was shown into a small room, with a bare concrete floor, containing nothing more than a single bed and a table. I was told to stay here until the gatekeeper came back and so, while I waited, I lay down on the soft, sagging mattress.

Four nights followed that were possibly the longest I had ever known. When the gatekeeper came back she had told me that I needed to stay in this room and not wander through the building. She showed me an alarm that I could press if I needed any urgent assistance, and explained that there was a toilet and shower at the end of the corridor. I was then told that her assistant would bring us our meals throughout the day. As she was telling me this, I had an urge to reply angrily, indignant at being forced to live in a place so similar to a prison. But, before I could do so, she spoke soothingly, encouraging me to be patient and explaining that, if I was to be kept safe, these measures were essential. After she departed, all I had for company was a copy of Krugman's book, which she had left in case I wanted to re-read it. I didn't see Drayton again until the day I left.

On the first day I spent in the room I had only a meagre lunch. Sitting down on the bed after I had eaten, I began to question why the gatekeeper had brought us here so far in advance of the induction gathering. Why had I allowed myself to be persuaded into staying here? But my meditation practice helped me to understand that these thoughts were just clouds in the sky: my mind was struggling to find a logical and rational explanation of why I had put myself in this situation. I tried using this time to test myself. How long could I rest quietly in this place where there was no certainty or control and where nothing made sense? The answer was not long; I quickly wore through my thin layer of patience and became agitated and restless. Was this test of endurance designed to see how committed I was to becoming a member of the community, I wondered. For, aside from the assistant, who came three times a day, I saw no-one else in this part of the building. The other two guests were evidently being kept elsewhere. Since Drayton had mentioned that the induction days were run only when enough recruits had been found, I wondered whether other guests were being held in the building as well. Perhaps there were gatehouses right across Arasmas that the community used.

Finally, Friday morning arrived and I was awoken at an unearthly hour; it was still dark outside. I didn't know what time of day it was but, after I had breakfast, the assistant told me that I needed to be ready to leave in 20 minutes. Drayton herself came to collect me. She led me downstairs, where I was surprised to find myself amongst at least a dozen others. They were all waiting by the door through which we had come on our arrival. Among the nervous faces, I saw the two people I had travelled with a few days earlier. I caught the lady's eye and smiled; her face softened as she smiled back. We stood there waiting for a while. Finally, Drayton received a message on her phone and immediately turned to open the door. We walked out into the chilly morning air, noticing a large black minibus waiting. Drayton wished us well, and we filed past and climbed aboard the minibus. I was the last to take my seat and I closed the door behind me. Drayton gave the driver some instructions before sending us on our way. As we drove through the empty streets of the town I struggled to keep my eyes open and, before long, was fast asleep again.

Only when the sun started to rise to the left side of the vehicle was I able to get my bearings. I worked out that we must be heading south. Once we had turned off the main highway, I didn't have a clue where we were; the driver seemed to be steering clear of main roads. We drove along winding country roads and I gazed absent-mindedly through the window at the limited views visible over the top of the hedge line. We must have driven for at least two or three hours, although no clock was available for me to check this. I guessed that we could not be too far away from Pugnillay for we were travelling through a forested landscape. However, the forests to the south of Sarum were vast and so it was difficult to know precisely where we were. Eventually the narrow, winding road gave way to a gravel track that twisted through a wild, untamed landscape. Then, rather abruptly, our driver turned down a rutted fire track that quickly rose steeply ahead of us. As we drove, I thought how fortunate it was that we'd had a dry winter because the minibus would have struggled if this track had been muddy. Our driver seemed to know the route instinctively, not pausing at any of the many forks in the road that we came to. Finally, the minibus came to a clearing. I was surprised to see three minibuses and four small jeeps there already. We parked alongside them on a flat grassy patch and climbed out of the vehicle. Our driver then led us silently along a footpath for at least a mile before we saw wood smoke rising up into the canopy of the forest. Coming abruptly to a second clearing, we saw a number of small white canvas shelters gathered around one large tent in the middle; these had clearly been set up specifically to house this induction gathering.

At the entrance of the main tent, an elderly, white-haired man was sat at a wooden trestle table; he took down our personal details as we filed past. Entering the room, I was quite surprised to see that there were at least thirty people gathered inside, although this still represented only about half of the arena's capacity. Long wooden benches that were laid out in orderly rows and a raised podium stood at the front. I wondered when all this had been set up, for I assumed that these tents could not be left up permanently. I walked through to take a seat, and like everyone else, looked expectantly towards the stage. The room was tense and silent as we waited; no-one struck up a conversation with their neighbour. Finally, after a couple more groups had arrived to fill the last remaining seats, the people at the back started to stand up, as though they had seen someone important come in. I stood up too, and in walked a tall, though frail, elderly lady. Her hair was white and wispy and she must have been at least 70. Arriving on the stage, she gestured for the crowd to sit. Although her manner was timid and quiet as she greeted us, her voice was booming.

'Good morning and welcome to you all. Thank you for agreeing to come and listen to us today, in this wonderful setting. I trust that you all had a pleasant and safe journey and that our gatekeepers have been looking after you well. My name is Kerala. I was one of the first to hear Krugman's words, and, over the years that have followed I have continued to study that wise little book and tried to follow its teaching. My length of service is the reason that I am talking to you today, and I hope that, like I did, you will make the commitment to join our community. But I must warn you that it will not be easy; that this commitment should not be made if you have a faint heart. The battle will be as much against yourself as against the systems that are designed to keep us in bondage. However, the harder the challenge, the greater the rewards and, believe me, the fruits of my years of study and practice are extremely sweet. What I find especially pleasing is seeing more and more people coming into contact with our message as time goes on. I want you to appreciate that you are here at an important time: the revolution is finally beginning to take hold.'

Continuing in the same rousing vein, she eventually built to a crescendo that brought everyone to their feet, clapping in excitement. However, while I joined in with the applause, I couldn't help but look around me and wonder what I'd become a part of. For, cynically, I'd noted that Kerala's opening words still provided no details. I had not received the reassurance I was craving and felt wary and doubtful – although I seemed to be the only one who felt this way. All the people around me had the same crazy look in their eyes, and I wondered why it was that everyone else was convinced by this cult's message.

As the morning progressed, a number of other community members gave talks in the smaller tents; I was left to flitter in and out of these as I pleased. Most talked about the sacrifices they had made in joining the community but, frustratingly, it felt to me like they had been warned not to give any details about the life and work of the community. I was enthused by the passionate way that these speakers described the leaps of faith they had made, but nothing they said helped get rid of my doubts. All I wanted was for them to talk about the present rather than the past – I also wanted them to say something about everyday life. Although I wasn't intimidated by being surrounded by a group of believers, I still could not bring myself to stand up and express my concerns. So when the morning's proceedings came to a close and the lunch bell sounded, I still felt a strong sense of resistance to the ideas of the community.

We were led back into the main tent, where a lunch table had been set up. There were a wide range of salads and hot potatoes, and a large saucepan of steaming hot soup stood at the far end. We had eaten so early that morning that I had felt famished all through the proceedings – even the biscuits I had eaten during the morning break had not filled me up. I filled my plate with food and took a bowl of soup as well, then went to sit on a bench and started eating. I kept to myself during the break; I didn't feel tempted to talk to people sitting nearby. When I had finished eating, knowing I had a few minutes left before the afternoon session started, I went to sit outside. Here I listened to more members sharing their experiences and, once again, I felt left with more questions than answers.

Then the bell rang and we went back inside to start the afternoon session. Kerala came back on the main stage for the final segment of the afternoon. The room fell silent as she spoke, for she'd quickly earned the respect of her audience.

'Today you should have got some idea from our members

about the amount of faith you will need in order to commit to our cause, and so I need to ask you to make a final decision before we leave here. If you do not decide to join our community then we will let you go, as we trust that what you've heard here today will not be repeated to your family or friends. Do not feel pressured to do anything you are not comfortable with. We would rather you speak now than later, as something will happen very soon that will make it difficult for people to leave safely. So if you wish to leave please make yourself known.'

Kerala fell silent and bowed her head. This was my moment; panicked, I could feel my heart beating fast. My mind was screaming at me to let go of all my doubt and frustration by simply standing up and walking out. I felt as though everyone in the room was looking at me and telling me to leave. Yet, as Kerala continued to hold the silence, something strange happened inside of me that left me frozen to my seat. For it was at this moment that I heard a voice, which didn't sound like my own, speaking kindly to me. This voice told me in a soothing tone that there was a very good reason why my doubts hadn't yet been addressed and that I needed to be patient and trust that, in time, everything would become clear. The voice told me that all was well: I was in the right place. It said that I shouldn't be afraid; it was safe for me to let go of my resistance because I would always be protected from danger. As this voice started to fade out I felt my panic dissolve in an ocean of calm and my heartbeat slow to a normal pace. The muscles in my shoulders and legs immediately relaxed as I felt myself settling into a state of acceptance. As no-one else in the room was showing any signs of wavering, Kerala finally lifted her head and continued with her talk.

'Thank you everybody. It seems as if our faith in each of you was not misplaced. Now that I know you are committed I can tell you about a grave matter. For you will remember that Krugman wrote at length about the systems that have been designed to keep us in bondage. However, what Krugman did not realise was that the modern world is not the result of a natural process of evolution – as he had imagined was the case. Instead, as our subsequent research has shown, at the time of the great turning a small group of individuals took advantage of this transitional stage in the country's history and gained tremendous power over the citizens of Arasmas. To help you understand this properly, I need to take you back to the beginning; before the great turning began.

'This was a time of civil unrest: the people of Arasmas had begun to rise up against laws that had held power for centuries. Belief in Pantheon was waning and it was becoming more obvious to Arasmasians that the real powerbrokers were those who owned land in Arasmas as this was still the time of the agricultural age when many people worked on the land. There had been a few years of drought, and although the citizens now struggled to grow enough to feed themselves, the landowners refused to lower their rent. Eventually, because of this, the citizens rose up against the landowners and reclaimed the land for themselves. There was now a power vacuum in Arasmas.

'It was at this time that a group of people formed a clan to fill this vacuum. They had realised how much money could be made from the emerging industrial revolution, and, in a very clever way, invested heavily in scientific research and innovation, and funded new industrial ventures. By the turn of the twentieth century the clan were the biggest employers in Arasmas. But how they remained in power was a secret. They did not wish to make this information public and so each business they owned was registered under different names. Whilst our economy may seem to be made up of many isolated fragments, every cent that you earn or spend today can be traced back to the clan's central bank account.

'The clan realised that in order to maximise their power and keep money flowing into their bank account, they needed to reform the education system so that emphasis was placed more on the left hemisphere of the brain than the right. Krugman identified this change in the system accurately, although he never understood its cause. For, if you think about it, in any kind of economic activity people only use the left hemisphere of their brain: for the only reason any business is created is in order to solve an unsolved problem and to make money from the solution. But it is not the left hemisphere itself that is the problem. There will always be a role for it in our lives; after all, we cannot possibly live without any economic activity. Our concern is that the clan want it to be activated constantly; they want people's lives to be ceaselessly, unnecessarily busy.

'And this is where I come to the matter of grave importance. The education reforms alone weren't enough for the clan. They also obsessively monitor everyone's behaviour, checking they are conforming to the systems they have put in place and making sure that everyone stays on their treadmill – earning and spending money all the time. The more economically active you are, the more power that the clan has over you. If you wish to regain your power, simply step off that treadmill: work fewer hours and make your life simpler. However, if you do this, you should eventually expect a visit from the group's agent. We don't know what happens to those rare few who defy the clan, but we do know that Krugman is not the only person who has disappeared over the years.

'How is that they monitor us, you may be wondering. Well, your bank statements and tax returns tell the clan how economically active you are, and your movements are also tracked. Also, as we found out only by chance, inside of you lies a small metal chip. This chip is inserted into everyone born in Arasmas. It is done around a child's ninth birthday, during a routine dental appointment. Now, all dentists are trained to insert these metal objects – there are two, one on each side of the mouth – into teeth. The reason given to patients is that these objects help protect the second molar; a tooth that they claim is particularly vulnerable. But in one of the metal objects is a chip. This chip transmits an electronic signal which can be picked up by the clan. They use these messages to monitor every person in Arasmas.

'So, because of this, it is quite possible that the clan have already been alerted by your unusual recent behaviour; they may already be keeping an eye on you. However, our own spotters have also been well trained, and we would not have brought you here if we weren't confident that you are not yet under suspicion. We believe that it is because we are so effective at spotting non-conformists that it is very unusual for people to disappear. However, it is still extremely risky to gather so many of you together in one place. One reason we have chosen this spot is because we know that dense woodland helps distort the signal. But the main reason that you are here today, and the reason why we needed to be sure you were committed, is that we have to remove these two objects from your teeth. It is essential for this to happen before we can go forward together. I promise you that this will not harm you: we have professional dentists among us, who have all the right equipment to carry out these operations.

'Once this chip is removed, you will have created some distance between you and the clan. It does not mean complete invisibility, however. If an agent was to walk past you in the street they would automatically know that your chip has been removed and would become suspicious. However, by careful planning, we've been able to create a small number of secret communes that do not exist on any map. We believe that these hidden bunkers can be found only by chance or through the foolishness or treachery of one of our own members. We guard against the possibility of treachery by monitoring potential members over many, many months until we are sure where your allegiances lie. Proper caution is instilled by rigorous training, with which we will provide you on your arrival at one of these communes. I can assure you that, such has been our carefulness, no commune has been discovered in the twenty years since our first one was built. So our time together must now come to a close, Please follow my colleague through the side of the tent to where our equipment has been set up.'

I had listened to Kerala in a state of spellbound silence; my body was still frozen in my seat, and I struggled to get to my feet in order to follow the others outside. Once I had managed to, we joined one of the queues that had formed outside each of the other canvas tents. It looked like this was where the dental operations would be taking place. My head was still spinning: what Kerala had said about this secret clan and its sinister motives had filled me with horror. It was so hard for me to grasp: I had always believed I was living in a free and democratic world, and to have this belief abruptly shattered was an enormous shock. I felt many emotions, but the main one was anger. I was angry that I was not being given time to process this new information, but at the same time I felt as though I was in some strange, surreal dream which I would soon wake up from. What on earth was I doing standing in this queue waiting to have someone perform an operation on me and why did I seem to be the only one who thought that this was completely crazy? But yet again the voice came to me to be patient and to trust that all would be well, and, once again, it told me that everything would soon become clear.

When it was finally my turn, I pushed my way through the unzipped canvas flap and saw a fairly young female sitting next to a long metal operating table. She smiled reassuringly and gestured for me to lie down. She then told me that first of all she would disable the chip and then she would remove it altogether. She stood over me, administered an anaesthetic and then waited for it to work. I started to feel woozy but remained conscious enough to know what was going on around me. After a few minutes she put a strange looking device into my mouth; I felt a strange tingling sensation when she pressed it down against one of my teeth. She then picked up a drill and proceeded to loosen and remove both of the metal chips. Afterwards she showed me the two offending objects before putting them in the bin. Holding out her hand, she then helped me up, and, making sure I was not too unsteady, directed me outside.

I sat down in the open air, joining a number of others also sat on the forest floor, and tried to compose myself. My mouth was still numb and sore, and my head was a little fuzzy. Finally the queue dwindled down to nothing and, just as the light started to fade, we were asked to head back to the minibuses. Our driver told us that we would be returned to our homes that evening and that someone would be in touch with further details about moving into one of the communes. He also told us to be extremely cautious and to lie low while we waited, as without the protection of our metal chip we were in an extremely vulnerable position. With this warning still ringing in my ears, I got off the minibus at Pugnillay train station.

Chapter Twenty-One

The evening light had long since faded by the time I got home. I could still feel the effects of the anaesthetic that had been administered. I had dozed on the ride home and didn't feel like making myself anything to eat. Instead I sat quietly and tried to absorb everything that had happened since those two men had approached me a week ago. A lot of things that Kerala had spoken about today had affected me strongly, but I didn't have the strength to think about them now and so I wearily put myself to bed.

As suggested, I kept a low profile over the following days. I even ignored my landlord. He was knocking on the door all weekend; I guessed he was wondering whether I was going to renew my lease, as it expired the following Saturday. He left a letter outside my door when he left on the Monday morning, and I wrote back a short reply explaining that I would be leaving the following weekend. On the Monday I also ignored a phone call from the bookshop owner, who I hadn't spoken to for a week. Fortunately I had enough food supplies in the flat to last me to the end of the week and so I had no need to go into the centre of town. The only time I did venture outside was to take a walk through the woods, in an attempt to try to calm my anxious mind. I also felt drawn to my little black book, and even completing just one page gave me a tremendous sense of release.

But I didn't remain in this state of limbo for long. On Thursday I was sat eating breakfast when I heard a package being pushed through the letterbox. I raced downstairs and immediately noticed that the envelope was unstamped and unmarked. Eagerly, I took a seat and ripped open the tightly sealed flap. Inside was a single piece of paper. On it was a map of the city of Baron, which I knew was a fairly large settlement lying around 50 miles north-east of Sarum. On the back was scribbled a train timetable, with one service circled in red ink. The departure date was in two day's time – perfect timing, as my lease ended on the same day. It seemed that things were coming together quite naturally.

The following day a second package arrived, containing a swipe card and details of the route I had to follow. I presumed that these must be directions from the station in Baron, as no names were mentioned in the description. By referring to my map I was able to work out more or less where my future home was located. They had clearly gone to great lengths to ensure that the location remained secret, and the note said that I needed to memorise and burn the information as soon as possible. I did this later that morning and, as I would be departing the following day, I started to prepare for the journey. The second package also contained a short list of items that each member should take, although fortunately I already had all the items mentioned. I went out and discarded everything else that was not on the list, apart from my black notebook and pen.

That night I slept only fitfully, and was woken early by my alarm. I had to catch a train to Sarum, which left just before seven o'clock. Locking the door, I noticed that my nerves were beginning to tighten a notch. As I walked to the station, I felt more and more on edge. My mind wanted stability, and yet I couldn't make myself turn around either. I clearly hadn't fully accepted all that had happened to me during the induction day the previous week. Nevertheless I arrived at the station in good time to buy a ticket. The early morning train was largely empty and I was able to have a whole carriage to myself; this, at least, calmed my fears about secret agents watching my every move. Once in Sarum I had to travel a short distance on foot to the northern terminus. It felt strange to be back walking through the city centre once again. I even caught a glimpse of my old office block, way off in the distance. It still seemed too far-fetched to believe that the freedom I had thought I was enjoying in that job was an illusion, and that really I had been living in a confined world created by a secret clan. Once in the station, I bought a single ticket that would take me to Baron and, as there was still some time until my departure, found a quiet corner from which I could view the departure board.

At last my train arrived and I got on. As we pulled out of the station, I looked out onto an area of the city that was unfamiliar to me. Only a handful of other people were sat in the carriage and, after taking my seat, I had scrutinised them intensely. At the far end were a young couple, who were totally engrossed in one another and oblivious to their surroundings. In the middle was a lady with greying hair set in a perm, and wearing a white woollen cardigan. She was also looking out of the window, and I could not believe that she was a serious threat to me. Finally, there were two men, barely out of their teens, sitting close to me. Although they were both strongly built and wore the uniform of the army of Arasmas, I didn't feel any discomfort in their presence either. Maybe it was because they looked too young to be given an assignment of halting a revolution, but most likely, it was because I didn't think that the army would be used. Perhaps this was only because my image of what a secret agent would look like came mainly from spy films.

As we approached the first station, a commuter town at the edge of the city, the two young men left the train. I guessed that there must be a large barracks here, although I had never heard of it. Eventually, the train passed through the outer fringes of the dormitory settlements that were dotted around Sarum and we started travelling through a flat, agricultural area: fields upon fields of grain and barley with hardly a dividing hedge between them. We had been travelling for just under an hour when we finally came to what looked like a major settlement, which I guessed must be the city of Baron. On the platform a large sign in bold letters confirmed that this was the case, and so I stood up and picked up my rucksack. I yanked open the stiff glass window and reached down to pull the handle before stepping off. Once on the platform, I looked up and down nervously, checking who had left the train and whether anyone was surveying me. But, apart from me, there was no-one on the platform at all, and I walked slowly away.

Since I had destroyed the map, I stood at the entrance and, taking a couple of deep breaths, tried to bring the route to mind. I then started to walk mechanically through the maze of streets ahead of me and was soon surrounded by rows and rows of ancient terraced housing. I kept checking nervously over my shoulder for signs of movement but nothing was behind me apart from the vague outline of my shadow. After walking for a good two miles to the eastern edge of this run-down city I arrived on a street that marked a clear division between the old and the new and came across buildings that looked totally out of character with the area around them. It appeared as if this part of the city had hastily been bolted onto the existing city border comparatively recently. The streets and the pavement were much wider and the newer tenement buildings were a lot taller, most rising to three storeys. Unlike the twisted muddle of streets that prevailed in the centre, here things were uniform and square – blocks, buildings and streets. This meant that it became relatively easy for me to find my way to the street and the block that was my final destination.

Halfway down the street, on my left hand side, was a narrow, dark alleyway. It was to this alleyway that I had been told to come to, and so, after taking a final nervous look behind me, I stepped in. There was little room on either side and I could imagine a person of a much bulkier disposition finding themselves completely wedged in. Halfway down the alleyway was a wrought iron gate: an imposing barrier against unwelcome visitors. I assumed that, to open this, I needed to use the access card I had been given. Holding it in my right hand, I swiped it confidently through the metal strip. I immediately heard the lock click open, and pushed against the gate. It opened easily, and I walked through.

Only when I reached the end of the alleyway did I understand why it was that I had been forced to grope my way along in pitch darkness: at the end I came up against a large oak door, which had been wedged tightly into the space. Before I had had a chance to knock, the door swung open automatically, revealing a set of steps leading downwards. It was quite bizarre; the only illumination came from a small lantern. I started to walk down the spiral staircase, deeper into the earth's crust. I had only taken one step when the door crashed shut noisily. My imagination started to run wild. But eventually I reached the bottom step, and, walking forwards, gave a loud gasp at the sight before me. The ceiling suddenly broadened and rose up to an enormous height; I found myself standing in a circular courtyard, which reminded me of a gladiatorial arena.

Around this courtyard were a large number of portholes carved into the wall, and these rose up, showing that this underground chamber had six levels. As I stood here on the cold and sandy floor, my mind drifted as I imagined myself standing here in front of a baying audience with lions and tigers circling me menacingly. The thought made me shudder. I walked across the arena to a large set of double doors that stood at the far end. On the way I peered through a couple of the portholes and realised immediately that these were the quarters that I would be living in. In each room was a flimsy wooden screen that could be pulled across if one wanted some privacy. These living quarters could easily be mistaken for claustrophobic prison cells, I thought. It seemed ironic that I was leaving what seemed to be a free world for one that appeared confined. Would I really find true freedom here?

Coming through the door, I was met by an elderly lady who was almost bent double. She was shuffling along and, with a tooth-less smile, lifted her head and cast her eyes over me. Strangely, she immediately gave me a warm hug, which took me aback a little. Then, following an awkward moment of silence, she spoke in a soft tone which echoed slightly against the high ceiling behind me.

'Good morning, Myrkais, and welcome to your new home. I do hope you will enjoy your stay here. Could you please follow me through so that I can sign you in?'

'Certainly,' I replied and followed her through the door into a narrow corridor. I was so nervous that I didn't feel able to start a conversation, and so I followed a short distance behind.

She turned into a room at the end of the high-ceilinged

corridor and walked over to a large wooden desk. From behind this desk, she brought out a wrapped bundle – my bedding, I assumed – and placed it on the desk. Gesturing for me to come forward, she asked me to sign against my name, proceeding to tell me that I was one of ten new members. They had been arriving at various intervals throughout the week, she said. I glanced at the list, and saw that I was the last but one to arrive. She then opened one of the drawers and pulled out a small folder, which she gave to me.

'This is the rule book. We have to abide by these rules in order to keep things in harmony, and I advise you to read it thoroughly. I am the Matriarch over all those who live here. The ten new arrivals take us to full capacity: 96 guests, plus myself and a couple of teachers. If you have any problems or concerns, I am the one you should come and see. It is my duty to make sure that everyone here is well-fed and well-looked after, so that spirits are kept high and the mission can be continued with. Now, unless you have any questions, I suggest that you spend some time settling into your new home. Lunch will be served at one o'clock sharp; you will find the dining room marked on the map in your folder. Your room is number 87; if you go up the stairs on the right outside my office, then follow them up to the top floor, you should find it easily. Do you have any questions?'

I shook my head and reached forward to pick up the bundle of bedding before leaving. Following her instructions, I climbed the iron spiral staircase, right up to the top floor. There was a narrow metal platform that curved around, following the line of the circular arena. The walls were made of dry, compacted mud; I assumed this must offer some protection from any water that might have leaked down from the surface. There were no doors leading into any of the rooms, only a thin red curtain that could be pulled across to offer some privacy. The numbers of each room were marked in black ink on the timber frames that secured the doorways from collapsing. I walked slowly and deliberately around the curving corridor in an anti-clockwise direction, watching the numbers decrease until I reached my room. The curtain was pulled across, but I lifted it up and squeezed my way inside. The floor was covered in timber and in the middle stood two metal poles that seemed to be preventing the ceiling from collapsing. The room was fairly basic: a bed took up half the space, and a small bedside cabinet and a battery powered light stood next to it. I guessed that the toilet and shower facilities must be elsewhere. I walked across to my porthole; the view across the cavern was a spectacular one. I stood there for a while, and eventually I saw the final recruit walking down the stairs and through the centre of the room, wearing exactly the same look of amazement that I'd had. I set about putting my belongings away in the cabinet and making my bed. Afterwards I decided to take a quick rest, but, before long, the bell rang for lunch.

I made my way to the dining hall, and there I met the nine new recruits. I assumed that the other residents must all be out doing the work of the commune. As I walked towards them, I realised that they were all faces that I had seen before, although I was surprised that I didn't recognise any from the minibus; I guessed they must have come from all parts of Arasmas. It made me wonder how many communes they owned and where the other inductees had been taken. I was also puzzled by how tiny the dining hall was – there was no way that one hundred people would be able to eat together at the same time. I could only assume that meal times must be staggered across the evening.

Taking a bowl of soup and two slices of bread, I became aware that I was feeling a little shy and hesitant about the prospect of engaging with those around me and so it was with reluctance that I joined my fellow recruits at the table. The experience reminded me again of those first few days working in the factory: how I'd grappled with the feeling that I was an outsider who didn't fit in there and how I had struggled to overcome this. A small part of me still wanted to wear a veil to help me fit in, but the stronger part no longer wanted to pretend to be something that I wasn't. While we were eating, the Matriarch came in and informed us that our dinner would not be served until eight o'clock that evening and that, accordingly, we would have the afternoon free. Soon after being told this, I left to go back to my room.

Once there I lay down on the bed and began to read through the folder of information I had been given. The most fascinating thing was a fact sheet that explained the history of this particular commune and how such an incredible building had been constructed. It was an unusual commune: most of them were in old farm buildings or on caravan sites, and so it had been a bold decision to place one in such a massive building in the centre of a major town. The site had apparently been chosen because transport links in this part of Arasmas were extremely limited, and so it had been difficult to find a site that would allow guests to travel about to do the work of the mission.

This part of Arasmas was an important strategic target and so they had had to come up with an ingenious solution. The project had begun nearly 30 years previously, when, in response to rising demand, developers had started to build in the town. The town planners had cleared a lot of old terraced housing in the town centre to make way for redevelopment, and some supporters of the mission decided to purchase a whole block. They had been very careful, not wanting to draw attention to themselves by making such a significant transaction, and it seemed that the clan had not noticed. Each block had three-storey housing on four sides of it, with a private square courtyard in the middle. The authorities had cleared enough space to allow a dozen of these blocks to be built. I couldn't even begin to imagine what this whole block must have cost – but the supporters had not stopped at buying it.

For it was afterwards that the most risky and ambitious phase of the project began. The first task involved raising the courtyard floor by an astonishing 20 feet above the first level, so that the purpose of the building could not be detected from above. New windows had to be put into the building that was still above the level of the new courtyard in order to maintain the illusion of a three-story building. Meanwhile, beneath the cover of the raised courtyard floor, workers began on the painstaking task of digging into the earth. This required many labourers and a significant period of time, but eventually the all-important depth of 20 feet was reached. Now the 40-foot shell was in place, it was a simple task to fit out this massive hole with timber frames and set up a home that would be fit for one hundred men and women to live in. Its successful creation was viewed, with pride, as a tremendous triumph in the movement's history. Once this was completed, the outer buildings were rented out to over one hundred trusted supporters of the mission. These were supporters who had been asked to sacrifice their own freedom by keeping their monitoring chip and continuing to act in an economically normal way so as not to draw suspicion to the site.

It was an incredible story and yet I found it difficult to believe that they had really managed to carry out all this work on the inner courtyard in secret. I also struggled to understand why they had gone to such lengths and such expense to create this home. Shifting my focus slightly, I turned to read through some of the house rules. These were designed to reduce the likelihood of conflicts arising – a serious risk, considering how many people were living together in such a confined space.

It was a long afternoon, only broken by the sound of the other guests returning to the commune and I could see that security was being maintained by the way that small groups of two or three people came in at staggered intervals. It appeared that our hosts had established a well-drilled operation. Finally it was eight o'clock and I went down for dinner. Walking into the dining hall, I noticed that, once again, the new members were eating separately; it appeared that a special meal had been prepared for us. We ate by candlelight and the calm atmosphere helped me to relax. Only after our plates had been cleared away and I was thinking about leaving, did I notice a gentleman standing in the doorway, wearing a long black and red robe wrapped around his body. He waited for the rest of our table to notice him and for the noise of conversation to die away, before stepping into the room. Everyone immediately realised that this gentleman was a high-ranking figure. He started to speak in an accent that was unfamiliar:

'Good evening, friends, and welcome. My name is Alamo. It is my responsibility, over the next couple of weeks, to teach you about the complex messages that can be found within Krugman's short book. But I will tell you about that later. I am here tonight to let you know that we will be meeting in the study room at nine o'clock sharp tomorrow morning. Breakfast will be available from eight. Please be downstairs promptly so that we can begin on time. As for the rest of the evening, I am sure our other guests will make you feel welcome – if they've not done so already. If you should have any urgent questions for me, you will find me in the small office directly opposite the doors leading out into the main arena. If not, I will see you all bright and early in the morning.'

With that, he walked slowly away; his robes touched the ground and gently swept across the dusty floor. Although the others on my table talked about retiring to the lounge, I decided to take my leave soon after Alamo had left the room. I walked past the lounge on the way back to my room and, hearing the noisy sounds coming from inside, I was glad that I had not tried to overdo things by forcing myself to interact and make some new acquaintances. It felt good for me to use this time to adjust gradually to this new way of life.

Chapter Twenty-Two

After breakfast the following morning, most of the residents left in small groups, at staggered times. I still kept my distance, although I was feeling brighter and more cheerful than the day before. I had slept well, for the building was surprisingly quiet at night and my bed was comfortable. The only thing I did miss was seeing daylight after waking up. Having eaten, I joined the others in the cramped study room and waited expectantly for Alamo to arrive. He was running a few minutes late and, when he did eventually appear, he seemed flustered. He was very different from the calm presence who had stood before us the previous day.

'Good morning to you all. Now, I am afraid I must tell you that my opening words will be a confession. No doubt some of you will have realised that we have been holding back certain pieces of important information. However, I can tell you honestly that we deceived you only from the best of intentions. The full truth that I am about to tell you may well blow your mind. That is why we felt it was important to bring you here before telling you, because only in this environment will you be fully supported and will you have the time to absorb what it is that I have to tell you.'

I listened to these striking words and immediately sat up straight in my seat. Was Alamo finally going to tell us the truth that I had been waiting for?

'Now you will remember from what you were told on your induction day that the metal chip was installed into your second molar in order to monitor your behaviour. This is one role it plays it is true, but what Kerala chose not to tell you was that this chip plays

215

another, more important, role in the life of those growing up here in Arasmas.

'The story begins about 80 years ago, when the members of the clan became concerned that their power was being undermined. It may sound bizarre, but the reason why they became concerned was that the economic problem had been solved. By this I mean that there was no longer any practical reason why anyone in Arasmas should have to spend their lives busily fighting poverty, and so, as long as the existing wealth of resources could be distributed fairly, there was no further need for more economic growth. Yet you may recall that in order to sustain the wealth and power of the clan, the economy needed to keep on growing. One way to explain this idea is by showing you what happens when I rub together these two stones in my hand. Can you imagine what is created when I do this? The answer is heat – and it is this heat that provides the clan with wealth and power. The speed at which I rub the stones together indicates the pace of economic activity. If there is no longer any need for the economy to grow, there is no need for these stones to be rubbed together, and therefore no heat is produced.

'Thus the solving of the economic problem sent shockwaves through the clan, for they would no longer be able to rely on the education system to control the people of Arasmas. They would soon see for themselves the big lie being told to them. So they turned to a team of professional scientists who worked for them. They eventually came up with an ingenious solution that would keep the fear of poverty present in citizens' minds, thus ensuring that the treadmill of economic growth stayed running. They did this by targeting the citizens who today we would identify as the middle class, for they were the ones most likely to become less economi-cally active. And this is where we see the primary reason for insert-ing the metal chip. The clan's ingenious solution involved a com-puter programme that could be transmitted through the chip: this programme was designed to interfere with the brain by sending distorted signals to the left hemisphere.

'As you know, Krugman discovered in his research that it is in the left hemisphere of the brain that we organise and make sense of the influx of data that comes through our senses whenever we engage with the outside world. Indeed it is through this process of managing sense data that the brain is able to solve all the problems that arise in everyday life. Having discovered how this process occurs in the brain, scientists working for the clan quickly realised that they did not need to change the outside world in order to convince the brain that there was still an economic problem; instead, all they needed to do was to interrupt the signal between the senses and the brain.

'So how did this programme impact daily life in Arasmas? Take a person who has a secure well-paid job at a respectable company, a nice brick house in a part of the city where there is no crime and who is happily married with children. Now you would normally expect that this lifestyle would give rise to pleasant feelings and that this would be the main type of information that would come through to the brain. If the person had grown up believing that having these things was a good thing, which is exactly what our modern education system teaches us to believe, then this human being would feel satisfied with their life and would not need to have an active left hemisphere busy solving problems. But what the computer programme did was to distort this signal so that instead of the emotion of satisfaction, the opposite arose; it is by sustaining this dissatisfaction that the wheels of industry are able to keep moving. This had the effect of turning the middle class into competitively driven beings always needing more and more. This need is insatiable because it seems that people's greed and desires are limitless.

'It is important to understand that it was not only a problem for the clan's bank account when those who we call middle class experience satisfaction. What Krugman himself discovered was that when the left hemisphere of the brain shows reduced activity, the right hemisphere comes to the fore. Now what happens when individuals activate this part of their brain is that they begin to grasp their sovereignty, find their freedom and live more spontaneously and fully in an intuitive and inspired way. These people can no longer be controlled by authority because their lives have become inwardly directed. It may seem difficult to believe but this is what can be gained when you give the right hemisphere permission to take charge of your life, and, because of this, the clan are very frightened of its power. One benefit of joining our commune is that we will seek to help you realise the potential of your right hemisphere and, by doing so, bring out the very best in you.

'Now, as you already know, the chip is inserted around a child's ninth birthday. The reason for doing it at this time is because it is around this time that neural signals between the senses and the brain start to be established and, because of this, the child's cognitive abilities advance quite rapidly. It is at this point that the child becomes less dependent on their parents to solve their problems and that the left hemisphere of the brain starts to grow. This is the critical point where, if nurtured properly, a child can easily develop into a mature and independent human being; meaning that there is a balance between the two hemispheres, with the right side the master and the left its servant. But, instead of this, we have an education system that prevents a child from finding this healthy balance by forcing them to develop their left hemisphere too quickly. Now added to this was a computer programme that further unbalanced children.

'But the group quickly realised that it would not be enough to design a programme only for those in the middle class, and so they devised another one for people categorised in the lower social classes. One is a programme for success and one a programme for failure. But how do these two programmes dovetail together? Well, if it is decided that you are middle class and so are to be given the programme of success, you will live in a state of constant tension. As I already mentioned, the education system teaches these people that external things such as wealth, status, possessions are the key to happiness. What the computer programme does is dangle carrots in front of the left hemisphere in order to keep the attention constantly preoccupied with attaining more and more of these things. Even if you have these things in abundance, the brain still receives messages telling it to strive for more. At the same time, the brain receives messages telling it that unemployment, poverty, deprivation and isolation lie in store if it ever becomes complacent. This is the stick that the computer programme threatens us with and it leaves us feeling deeply insecure. The beauty of this system is that it controls us from within our minds. There is no-one actually dangling carrots and holding sticks before us, and so there is nothing that the person can rebel against, even if they realise that they're being manipulated.

'So what about the programme for failure? The clan realised that an individual who is assigned to the first programme needs to see that the carrots of success and the sticks of failure are not just images but are actually real possibilities. It was easy to show that it was possible to be richer, but it was more of a challenge to show that destitution was possible, when it was obvious that there were enough resources in Arasmas for everyone to live a life of abundance. The clan remembered all too well the landowners who had been overthrown in the events of the great turning, and knew that if they kept people in poverty they would not remain in power for long. Their eventual solution was to convince the lower classes that they were not worthy of receiving a fair share. The programme instilled this belief by sending the message that whilst their education and their economic system provided them with the chance to prosper; genetic malfunctions and cultural barriers meant that they stayed in their impoverished position. The left hemisphere of the brain is informed that this problem is simply too big to be solved, and, as a result, the child is left feeling helpless and disempowered, aware they will be unable to fulfil their potential. They come to feel that the difficult circumstances they were born into are just too great to overcome.

'What we've discovered is that these two programmes depend on one another: if one is destroyed, both are destroyed. Our task in these communes is to try to destroy them. Now you may wonder how it is possible to destroy these programmes, or more likely, think that the work of the mission involves going around and putting people through the dental operation that you went through at the gathering. Alas, we quickly realised that would not work, because although we are able to disable the chip, we cannot remove the imprint the chip has made on people's lives. Every one of us has experienced a lifetime of conditioning and it is not enough just to wipe the slate clean and start from scratch. Look deep inside yourselves and you will see that having the chip removed has not changed your personality and character one iota. So what is essential if this mission is to succeed is working on the psychological level to help people overcome their lifetimes of conditioning. To begin with, we have to work on ourselves; this will be a core part of your training programme here during these first few weeks. Then, once we have done sufficient healing work on ourselves, we will be strong enough to go out and heal others.

'You are joining us at a very exciting time, because we know that when enough people are psychologically healed then the programmes will simply implode. It will be a bit like a lifelong alcoholic who suddenly wakes up one morning, takes a sip of whisky and finds the taste so disgusting that, for the rest of his life, he never has the urge to touch another drop. With the left hemisphere suddenly silenced, the right hemisphere will be allowed to resume its rightful role of master, and all outer forms of authority will end forever.

'However, before we take a break, I need to talk to you about one final important matter. For what we've also discovered over these past twenty years is that while it is very difficult to do this healing work with those wedded to the programme of success, it is a lot more straightforward with those who have been given the programme of failure. Telling you what we've learnt about the challenges of destroying the programme of success will also help to update you on the changes that have happened since Krugman was writing. For what happened shortly after his disappearance was that this programme started to break of its own accord, due to external events. It was because the growing economy was starting to come up against the natural limits of the planet. We were fast running out of oil, the fuel that had driven the modern world, and this presented a challenge for the clan, who needed to keep the economy moving. This information started to filter through, as more and more people in the middle class became aware that the resource-intensive cycle of producing and consuming more stuff was unsustainable. This began to undermine the messages coming from the education system and the programme, and it troubled many of the more sensitive citizens. Suddenly the carrots being dangled before them seemed a lot less attractive. To those of us in the mission at the time, it seemed that the programme of success would break down on its own accord and that our work would be complete.

'But, alas, we discovered something startling. Rather than breaking free of the clutches of the programme and tapping into the power of their right hemispheres, people in the middle class instead sought solutions from the system that had caused the problem in the first place. It became clear to us then that the people in this group had far too much to lose by discarding the old world to take the risk of discovering the new one. In contrast, those who follow the path of failure have nothing to lose and everything to gain from a new alternative. This is why it's easier to work with these people.

'So those entrusted with keeping the system going had to come up with an answer and their solution was, to be fair, another stroke of genius. For, literally overnight, they altered the computer programme and completely changed the carrot that was on offer. Rather than telling the person in the middle class that they had to keep working in order to stay ahead of the game at the moment, they now needed to instead work hard in order to protect them-selves from potential future losses. It was a masterstroke that marked the end of the industrial revolution. Out of its ashes rose a new economy, one based on risk avoidance. A whole host of financial services were introduced, from housing mortgages to insurance to pensions to investments and savings, and everyone had to keep busy working in order to support these industries. The reason it was such a masterstroke was that the new financial, service-centred, economy was very clean and needed a lot less oil to sustain it. For not only was it housed in brand-new glass office blocks rather than dirty factories but its products were essentially numbers on pieces of paper that could be sold electronically and viewed on computer screens. These numbers on a screen have, very quickly, acquired tremendous power over many people's lives. These people now pour their hard earned wealth into this new economy, in the belief that, by doing so, they would be financially well-off in the future. Sacrifice a little today for a lot tomorrow was the new message coming through from all angles of society.

'That brings us pretty much up to date. However, no matter how ingenious the programme is, it will have to adapt if the clan wish to stay in power, for the situation in Arasmas is constantly changing. The current threat to the programme comes from those who are now approaching retirement, having dedicated most of their professional working life to this new economy. These are a group of people who are incredibly wealthy, but they are also people who have only a low quality of life and suffer from many health problems, mainly because they live in an imbalanced world where only one part of the brain is prioritised. This group of people are also now able to look back and see that their anxiety about the future was unnecessary; because of this, they are full of regret at wasting the best years of their life. The sad irony is that these people may have plenty of money but the things they really need for their retirement are those which money cannot buy: namely good health and loving relationships with those closest to them.

'But unfortunately we do not think that this will cause the clan any serious cause for concern. One of the consequences of allowing the world to become dominated by the left hemisphere is that we now only listen to those who are young and exuberant, no longer valuing the wisdom of our elders because their humble voices would only remind us of our impotence. As long as this ageism continues, this potential threat will probably not become a seriously destabilising force.

'So this is where we are with regards to the programme of success and this is why we are focusing our attention on destroying those who follow the programme of failure. This is more straight-forward, because we only have to do one thing to cause it to implode. That is, we simply have to find a way to help their children feel hopeful and optimistic, to convince them that they are not necessarily doomed to failure because of their genetic background and upbringing. We have to give these people the belief that they do have the freedom to think for themselves, and that they can make the most of their life rather than meekly accepting the world they've been brought up in. Strangely, one of the biggest obstacles to achieving success with the lower-class children is that, once they have achieved this feeling of empowerment, these children often suffer guilt because they worry about abandoning their roots. These young adults often find it hard to accept that just because their parents and grandparents lived a life of hardship and sacrifice; it doesn't mean that they have to go down that same road too. These wounds also have to be healed, but we will talk more about it in due course.'

Alamo finally paused for a moment, as if to catch his breath. I felt that he was well aware that we might be overloaded with confusing information. I didn't know about the others in the room, but my head was spinning after hearing all these different ideas and theories. After the pause had lasted for more than a minute, Alamo eventually looked around at the ten pairs of eyes facing him, and, before continuing, flashed me a brief smile.

'I know what I've said may be a little difficult to digest and so I've put it down on paper so that you can absorb it all in your own time. Don't worry if you are left feeling confused, for there will be plenty of opportunities over the coming days for you to ask ques-tions and for us to explore this topic until we are all together in a place of mutual understanding. What I suggest is that we meet this afternoon after lunch and that you take the remainder of the morning to rest. Lunch will be served at one o'clock sharp.'

With that, we all stood up to leave. As we all filed out together, I took a copy of the paper from the desk. Going back to my room, I flopped down onto my bed and put Alamo's piece of paper down on the bedside table next to me. Had this morning provided any further clarity, I wondered, or had it merely left me with more questions? The longer I laid there, the more complicated things seemed to be; I felt frustrated by the fact that the longer I searched, the less I seemed to know. All this talk of a secret clan and computer programmes that were controlling my brain still seemed a little too far-fetched to believe; my mind whirred as I tried to square this new information together with everything I had learnt over the past few years. How did this relate to my decision to leave my old life as a mortgage advisor? How did this relate to the lessons I had learnt from Cipher's death? How did this relate to the lessons I received from my time with Chris and Tommy? How did this relate to the time I spent living in and around Pugnillay?

While I was asking these questions, I became aware that it was only the left hemisphere of my brain that was struggling to piece everything together and demanding an answer to these questions so that it would have some control over the jumbled mass of information that it was being asked to digest. All I could do was to breathe deeply and try to let these clouds pass across the sky. While doing so, it struck me very forcefully that this metaphor was actually a very good way of expressing what Kerala and Alamo had told me about the two hemispheres of the brain. I was reminded again that it had been my meditation practice that had helped me to lessen the effects of my own conditioning, and had left me less obsessed with trying to control the clouds in the sky.

After lunch Alamo gave us some time to explore his paper, but I was feeling strangely disengaged, and refrained from getting involved in the heated discussions and debates that some of our group were conducting. I suppose that this reminder of my meditation practice was helping me to reduce my left hemisphere activity and was helping me to relax more easily and to accept that I didn't know everything and didn't need to figure everything out. However, there was still one question that I needed to raise, although I decided it would be better to speak to Alamo about it in private, rather than bringing it up in front of the group. So after dinner that evening I went to his office, hoping to find him there. I knocked on the open door, and Alamo looked up from the newspaper he was reading, gave me a warm smile and beckoned for me to take a seat. Giving me his complete attention, he encouraged me to say what was on my mind.

'Alamo, there was one question from your talk this morning that I am still thinking about. You said quite clearly that it is very difficult to heal those who have been following the programme of success because they have the most to lose from letting go of the modern world. But I believe that I was following that programme for many years. I'm curious to understand why I'm the exception to your rule.'

'Myrkais, thank you ever so much for coming to me this evening. I've been waiting for us to have this conversation, because you are indeed a very special case. I remember when you first showed up on our radar, nearly four years ago now. We didn't dare get in contact with you then because we assumed that the way in which you went about letting go of your old way of life would surely bring you to the attention of agents. But we have kept our eyes on you over the years, and it seems that you have somehow managed to slip through their net. What I can tell you now was that your case triggered a heated debate among the leaders of our commune. Some thought you could be a tremendous asset to our cause but there were others who thought you would be a liability. Then when you reacted to our two spotters in the manner that you did, we really did feel that we had blown it. You need to understand, Myrkais, your upbringing has given you a very active left hemisphere and we know that working through this has been a real struggle for you. You're tremendously courageous to have had enough faith to stick with it despite all the challenges you've faced over the last few years. That courage is what makes you an exception to the rule, Myrkais, and you'll need to hold on to that courage over the coming days, weeks and months.

'For your presence here will be a challenge for you and for us, and, because it is part of your conditioning to challenge and question everything we do here, your left hemisphere will not accept our teachings quietly. But we do realise the steps you've taken to overcome your conditioning, and we also think that you have a lot of knowledge and experience to offer. This is why we eventually decided to take the risk. I can tell you Myrkais that you are more of a liability than anyone else in this commune; this is because the programme of failure does not lead to such a strong left hemisphere. These people generally feel very angry about their life; and we offer them hope and an avenue down which they can channel that anger. They are happy with this and often don't ask too many questions.'

'Is this why I feel like I don't belong here? Is this why I am finding it difficult to connect with the people who live here?' I asked.

'Of course it is, Myrkais. In all the years that we've been operating the mission, we have only ever had a small number of people opt out from the programme of success to join us. But even amongst this small number you are unique. For the one thing that was common to all the members of this small group was that they had all either experienced the death of a loved one or gone through a near death experience of their own. The shock of these experiences overrode the messages from the programme and caused them to re-evaluate their life. What is special about you is that you made the choice to change your life without receiving any shock to your system.'

I listened to Alamo speak; it felt strange to hear someone giving this perspective on my journey. I felt compelled to tell him how shocked I had been by seeing Jen's boss, and that, for me, this was like facing a near death experience. But still Alamo refused to play down my courage, saying that many people see these sights on a daily basis but are not sensitive or aware enough for it to get through the defences that the programme sets up to protect itself. He went on to tell me that even those who have had near-death experiences rarely make significant changes to their lives.

A silence descended as I allowed his words to sink in. I felt grateful for having had this conversation and really appreciated Alamo's promise that he would always be there and that I didn't need to struggle alone. But there was still one final matter I needed to raise.

'There is something else I need to talk about: the influence of my father. You see, Alamo, I think that I was very close to being given the programme of failure, but that my father's courage allowed me to escape the path I seemed destined to follow.'

Alamo nodded his head before replying.

'We know about your father, Myrkais. It isn't a surprise to us that he has been such a big influence on your life: your courage had to come from somewhere. You were born into that family for a rea-son, and the truth is that your father had the rare and precious ability to overcome his conditioning and the programme of failure he was destined for. But he chose not to use it and, believe me, there is not one day that passes when he does not regret that decision. All he could do to heal that pain was to make sure that his only son didn't make the same mistake as him. That's why he moved you to a different school.'

'Is that why I've found it so hard to go and see my parents? Because I know that my father will be disappointed to see that I've thrown away everything that he worked so hard for?' I asked.

'Of course it is Myrkais. But while it was your father's destiny to do what he did, it was not the purest act of love. For he believed that he knew what was best for you and he thought that the programme of success was preferable to the programme of failure. But only the right hemisphere of your own brain can tell you what is best for you, Myrkais and not the left. The reason you are here is because you know that the truth lies beyond both of these programmes, and that one is not preferable to the other. But it will be difficult to explain this to your father. Maybe all you can do for him at the moment is to send him your love.'

After hearing this, I took my leave and returned to my room. I felt reassured, knowing now why I felt different here, and this softened my resistance to the commune. I also felt called to return to my black notebook in order to release all that I had absorbed during the day. This time the writing covered four pages and, as usual, it flowed naturally, ending at the bottom of each page and beginning again at the top of the next. After writing, I felt calm and, soon after, slipped into a peaceful sleep.

Chapter Twenty-Three

I didn't have much time to fully absorb my conversation with Alamo, for, soon afterwards, he introduced me to something that removed any lingering doubts I still had. He only had to say one word for me to crack and commit myself fully to the mission. That word was Satyagraha.

Alamo had begun to change tack. The theme of his lessons had begun to move away from the theoretical basis for the mission's existence and towards the practicalities of its work. But, when I heard him casually say that the commune was set up to abide by the principles of Satyagraha, I nearly jumped out of my seat. I listened for his definition of this word with eager anticipation. Obligingly, Alamo went on to explain that Satyagraha was a term coined by the leader of an independence movement that had been formed in Aidni when the continent was under the control of foreign rulers.

'Rather than overcoming these rulers using the traditional methods of violence, this movement cunningly took a different approach, based on the understanding that fire cannot be fought with fire. Instead the leader of the movement established a set of principles that he thought would help douse the fire: Satyagraha was the title he gave to them. Satyagraha can, therefore, be loosely translated as 'one who acts by force of truth.' I want to explain the main principles, as these define different methods that you will need to follow as part of this commune.

'The first and most fundamental of these is that each one of us must know Satya: by which it is meant that each one of us must know the truth. This independence movement understood that the darkness in the world cannot be dispelled by more darkness, and that it can only be dispelled by the light of truth. Much of what I've been introducing you to so far has been concerned with shedding light, and trying to give you a greater understanding of what is going on, both in yourselves and in Arasmas as a whole.

'In addition, Satyagraha also provides guidelines about how to conduct ourselves in our daily lives so that our body and mind do not become polluted and cause us to lose clarity. We need all the strength we can muster to hold the light of truth in this world. For this reason non-violence is central to the principles of Satyagraha. You will have noticed that we abide by a vegetarian diet here in the commune, and that there are also guidelines regarding the consumption of alcohol and other intoxicants, as well as guidelines regarding sexual conduct. As part of the psychological healing work we will be doing on ourselves, we will also try to help you to reduce the amount of mental pollution you suffer from, in terms of the negative thoughts and emotions which serve to block out the light of truth. Finally Satyagraha contains guidelines regarding healthy communication and relationships: an especially important subject considering that we live in a confined environment in which tensions can sometimes arise.

'Applying these new ways of communicating is also key to the work we do in the mission, as it is through dialogue that we heal ourselves and help those from the lower class to overcome their feelings of despondency and helplessness. But you will explore all of this in due course. In the meantime I suggest you take the time to read through this folder of information: it contains all you will need to know about Satyagraha and the daily rhythms of living in this commune.'

I took one of the folders from the pile and returned to the sanctuary of my room. Most of that morning was spent reminiscing: I remembered everything that the old man I had met by Lake Lawdi had told me. Now I finally knew what it was that I was searching for and I felt certain that I was on the right track. By joining the movement of Satyagraha, had I finally found my true calling in life? I began to leaf through the folder and saw that it contained many different types of information. Towards the beginning, there was an interesting article that described the roots of Satyagraha in detail. There were papers on vegetarianism and healthy living and also an interesting article on energy hygiene. This article talked about the importance of taking responsibility for one's thoughts and emotions and suggested ways to protect oneself from being influenced by the thoughts and emotions of others. Finally, at the back of the folder, there was information about the daily rhythms of life in the commune. I saw that I had been signed up on a number of rosters; I would have to help with the breakfast shift once a fortnight and would have to cook dinner once a fortnight. There were also regular cleaning shifts for which I had been signed up.

But it wasn't only that morning's talk that helped me to feel more settled and at home in the commune. For, over the days and weeks that followed, Alamo set about establishing healthy relationships in our little group, helping to create a small, but vibrant community. He would often do this by making a subtle change that would, nonetheless, have a dramatic impact on the way that the group interacted with one another. For instance, on one occasion he rearranged the study room so that instead of us sitting in rows, the chairs were set out in a circle. He then explained the importance of the circle to us: apparently it symbolised unity and equality in ancient tradition. Alamo also showed that when the chairs were set out in rows this created a triangle, a symbol of hierarchy and authoritarianism. He explained that this symbol was not conducive to forming healthy relationships.

So, as we sat together in the circle, Alamo also showed us the powerful effects that speaking from the heart could have on both the individual and the group. Continuing, he told us of its importance in the healing work we needed to undertake. I felt as though I had joined a therapy group, but, when I let go of the stigma I attached to such groups, I found it tremendously nurturing to be able to speak freely into the circle. It was in these sessions that I was able to truly let go of the feeling of separation that I'd spoken about with Alamo and to discover feelings of connection. It helped me to realise that despite the differences we were all part of one race.

Having given us the tools to enable us to form healthy relationships with each other, Alamo went on to teach us about the different psychological defences that all of us put in place to try to protect ourselves. According to Alamo we build these defences because of fear. He also said that it is this fear that gives the clan the ability to gain power over us. In very stark terms, Alamo told us that we were able to free ourselves from these defences and that if we made this choice then the left hemisphere would no longer have such a strong influence over our minds. He promised us that when this happened, the computer programme's stranglehold over us would be at an end. Alamo went on to tell us that we cannot see our defences at work, but can only recognise them when our behaviour is reflected back to us by our interactions with others. I realised that this awareness of my defences could help me to work through other personal issues.

He taught us to become more aware of what caused our defences to be triggered within the group setting. Forced to think about this, I felt myself becoming more sensitive and able to understand the subconscious reasons for my behaviour. Not only was this important for my own personal development and growth, but I knew that it would also be crucial in carrying out the work of the mission. He told us very forcefully that we could not help others escape from the programme if our own psychological defences were always being triggered.

So as I began to live more fully from the heart, I discovered a new way of being. I was slowly becoming softer and more open and was also discovering a lighter and more humorous side to my character. While doing so, I became more aware about how serious and worrisome I had become in my quest to fix and control everything. I felt a lot freer now and knew I could be completely honest and heartfelt with the other people in my group.

Apart from relaxing our psychological defences and learning

to live more fully from the heart, we also started to learn about the methods of communication that the commune used to engage with the outside world and to help encourage change to take place. We were told that the primary targets were the parents and teachers of children between the ages of eight and eleven. But we were also warned that there was no magic formula of words that could impose feelings of optimism that would override the messages from their programme and that could then be transferred to their children. Alamo was very insistent on this point, explaining that we needed to illuminate the way forward rather than telling them about it explicitly. This was a fundamental aspect of the principles of Satyagraha, he said.

So what we were trying to give was the gift of empowerment and we worked very hard learning how we could do this. Essentially, the first thing to do was to get into a loving and open frame of mind and to give the other person your fullest possible attention. We were told, again quite forcefully, that if we had even one ounce of fear in our hearts that the defences of the other person would be triggered, meaning that any chance of a deep connection would be lost. We were told that the next important thing to do during the conversation was to imagine a light surrounding the other person that would allow them to uncover and access their highest wisdom. We were urged to encourage everyone to be the best person they could be, and to live more fully and more truthfully.

At the same time it was important that we abandon any desire to impose our own thoughts and beliefs on the conversation and to let go any desire we might have for a particular outcome to result from it. Instead our role was simply to listen and to ask questions. These were not prescribed questions and we were reminded of the need to stay in touch with our intuition and to trust that the right questions would come at exactly the right moments. There was though one rule to follow. For these had to be open questions that would enable the other person to break free of the restrictions that the programme puts in place in order to prevent freedom of thought and creativity. We were taught that by asking these questions, we could help the other person to bypass the left hemisphere and encourage them to access the power of their right. After being taught the technique, we spent many hours in our study room practicing this on one another.

In addition to this, we were taught the technique of indirect communication. Alamo insisted that it was not always necessary to initiate a conversation with the other person; many powerful effects could result from simply sitting nearby and seeing the very best in that person. Alamo explained that sometimes a person's defences were very strong and that, to bypass them, a more subtle approach was needed. He also explained to us that a lot of our time would be spent working with the energy and atmosphere of the particular person's surrounding environment, as much as with the person themselves. Alamo gave us some tools to help us with this work and let us have time to practice these techniques.

By the time our training came to a close, I was communicating much more effectively with those around me; indeed, everyone in the group had felt their energy levels increase. We were now working together in a mutually supportive way. For the first time in a long time I felt part of something that stirred real passion and longing. The work we had done to develop trust had also lessened the need for me to wear my veil in the group. I felt as though I was right back in that time of pure childhood innocence when the days were long and joyful and my friendships were natural and uncompetitive. I could also feel that there was limitless optimism within the group, as we prepared to take what we had learnt into the outside world. Although our leaders didn't tell us exactly how close we were to reaching the critical mass, there was a palpable sense of anticipation throughout the commune, suggesting that the time was drawing near.

Having spent more than two months training, I was feeling restless and longing to return out into the open air. Although we had been allowed to spend an hour outside every three days, and had been given vitamin tablets to help overcome the deficiency of sunlight, this hadn't been anywhere near enough to satisfy my needs. So there was a palpable buzz of excitement when, one day, Alamo came in and told us that our training was complete and that we were now ready to become fully fledged members of the commune. He told us that his last task as teacher was to divide us into five pairs and that having observed all of us over the past two months, he had been able to work out which pairings would be most effective. Alamo then explained that he was going to give each pair a broad geographical area to work in and that it would be down to us who we decided to befriend and how we wished to work with them. It seemed that we were suddenly being given a lot of responsibility, but he did reassure us that he would remain our guardian and that we would all be able to arrange regular catch-up meetings. With that, he read out the list of names. My name was the first to be read, and I was paired with a lady by the name of Araya.

Araya was someone who I had not really had the chance to connect with intimately. She was of a similar age to me, with a wild gypsy spirit. Alamo explained that he had paired us together because he felt that Araya's bubbly character would help in initiating conversations, while my more steady character would help maintain focus. After listing all five pairings and splitting us up, Alamo walked around to give details of each pairing's assignment. He came around to us first.

'I want you to work in and around the old mining community of Lonarch, which is about an hour north of here. I have a map, a copy of the train timetable, and some basic information about the town to help you find your way around. This is a community that, relatively recently, has developed a particularly high concentration of those given the programme of failure because of the vicious cycle of decline that has taken hold of the town, following the collapse of the coal mining industry towards the end of the last century. Despite numerous regeneration initiatives since, it has never been able to free itself from the clutches of negativity and a sense of hopelessness is now quite embedded within the psyche of the youngest generation. It is a harsh environment and so it will be a difficult challenge. However, it could also be an incredibly rewarding one, for it is one of the few remaining places where we have wanted to have an influence on but haven't had the numbers to do so. I picked the two of you because I feel you are the most capable of having an impact here, so I hope, for the sake of the mission, that you can support each other to fulfil your, and our, highest potential. Is all this quite clear?'

We answered together that it was perfectly clear. Alamo went on to tell us that we had been allocated a daily allowance to help pay for travel and any other expenses that might result from the mission, and that we would each also be given a mobile phone to use to support our work. Alamo invited us to visit the town today in order to get a feel for the place. He then gave us one final warning, telling us how difficult it was to remain in an open, loving state when in the outside world. We were advised to keep an eye open for people and places that didn't feel right and to report anything suspicious to the Matriarch. After that Araya and I left the room, and Alamo went to speak to the other four pairs.

Chapter Twenty-Four

After Araya returned from the Matriarch's office, bearing money and mobile phones, we walked out together into the fresh mid-morning air. Both of us breathed in deeply, appreciating being in the outside world once more. The bright June sunshine was welcome, and we walked purposefully towards the station in order to catch the next train north.

We arrived into Lonarch at lunchtime and decided to head towards the main street and try to find a bar where we could get a bite to eat. We agreed that it would be useful for the two of us to get to know each other on an even more personal and intimate level, given that we would be working so closely from now on. We both felt uncomfortable talking candidly in the street, so we looked instead for a quiet corner where we would be left undisturbed. I took some money from Araya and went to the bar to order sandwiches and drinks for us both. My new found-sensitivity was jarred by my conversation with the barman. He seemed to be feeling a lot of anger and negativity.

At that moment the full extent of our task struck me and I felt weak and overwhelmed. However, after I expressed these feelings to Araya, she did a lot to reassure me, as she gave loving attention and support. After that, I was able to appreciate why it was so important that we were here working in partnership and not alone.

Having found us a quiet spot, Araya became increasingly vocal, describing, in greater detail than she ever had previously, her own difficult background and upbringing. I sat and listened attentively, inviting her to share all her wisdom. Although we had been in the same induction group, the reason I had not really connected intimately with Araya over the past three months was because, when it had been the time to talk about our past, we had typically been split into separate smaller groups. As it turned out she was not really of similar age but a few years younger than me. However, her life had been very different to mine. She told me about her difficult childhood, in the industrial city of Arran in the far north-east of Arasmas.

'Much like the town we are in now, Arran had been solely dependent on one industry. I had only just been born when that industry collapsed completely. Unable to support his family and with no new prospects for work, my father was devastated, taking his own life not long after my first birthday and just before the birth of his second child. My mother struggled on gallantly but was not able to help me and my sister escape our difficult circumstances. She was proud and stubborn and always refused to ask for help from friends and family or to make a fresh start in a more promising place. It was not the easiest upbringing for a young, vulnerable child to endure. Even after my mother passed away when I was 23, because she was exhausted and broken by life, my sister displayed the same stubbornness by staying on in Arran. But I was always more of a free spirit; I'm proud to have rediscovered this identity again, despite all that I've been through. I feel I'm being rewarded now by being a part of something that is helping to heal the many traumas I've experienced in my short life.'

I interrupted her flow to ask when it was that she had discovered that her freedom of spirit was obviously stronger than any programme that was seeking to control her. Looking deeply into my eyes, she confidently gave her answer:

'It must have been at that crucial age, around eight or nine. I remember being in my class at school one morning. I can't remember what we were being taught, but I know I was bored almost to tears being there in that grim, miserable place with an uninspiring teacher completely drained of any passion for life. Finally, it was time for our mid-morning break, and something deep inside of me, some gut instinct I guess, took hold of me for a moment. I just started walking and walking and walking. It was complete madness, I knew; I had no idea where I was or where I was walking to, but I remember feeling calm and knowing that I had to trust this instinct that had taken me over. Now, Myrkais, if you don't know the area it will be hard to picture, but you don't have to travel very far out of my hometown to find yourself surrounded by a majestic landscape of open countryside and distant mountains. And here I was, a child who'd never set foot outside the town before, suddenly enveloped by such beauty. I stood there, I don't know how long for, and just let the natural surroundings ooze into my blood. It was so inspiringly beautiful that it gave me a reason to live. It sounds strange hearing myself say it now, but there was something in that landscape that was so vast and mysterious that it gave me hope that there was something bigger out there waiting for me. And yes, I did go back to school. I think I did this mainly because I didn't wish to upset my mum, who I knew was suffering. But every once in a while I would feel the need to walk back out to that spot in order to revitalise and cleanse myself.'

I felt totally captivated by Araya's story. In many ways it reminded me of the cleansing experiences I had had in the mountains and in the forest, and I felt inspired to hear that Araya had been able to overcome her difficult circumstances after finding something in nature.

'What happened when you finished school?' I asked, full of curiosity.

'I stayed in Arran for a few years, working in a series of temporary jobs in order to support the family. I guess I still felt a strong sense of duty. I knew I should stay and look after my mother even if I wanted to leave the town and travel the world. But that was the naïve innocence of youth and, by the time she'd passed away, I'd become much less of a free spirit. My sister had already married and started her adult life and my maternal body clock suddenly kicked in, telling me that I had to do likewise. I did move away from Arran, though, and soon after I married a man, after a whirlwind romance. Unfortunately though, things between us started to sour after we found out that we wouldn't be able to bring children into the world. Although we stayed together for a few years afterwards, there was a lot of bitterness, and we split up five years ago. It was only then that I started to remember my longing for freedom. It was this longing that eventually brought me in contact with Krugman's book and that was that.'

A silence fell before Araya turned her attention to me, asking me to tell my own story to her in a little more detail than what she'd heard before. Although I had taken the initiative and shared a lot of stories about my personal life in the smaller group, this was quite possibly the first time that anyone had ever asked this question with an apparently genuine desire to know who I was beneath the surface. I realised how significant her question was, but didn't feel this burdening me in the way I would have expected. It seemed that I no longer needed to be defensive or aloof and I felt quite calm about responding openly and honestly. As I told my story, Araya seemed genuinely struck by what I was telling her, surprised that someone who had been following the programme of success had been able to break free. I still saw it as only a modest achievement and suggested that the impulse that had led me here was no different from hers.

Araya strongly disagreed:

'Yes, but my impulse first came to me before the programme had affected me. Yours came to you after you had spent more than 20 years wedded to it. Surely you can see that this required a lot more courage?' There it was again: the word courage that Alamo had also used. I did not know what to say, for I still could not fully accept that my defection from my old way of life, which, to many people, was a completely insane decision, could really be called courageous. However, I was at least now aware that my actions only appeared insane to those who were still in the grip of the left hemisphere and that I no longer had to concur with this view. It no longer seemed a concern of mine what other people thought of my behaviour.

We left the bar and took a walk through the centre of the town, trying to get a feel for the place. As we walked we talked discreetly about how we could approach the task we had been set. I suggested to Araya that the best thing would be to try to connect with one of the teachers at a local school, and she agreed. Seizing the moment, we looked at the map and picked out one of the three junior schools in the town to go and check out. But, because we arrived during school hours, we were only able to look at the buildings and so it was difficult to get a feel for the place. However, since we had walked through a housing estate to get there, we were at least able to get some idea of the psychological profile of the typical person that was living here. I was ready and willing to call it a day here and to catch the next train back to Baron.

But Araya said that she had the feeling that we needed to stay a little longer: to wait for school to close and the teachers to leave. Pulling out the train timetable from her pocket, she showed me that we had plenty of time: we could take the train that left Lonarch at a quarter past five and still be home for our dinner slot. She seemed to be keen to put her training into practice right away and obviously did not want to wait for tomorrow. Reluctantly, I agreed to stay.

We did not have to wait too long before the school bell went and children came pouring out of the building. There were not many parents waiting, and most of the children walked or cycled away unattended. We continued to wait outside the school until the teachers came out as well. Our choice of who to target was made for us: every teacher apart from one was walking towards the parking area and driving away. The solitary figure walking out on foot was a plump young female, probably in her mid-twenties, who was striding purposefully down the road. We followed behind at a safe distance, feeling optimistic that we would get the opportunity to speak with her when we realised that she was leading us back to the main street in the town centre.

My initial impression of the centre of Lonarch hadn't been a positive one: I had felt that it was dull and bland. The high street was lined with the same stores and signs that could be found in many other towns all across Arasmas; it was as if it had been cloned. I did not see one independent store, but I did not doubt that the younger generation saw it as a sign of progress that many of the familiar outlets had deemed it worthwhile to set up in this depressed part of the world. But this was just my first impression and I knew that, at some point, we would have to explore the history of this town in order to properly get to grips with its people.

But today, thanks to Araya's insistence, we were boldly starting the work of the mission. We were pleasantly surprised when we saw our intended target step into one of the coffee houses just off the high street. I held Araya back at the door and watched to see if she would take a seat or not. When we saw her drink being prepared in a china mug, we nodded to each other and swiftly went inside. Standing just inside the doorway, I suddenly felt unsure about what I should do next.

By contrast, Araya seemed to have complete trust in her training and walked boldly over to the lady, who had just sat down, asking if she could join her. I was left at the counter, presumably to order both of us a drink, and could not help but marvel at her brash confidence. By the time I came over to join them they were already deep in conversation and paid me no attention. However, this did give me the space I needed to take a deep breath, control my racing pulse and observe how Araya put her training into practice. It also gave me the chance to visualise a light above Araya's head that could give her the strength to hold the conversation with loving attention. I was mightily impressed at how adept Araya was at relating empathically; she clearly was aware of this lady's feelings and needs, and this encouraged her to respond with complete honesty and openness, despite the fact she was talking with strangers. Maybe Araya could empathise more easily with this woman because they were from a similar background, but I still found it incredible to see that the communication techniques we had been taught really were able to bypass the natural self-protective mechanisms we all put in place between ourselves and others.

The initial exchanges showed that this lady was feeling

extremely frustrated and ground down by her job. She talked about the difficulties that the added responsibilities and paperwork brought, and about how difficult it was to create a healthy and loving atmosphere when most of her time was spent disciplining children who seemed unwilling to learn. However, there was a moment when her mood seemed to shift and she became more optimistic. Araya had told her nothing, simply sitting and listening attentively as she had been taught to do; and now and then repeating what she had heard to reassure the lady that she was being listened to. But there was a point where I sensed that Araya was wavering and that the energy of the conversation was moving in my direction. It felt as if both of them were inviting me to step in and help the conversation to flow again.

It happened when the lady started to request solutions for the situation she was in; Araya had lacked the knowledge to pose the right questions that would help her find her own solutions. At that precise moment, it became clear why Alamo had paired us together: my calm and steady presence helped me access the wisdom I needed at that moment. This helped her to see how she could bring her optimistic spirit into the classroom; I then gave her some advice on how to protect herself from all the pressures that makes teaching such an exhausting profession. We also encouraged her to remember the passion that had inspired her to be a teacher in the first place.

The lady seemed to genuinely appreciate the support we were giving her, although she seemed a little dazed as well. But, before she could ask us any questions, she suddenly looked with horror at her watch and had to make a hurried exit. Getting up to leave, she said to us that never before had anyone given her the chance to express her frustrations in this way and she wondered how she could thank us. Araya told her that we asked for nothing in return and just wrote down our contact number in case she ever needed to get back in touch.

After she had left we finished our drinks in silence, taking in everything that had just happened. Finally, Araya looked into my eyes.

'We should be making a move if we want to get the train home in time for our evening meal,' she said.

I nodded my head, and, getting to my feet, replied.

'I think we've earned it.'

Chapter Twenty-Five

Wednesday, March 12ᵗʰ 2031

 had been part of the mission's work for just under two years when I stumbled across something new that sent my world spinning into flux once more. This incident sent me tumbling into a state of rage, because these two years had passed so happily. I really didn't want this peaceful period to end, but to an end it had come.

Until this moment it had felt that my joy was sustainable and would last. I thought this because I knew that it wasn't as intense as the joy I'd experienced during those few weeks spent with Chris, Tommy and the others. That period of joy had been stimulated by stepping out of the natural rhythm of life, whereas the happiness I had been experiencing during my time in the commune was more heartfelt and real. The key to it had been simplicity and the starting point was the purification of my mind and body – an essential aspect of the principles of Satyagraha. This change in lifestyle had removed so much emotional weight from me and left me feeling lighter and freer in my body and clearer in my mind. I don't think the left hemisphere of my brain had ever been so quiet, and, as a result of the personal healing work I had been doing, I was filled with all the energy that I had previously lost to excessive thinking. I was in the full flow of the river and not holding onto the river-bank; but it was so different an experience to how Tommy had described it.

But even more important than this was the joy I got from the relationships I shared with those living in the commune. This connection was partly the result of the formal sessions of personal sharing that our group of ten continued to do each week. But it mainly resulted from impromptu conversations at mealtimes or in the evening; never before had I felt so connected with other people. My defences had been lowered, helping me to stay connected with life itself.

However, even more significant to my happiness was the relationship I had forged with Araya. After spending every day together these past two years we had formed a deep and lasting bond. It was a precious gift for me to find someone in whose company I felt totally at ease to speak from my heart and to be completely open and vulnerable. Despite all the layers of my conditioning, she had helped me to bring my soul through to the surface. It was not only a joy and privilege to spend my time being with Araya, it was also a joy to be working with her and I was happy that our partnership worked so smoothly and harmoniously.

Because of the strength of our relationship, the work of the mission seemed remarkably easy and it felt that, even in the short space of time we had worked there, we had had a tremendous impact on the town. However, while Alamo always praised us both highly for our work, he also helped to keep me grounded by warning us both about the dangers of complacency and false pride. He encouraged me to see that the ease with which things were shifting was not down to our influence alone but was also a promising sign that the time of transformation was close.

But then something happened that knocked me off balance and allowed my left hemisphere to come roaring back into play with a vengeance. It happened on a particularly bitter Wednesday morning, during what was an unusually late spell of cold weather. The heating within this underground pit was not effective at the best of times and it certainly was not designed to deal with temperatures as low as this. I was lying prone on my bed, my head was throbbing and my nasal passages were full of phlegm. It was hardly surprising that I had been laid low with flu because disease spreads easily in such a confined space. Even though my body and mind had been purified, I was still susceptible to illness. At this point, I had not been outside for four days and had had no choice but to leave Araya to deal with the work on her own. I spent most of this particular Wednesday morning drifting in and out of consciousness; it was getting on for midday when I properly woke up. It was a quiet time in the commune; the breakfast team had long since left and the afternoon cooking team had not yet arrived back to begin their work shift. It felt as though I had the place to myself, although there may have been others in the building also convalescing. Nonetheless, it did seem especially quiet today.

Having been awake for some time, I went to get a hot drink in order to try to soothe my throat and unblock my nose a bit. Rising unsteadily to my feet, I took a deep breath to regain my balance before going down to the canteen. Standing by the urn, I poured some hot water into a mug and added some herbs that the Matriarch had given me, which had helped relieve some of my symptoms. I was just about to turn back out of the canteen to my room when I heard voices coming down the corridor towards me. I reacted instinctively by stepping back into the room, and three men in smart suits walked briskly past and turned into a room towards the end of the corridor. I had not been able to pick out any of their features as they strode past but I immediately picked up a bad vibe.

With an unashamed curiosity, I tiptoed down the corridor after them and saw that they'd left the door slightly ajar. I peered carefully through the gap, and was unable to restrain an audible gasp. Nervously I pulled myself back in case they had become aware of my presence. I could not quite believe what I had seen, for I had looked directly into the ageing face of a man who I had instinctively recognised: I was quite certain that the face belonged to Dr Small.

Dr Small was a man who had been friends with Krugman himself, and was one of the first people to take the movement forward after he had disappeared. I recognised his face because his picture adorned the wall of the main study room and I assumed that the two other men in his company must also be senior figureheads in the resistance. He must now be well into his eighties, I thought, and stepping forwards again, I peered through the gap in order to study more closely this powerful and respected figure. He did not have the same dominant look as he had in the picture: he had a wizened face and his hair was now a ghostly white. But the one thing that captivated me was the sparkle that radiated from his tiny jet black eyes, which had clearly lost none of its impact with age.

What I was struggling to fathom was why these three men had come here for a meeting. Alamo had once told us that the senior figureheads had their own private base, far away in the mountainous north. Moving a little closer, I was able to pick up some of their conversation, and I couldn't resist the opportunity to stay and listen to what they were discussing.

'Are we still making good progress?' asked the man to my left, whose back was facing towards me.

'Yes, we are. We believe that we're back on track with the end of the year remaining our projected completion date for the project, as we had originally planned,' Small replied.

'Do you really think we will have reached the critical mass by then? The signs on the ground still seem to suggest that progress is sluggish,' the third man, who was facing side-on to me, probed.

'Yes, I know, and that has caused some serious doubts. But the data we have received still suggests that we are close to completion. However, perhaps the impact will be more sudden and dramatic than we had previously envisaged. If so, then this should be a cause for joy on our part because it will take the clan more by surprise than a drawn-out collapse would. Do you not agree, gentlemen?'

'Definitely. But at the same time, you do understand our concerns about the lack of a strategy for after the implosion,' the third man responded, in an urgent tone.

'That is why I came here to speak with you today: this strategy has just been finalised by my closest aides and I wanted the two of you to know about it right from the beginning. You two have been the ones who have posed the most questions regarding the lack of a cohesive plan, and I respect you for your persistence regarding this.

I know you were impatient for clarity, but I am sure you can appreciate the difficulties we've faced: we have struggled to gather sufficient information to predict the effects of our revolution. However, we believe that we now have a clearer sense of what is the most likely scenario, and I can speak to you about it today with confidence.

'The first thing I have to tell you is that whilst the implosion will be dramatic, we do not believe that it will be terminal. As you know, top programmers are already fighting against the threats that are starting to emerge, and these programmers will not let the programme die without a fight. We believe that they've already prepared an alternative strategy so that if the programme of failure does go into meltdown they will have a chance of saving both programmes before it is widely realised. If this was successful, only the critical mass, which makes up about five percent of Arasmas' population, would be lost from the clutches of the clan's control.

'However, our view of this alternative programme is that it is not of the same quality as the original one. We feel that people in the low group will soon develop more and more doubts and questions that this new programme will not be able to address. We believe that this will have a domino effect and our view is that they can only keep the programme in place for another six months to a year after this date, and that this won't give them enough time to devise another alternative. We believe that after this time there will be enough free people in the low group to properly begin the process of destabilising the middle group and undermining people's confidence in the economic system. We are sure that the programme used to control this group will not be able to withstand this sort of destabilisation, but we envisage that process could take up to five years to run its course. For this period of time, we will tell everyone involved in our mission not to go into the outside world; we are already beginning to stockpile supplies in our bunkers to make sure that we will be able to hold out.'

'What do you think they will do to try and regain their position of authority when the destabilisation starts to happen?' the second man asked. I sensed a tremor of uncertainty in his voice as he spoke.

'Our guess is that in desperation they will resort back to the oldest trick in the book: they will persuade the military to declare war on Aidni.'

'But how would this action help the clan to stay in power?' the third man interrupted.

'Surely you understand that fear is the one thing preventing us from freeing ourselves of all forms of authority. Well, authorities employ two principal methods in order to create fear in their people. Frightened people are easier to control, after all. The first way is to show people that only the authorities are able to fulfil all of their material needs. The second way is to show people that only the authorities are able to offer security and protection. To do this, they have to create an enemy which is supposedly a threat to the country. They can pick a fight with any of the rogue people and tribes roaming Aidni, and, by doing so, the clan will remain in control a little longer. Of course all the expenditure on military equipment will also help to keep the wheels of industry turning. But, of course, let us not forget that the real reason why the clan needed to devise more sophisticated methods of mind control was because neither of these two methods offers lasting power over the people. They cannot sustain a war on Aidni indefinitely.'

'So what happens when the people of Arasmas start to question why we are at war with Aidni and revolt against the authorities? What then?' the third man asked.

'At this most critical moment we will finally reveal ourselves and offer the people a means to express their frustration with the authorities. We must initiate a violent assault against the clan in order to finally destroy this poisonous society. It will be the time to initiate civil war. All of those still attached to the ways of the modern world will want to stop us, and no doubt the battle will be bloody and violent, but the prospect of freedom surely means that violence will be a price worth paying. Because remember, gentlemen: we hold the moral high ground, and we are carrying the light of truth with us.'

At this point Small stood up, and, with his clenched fist, he hammered it forcefully on the table. 'Then I will finally fulfil my own personal destiny. After all these years in the shadows, I will be able to stand once again before the Director of the clan and look this broken man in the eyes. He will know that it was I who had plotted this, that it was I who had defeated him.'

My eyes widened with shock. I watched Dr Small take a deep breath before calmly returning to his seat. The two men in my company had, surprisingly, remained calm at this dramatic outburst and did not seem perturbed by the wickedness that had entered the room.

But then the man with his back to me posed a question to Small. His reply pierced my heart.

'Do you have any idea what will happen once the power of the clan has dissolved?'

I looked directly into Small's steely eyes and was shocked by the look of distaste that he shot at the man who had asked the question.

'Afterwards? Is that something we should really concern ourselves with? The mission will have succeeded, and everyone will have been freed from the clutches of the Director and the rest of the clan. Surely that is all that matters to us; surely that is our only purpose? All I can take responsibility for is what will happen to me personally. I would urge you to start making your own plans for escape, for, no doubt, some people will want revenge on those of us involved with the mission. For myself, I dream of disappearing to a remote paradise on an island off the western shore of Adanac. I imagine golden white sandy beaches and I see myself sharing champagne with my closest allies in the hot sunshine. Maybe you two would like to join us there? Or do you have your own dream endings in mind? Gentleman, I accept my fate: as no doubt at some point someone will track me down and kill me, if the sands of time do not take me first of course. But I will have at least secured my place in the history books as the saviour of Arasmas and my life's work will be done.

'You too must have known when you signed up for the mission that death was a likely consequence, yet I see that the prospect still scares you and makes you hesitate. But please, gentlemen, don't hold back now. Your help is vital, and surely you can see that it is better to die bravely than to live as a coward. Come and join me in a prayer that one day the power of the clan will come to an end and light will shine over Arasmas once more.'

As they started praying together, my fever swept over me again and I began to feel dizzy and unbalanced. I left as quietly as I could and went back upstairs to my room. My head was spinning, only partially because of my illness. I lay down on my bed, sweat pouring off my brow; I tried to hope that what had happened had been nothing more than a feverish nightmare. But, deep down, I knew that this was not the case. All I could do to try to calm myself was to take my notebook and pen and begin to write. This time the writing covered four pages and, as usual, it flowed, ending at the bottom of each page and starting again at the top of the next. Afterwards, I dropped the notebook and slipped into a state of unconsciousness.

Chapter Twenty-Six

As my body returned to full health I felt more able to think about the conversation I had overheard. My illness had dragged me down into a state of negativity, causing strong emotions that I just didn't have the strength to overcome. The first question I needed to answer was: why had this incident so damaged my faith in the mission? After reflecting on this, I realised that although on the surface it was a noble endeavour, this was an illusion; by digging down a little deeper I had uncovered the truth. This truth was that all I was doing was helping one man to carry out his petty desire for revenge against the leader of the clan. Was this really a calling that I could feel passionate about?

I felt so angry. Part of this anger was directed inwardly: I felt frustrated that I had allowed myself to become a pawn in their political game. But mainly I was angry that after hearing Dr Small my happiness and blissful innocence had given way to dark and sinister feelings. The power of Satya was clearly being abused and the noble principles of Satyagraha to which we had committed ourselves seemed well and truly tarnished by Dr Small's desire to engage us in violent battle with members of the clan. The hypocrisy of it all was what hurt the most.

Whilst Dr Small was only one man among all the hundreds who were also involved in the mission, I knew that he had a lot of influence. Why had I never before asked what would happen after our society was free from the clutches of the clan, I wondered. I felt that I should have been wiser than to believe that we would find freedom; after all, our history was littered with revolutions that promised heaven but led to hell. Why did I think that this one would be any different? Cynicism was seeping back into my veins; I bemoaned the fact that all human civilisations were flawed and riddled with imperfections and injustice. At this moment it seemed to me that freedom would be impossible to deliver.

But I felt unable to tell anyone what I had overheard and so I carried the burden of the truth around with me for a while. I think everyone close to me picked up that something was amiss, as, over the days and weeks that followed, my behaviour changed and my enthusiasm evaporated. Even with Araya I could not express what I knew and strains started to emerge in our relationship. Little did she know that I was trying to protect her and the others in the commune: deep down, I knew that this mission had given them a glimmer of hope and I didn't want the responsibility of having to blow out the flame. I realised that I would not be thanked for having taken on the role of whistleblower.

But the longer I stayed in the commune, the more difficult it became. My conscience wouldn't let me forget what I had heard and I knew now that by healing people, we were only making the situation even worse than it was at the moment. I was damned if I did and damned if I didn't. All this heaviness within me created a growing sense of resistance to the work of the mission, and my loss of focus meant that our conversations with the people of the town were becoming frequently unsuccessful. Deep down, I knew it would not be long before Araya would start to feel suspicious about my loss of passion; I feared that I was causing irreparable damage to my relationship with her. The only option I had was leaving and I started planning for my escape by putting aside some spare money. Although I had some money left in my bank account, I was wary of using it, worrying that an agent could be watching my transactions.

I was unsure where to go, so I walked down to Lonarch train station. It was a major junction with trains from Sarum passing through, heading to the north east of Arasmas, and trains from Eton, the capital, also passing through, heading through to the north west. Looking at the train timetables I saw that not long after our usual train arrived into Lonarch in the mornings, there was a service passing through from Eton; this train went right through to the end of the line. A station towards the end of the line grabbed my attention; a place named Nabotan. I felt an urge to go there so as to get as far away from the commune as possible. There was no doubt my fellow members would come searching to find me in case I fell in the wrong hands. It had taken me nearly two months after hearing Dr Small's words to pluck up enough courage to leave. Yet it was not the fear of capture or the hopelessness of my future that'd caused me to hesitate, it was my feelings for Araya.

After I decided to leave, I had discovered just how deep my feelings for Araya were. The first evening after making my decision I had gone to bed early, but was unable to sleep; my stomach churned and I felt restless. Initially, I had put this queasy feeling down to the fact that I was entering a time of transition and change; I sensed that my body was resisting the unknown future that lay ahead of me. But the churning didn't stop over the days that followed, so the sleepless nights continued and my appetite deserted me.

But the more that I tried to figure out the reason for my unsettledness, the less convinced I felt that it was because I was reluctant to leave the safety and security of commune life. The more I reflected, the more I came to realise that what I was experiencing was not a sensation of fear but a sensation of love. The distinction between the two was a subtle one: it seemed that the feelings of love and fear were walking side-by-side inside my heart. But despite this, I could tell it was a feeling of love because I felt it pulling me towards something; fear always feels like a push. I realised that it was this pull of love that was churning up my insides, and when I asked myself what it was that I was being pulled towards, the answer I received was that it was Araya.

I felt tormented by my realisation of how deeply I longed to be with her. I had known it would be a wrench to leave her, but had never before appreciated quite how strong my feelings for her were. But, over the days that followed, I couldn't decide whether this attraction I felt was just a result of the bond that had developed between us or whether there really was something more profound there. The more I delved into the deepest recesses of my heart, the more I realised that the love I felt was a combination of the two.

This led me to cast my mind back to Jen and our relationship. Although, over the years we had spent together, I had learnt to find the real Jen that lay beyond the image she had to portray at work, our connection was quite superficial in comparison to the connections I had established with people here in the commune. I accepted that this was largely down to the failure of our education to give us the ability to relate on a deeper level, but at the same time I accepted that my feelings for her came from my head rather than my heart. It left me sad to realise that the grief I'd experienced in leaving her had been more because of the blow to my self esteem than because of the loss of her love. But the feelings I had for Araya were very different; her presence in my life had helped me to live more fully from my heart, to live with real passion and a strong sense of purpose. But was this a reason to tell her how I felt?

The prospect of doing so filled me with doubt. For one thing I'd learnt by living here in the commune was the beauty of an unconditional love that I could share out with all people. I believed that this kind of love was more powerful, more important and much healthier than a romantic love between two people. I had always seen Araya as a soul mate rather than as a lover, and I was reluctant to combine the two. As well as this, I was aware of how attached Araya was to the mission and that she would not welcome it if I made her choose between the mission and me. Fear of rejection also played its part in this heady and confusing mix of emotions.

In response, I meditated, working to try to let go all of my fears and doubts and also to let go of the beliefs that were preventing me from finding the Satya I needed to help me with this situation. I let go of my desire for the outcome I wanted to happen: Araya leaving the commune with me and for us to continue our relationship. With as much patience as I could muster, I waited for clarity and wisdom to emerge to help me to make the right decision.

The answer came to me eventually: it was that this situation was a test of how willing I was to trust. I had to trust that Araya would discover the truth for herself before it was too late, and it was not my place to interfere in that process. I also had to trust that I would have the strength to continue on my journey alone. I needed to let go of the bonds of dependency that had formed during my time in the commune. Finally I had to trust that letting her go was the right thing to do, having faith that if, when apart from one another, we discovered that our love was genuine, and that we truly were soul mates, circumstances would one day bring us back together.

However, when it came to the day of my departure, a stifling hot day in early June, I knew that I could not just vanish without saying something to her. It took me a long time to think of the right words to say; I knew that it would not be an easy conversation. We left that morning to catch our usual train to Lonarch; I had taken nothing but the clothes I was wearing, my notebook and my wallet. I was quiet on the journey, trying to gather my thoughts, and Araya seemed a little distant too. Finally, as we approached Lonarch, I asked her whether we could take a moment to talk before starting our day's work. She agreed and I led her to a small park next to the station. We sat down on a bench, shaded by an old oak tree.

There was a long silence, as I tried to summon up the courage to speak. During this pause, the words I had rehearsed finally came to mind.

'Araya, it has been a unique and privileged experience to have spent these past two years with someone whose presence touches me so deeply. I've never felt anything like the emotions you evoke in me. I'm reluctant even to label them, for words cannot do those feelings justice. Honestly and genuinely, I do not need you to try and reciprocate these feelings: I am not asking anything of you. I'm sharing this to let you know what is going on inside of me. I'm doing this because I believe that if this feeling is truly genuine then I have to be willing to let you go and to be separated from you. I believe you are my soul mate, Araya, but it would be too easy to

257

taint the love I feel for you with feelings of romance and desire. I have faith that if this love is real that our paths will cross again in the future. If our paths do not cross then I know that my feelings for you were just false and dishonourable ones.'

After I said these words, a long, heavy pause followed. Araya closed her eyes before replying.

'I believe that our feelings are mutual, but, unlike you, I know that my feelings are only of pure love not of desire. I also believe you are my soul mate, Myrkais, and so I'm left feeling devastated by what you have told me. Myrkais, I cannot understand why we cannot hold on to our feelings of love by staying together rather than being apart.'

She clasped my hands with hers and looked deeply, piercingly, into my eyes. The look she gave me showed the deepest love, and it tested my resolve. I had to bow my head and avert my eyes, for I knew that I was not telling her everything. Eventually responding, I spoke softly:

'I know it is difficult to understand, but I have to follow my instincts, and this is what they are telling me to do. All I ask is that you also stay true to your instincts even if this means making difficult decisions, especially regarding any attachment to your work here.'

Araya was clearly perplexed by my final statement; this showed in her eyes. But I did not give her time to ask me what I meant. Instead, I asked her to close her eyes and embrace me. It was hard to let her go but, as I moved away, I asked her to stay where she was with her eyes closed. I got up to walk away, but before I did, with real tenderness, I bent down, took her hands in mine once again and kissed her gently on the lips. It was a wrench to pull myself away from her and, as I walked off, I struggled to resist the temptation to look back.

Chapter Twenty-Seven

There were tears in my eyes as I sat on the train, my face pressed to the window. Dreamily I looked out at the rolling hills passing by, although Araya was still at the forefront of my mind. It had been wonderful to hear, but her assurance that the feeling of love was mutual only made it more difficult to leave her.

I was on board an express train that whizzed through many stations without stopping, but it still took most of the day to get to Nabotan. When I finally arrived I discovered that it was a small fishing village, sitting nestled in a cove giving it shelter from the elements. This was a very rugged and wild part of the coastline; there seemed few settlements in this part of Arasmas. The town was bathed in warm sunshine, giving it a cheerful air, although, as I left the train, I quickly sensed that this impression was a deceptive one: the faces of the people walking past showed clearly that this was a hard place to make a living. I guessed that, apart from occasional tourists, that the fishing industry must be the lifeblood of this quaint old village.

It was getting late in the day and I wasn't sure what my next step would be. As I had spent most of my money on the train ticket, I was reluctant to pay for a room. Instead, as it was a warm evening, I thought I would find a sheltered spot on the beach to rest. However, walking past the village general store, my attention was captured by a notice pinned on the window. The notice said, simply and intriguingly: 'Help required in exchange for meals and board. Please place all enquiries with the General Store.'

At that moment a man walked out of the store and for some

reason my intuition gave me the feeling that he was the one who had placed this notice. I called out to him:

'Excuse me. Do you know anything about this notice in the window?'

The man turned around with a surprised look on his face.

'Yes, I have only just placed it there. Are you interested in the position?'

'Yes I am,' I answered without hesitation. 'My name is Myrkais,' I added walking over and holding out my hand.

'John,' he answered simply as he held out his in return.

John went on to explain that he lived on a small island called Diarra and that he needed a second pair of hands on his allotment. It sounded to me like the perfect hideaway. I enthusiastically agreed on the spot; but John was more cautious as he said he would take me over to have a look around first. We strolled down to the jetty together to the place where his small motor boat was moored. Taking a look across at John I could not quite place him amongst this backdrop. I could tell he was not a local because, unlike the other people in the village I'd seen passing through, he didn't have a weather-beaten face. The glasses he wore made him stand out even more. Instead, he had a smooth, chubby face, and was rather heavier than I would have expected from someone working in an allotment. He was young as well; probably a good ten years younger than me. It immediately made me wonder how he had come into possession of an island and why he had chosen to live there.

We didn't speak much on the journey although, from the few words he did say, I recognised his accent as being from southern Arasmas. Before long, we rounded the headland and I caught my first glimpse of Diarra. It looked like nothing more than a big slab of black rock jutting out of the water. Pointing it out, John told me that it was only a small island, a mile long and a mile wide. Even in the late summer sunshine it appeared to be an inhospitable and foreboding place and I wondered how John had managed to set up his home there.

We soon pulled up against a huge rock that had been transformed into a landing post. Some iron rungs had been fitted, providing us with a ladder to climb up to solid ground. After helping John tie up the boat, I climbed up, and he followed. As we walked, he explained to me that the old stone cottage where he lived had been built by a company who had constructed a lighthouse on the far side of the island. The house had been intended to provide a home for the lighthouse keeper and his family. He told me that the lighthouse was now redundant, but the cottage remained, and he had bought it two years before. John led me into the cottage and I was immediately struck by how cool it was inside. When I mentioned this he immediately pointed to the thick stone walls, telling me that they were designed to keep the house cool in summer and to keep the heat in during the winter.

He gave me a brief tour of the house. There were two bedrooms and a bathroom upstairs and a lounge and kitchen downstairs. Apart from a couple of electric heaters the main source of heat was a wood stove that stood in the lounge; John told me that this also heated the water for the bathroom and kitchen. I was surprised to see that there was no toilet in the bathroom, and, when I asked him about this, he told me that there was a compost loo in the back garden. John explained that the plumbing system used rainwater, which was brown in colour because it drained through the peat bogs at the back of the house, although he insisted that it was safe to wash in. He went on to show me the filter that was in place, which meant there was now also a supply of drinking water.

John then took me around the small allotment he'd established at the front of the house, which he said helped him to live a largely self-sufficient life, before taking me back to the house. Ducking frequently to avoid the many low wooden beams, we walked through into the lounge and John invited me to take a seat, while he went into the kitchen to put the kettle on. On his return, he sat down and asked me hesitantly whether I wanted to stay or whether I would prefer to be taken back to the mainland.

I was surprised that he seemed worried that I might have been put off by what I had seen, and I tried to reassure him that I was willing to stay. Indeed, it did seem the best possible option for me at that moment. Finally John asked me a question I had long been expecting: when did I want to go back to the mainland to collect the rest of my belongings? I had already thought of a plausible explanation to explain my lack of possessions: I told him that I'd had a bitter falling out with my wife and that she had locked me out of the house the previous night. I explained to John that I had decided not to try to resolve our differences and that, instead, I was looking to get away in order to make a fresh start elsewhere. I told him that I had stayed with a friend the previous night and then simply jumped on the train the first thing that morning.

John simply nodded his head, asking no further questions. This seemed slightly odd, given that he had invited a complete stranger to live in his house. Instead he kindly offered to lend me some of his clothes until I got myself sorted out, before going upstairs to make the bed for his new guest. After eating a fresh salad for dinner, I said to John that I wished to retire early so that I would be ready to begin work first thing the next morning. In truth I wanted time alone to absorb all that had happened and to turn my mind towards Araya. Another sleepless night followed; the churning sensation in my stomach still had not eased. Fortunately, I didn't need to go outside to use the toilet during the night, and I did manage to get some sleep before John woke me up at six o'clock.

The soft, sagging mattress had made my back ache, and I felt reluctant to get out of bed as the room was cold. When John had finished in the bathroom, I did force myself to take a shower. It felt strange to be bathing in brown water, especially as the water was cold. John had told me that he didn't want to waste wood to have hot water through the summer months. Returning to my room, I saw that he had laid out a set of work clothes for me to wear, although, as John was a few sizes bigger than me, they were a very loose fit. I walked downstairs and saw that John had already laid out some freshly boiled eggs and toast along with a pot of herbal tea.

I didn't have long to enjoy my breakfast, for John explained that his goat needed milking and he wanted to show me how it was done. For the rest of that first day, John gave me a thorough tour of his garden, showing me all the varieties of fruit and vegetables he had planted during the spring. Chickens roamed freely through the garden; we spent some time searching for eggs. John explained that he let the chickens roam free because they were helpful little gardeners, working the soil with their claws and fertilising it with their manure. He had many other odd and eccentric methods of gardening, and later that evening showed me his large collection of books covering subjects such as basic organic farming methods, permaculture and bio-dynamics. John advised me to read these if I wished to learn more about his style of gardening, and, as the evenings were often long and quiet I borrowed many of them.

I was given a lot of free time, enabling me to go off and explore the island on foot. Although Diarra looked like just a slab of rock, the environment was actually quite varied with a lot of interesting geographical features. The rocky terrain that predominated around the edge of the island gave way to spongy marshland in the centre; there were also a couple of sandy coves on the far side where the island was most exposed to the elements. There were few trees on the island, hardly surprising considering that the island was battered by strong winds, and this left the landscape looking rather barren. John never joined me on these walks: he said that he was not fit enough to properly explore the island and he preferred to stay close to the cottage. However, as he was not yet completely self-sufficient, he did have to leave the island once a week in order to collect supplies from the mainland. I would often join him on these trips, as they helped me release my feelings of isolation.

As the summer wore on, I got used to the lifestyle of the island. It felt good to spend a lot of time outside among nature and work-ing with my hands. Even though I knew that Arasmas would soon be dragged into civil war, I felt very distant from any turmoil on this remote island. But I wasn't able to let go of my thoughts for Araya, and I knew there was still a lot of pain to be healed.

But while I enjoyed my time in the garden, I found living with John a trying experience. The first time I met him I knew instinctively that he was carrying a lot of anger and emotional baggage; I knew that he was hiding from something and that was why he had come to this island. He was incredibly stubborn; a man who always wanted to be in complete control, even when doing the simplest tasks. If I did anything slightly differently from how he wanted then he would just quietly take over from me. This was something I found to be a real drain on my energy levels. In those moments, I wondered why it was that he had invited me to stay.

I did ask him once why, after two years living on the island, he had decided to advertise for help. His answer was interesting:

'It is because I recently discovered, on the Internet, that there are networks of people who, like me, are trying to live more and more outside of the system. But what they, and I, realise is that it is not efficient to try to meet all one's needs by becoming self-sufficient. To give an example, my clothes are starting to get really worn and I would like to get hold of some wool to make some new ones. Now it doesn't make sense for me to buy sheep just to provide me with the wool I need. At the moment I have to buy my wool from the general store in Nabotan, but I feel really uncomfortable using money. This is where the network comes in: they trade in goods rather than in money. So this is where you come in: I need assistance in order to be able to produce a surplus of food so that I will be able to trade and buy the things I don't have.'

His response made me think about the clan and how John was trying to live outside of their control. I doubted whether he knew the truth and I didn't think I should tell him all I knew, as I doubted his trustworthiness. It was strange. I had received training to help people shift their anger, and yet something was still holding me back from sitting down with John and listening to his story. I knew that this was partly because I was dealing with my own issues at the moment and so I felt too imbalanced to support him as well. His controlling nature didn't make me feel inclined to try to overcome the emotional distance that lay between us either. Instead I tried to appease him as much as possible by doing what he told me to and by keeping a safe distance. Doing so did not bring me any peace, though.

The evenings were the hardest; this was when I felt most weak and helpless. I would become lost in my own thoughts and craved the support of the commune. I missed the intimacy and the deep connections I had experienced with the people there, but most of all I missed Araya. I found myself cursing Dr Small for having politicised and tainted the mission's noble work. I no longer knew who I was or what the future would hold for me. All I had to look forward to was a cold winter of hard labour in the company of a man who I couldn't bear. During these long evenings I would long for the morning, when I could put my hands in the soil and let the darkness dissipate.

Life became more difficult as we moved into the winter months. As the weather worsened everything about life on the island suddenly became more trying. The island was constantly pounded with cold, driving rain, making working difficult. For a couple of weeks we were stranded on the island as John deemed it too risky to take the boat across to the mainland through the gales. Our stove needed timber, which John usually collected on the mainland, and so during this period we had to live on the supplies that he had stockpiled. But even when we had plenty of wood, there was nowhere to put it where it would stay dry. Lighting fires with cold and damp wood was a real ordeal, and I became increasingly frustrated that John wasn't trying to find a solution to this problem. Even with the fire lit and the electric heaters on the house was still cold, for the windows were not double-glazed and draughts would blow all through the house. I complained inwardly about having to use the poorly-built compost toilet and having to wash with peaty water.

As the days shortened and we moved into the depths of winter, I was even able to watch how my behaviour changed. I now seemed to be acting according to my basic instincts, almost as though I was focused only on staying alive. Sometimes I would catch myself anxiously watching John when he cooked dinner to check if he was giving me a fair share; at other times, I would rush into the shower before him in the morning so that I would get hottest water. I even found myself leaving work undone, hoping that he would take on more than his fair share. Even though I knew that my behaviour was only increasing the strains on our relationship, it was hard to resist my impulses. Whenever I caught myself doing something like this, I must admit it was strange to observe because it was most unlike me to be so selfish. Living like this made me pine even more for the commune and its atmosphere of love and co-operation.

After these harsh, trying weeks I was grateful when we moved into February and the first shoots of spring started to appear. This was the busiest time for the garden, and the added work proved to be a welcome distraction. However my body was weak and I was feeling deprived of sunlight. The lack of sunlight was one of the most difficult aspects of a northern winter and it reminded me of the winter of discontent that I had endured after I had left my old life in Sarum. The thing that I was reminded of the most was how much a life of poverty had caused me to lose all of my clarity and wisdom.

On reflection, I could accept that the modern economy that the clan had created was not the evil force that the mission had made it out to be. It was not something that should be conquered so that we could return to the old ways of living. Technology and science were gifts that had helped to make our lives simpler and had helped the human race to evolve so that life was no longer merely a struggle for survival. The lesson I had learnt before was that renunciation of the programme of success in favour of a life of poverty was not wise; now I could take a broader view and see that the renunciation of the whole of the modern world, which was what John seemed to be doing, was also not a wise path to follow. When I realised this, it became clear to me that the time had come to leave the island and to find a new direction.

But the question I was still left with was how I could be in the world and yet not be of it. How could I possibly use the advantages of the modern world to make my daily life simpler and yet have the time and energy to address the most fundamental problems of being human? I knew I still hadn't fully reconciled the abyss that lay between the left and right hemisphere of my brain. I also knew that whilst I'd had glimpses; I still hadn't truly discovered Satya.

I hoped that I would receive guidance from somewhere, but, for the moment, all I could do to help release my confusion was take my notebook and pen and begin to write. This time my writing covered three pages and, as usual, it flowed naturally, ending at the bottom of each page and starting again at the top of the next.

Chapter Twenty-Eight

A couple of days later something strange happened. It was the middle of the week and, as John had gone to the mainland to run some small errands, I had been working alone on the island all day. I was preparing dinner when he returned. He told me that he had been to the post office and had picked up a letter that had been waiting for me there. I was surprised to hear this, as I had not told anyone where I was living. Part of me was hoping that it was a letter from Araya, maybe saying that she had escaped and found out where I was. But there was also a part of me who was afraid that I had finally been tracked down, either by agents or by members of the commune. However, it didn't seem very likely that an agent would send me a letter I had to admit.

After we had eaten and John had gone off to do the dishes, I took the letter upstairs. Although I had been trying to stay calm, my heart was pounding with a mixture of anticipation and apprehension. While walking upstairs I looked at the envelope and felt disappointed, as I immediately realised the writing was not Araya's. In fact, I didn't recognise the handwriting at all. Neither had I heard of the town where the letter had received a postmark. When I got to my room I nervously tore open the letter, and a small piece of paper dropped out onto the bed. In handwriting that was barely legible, it read:

'I can give answers to questions you don't even feel the need to ask. I will be waiting in the café at the back of Wagsale's centre of worship at two o'clock sharp this coming Sunday afternoon. If you want to go a little deeper down the rabbit hole then meet me there.'

My first thought was that this was a trap set by people who wanted to capture me. But again my instincts pulled me in a different direction; I was struck by the coincidence that I had received this letter so soon after my realisation that I had to leave the island. There was still a part of me that longed to trust in the kindness of others. I had spent far too much time recently in the company of the mistrustful John. I had to trust that through the power of a genuine heart and open communication my difficulties could be resolved, for, deep down, I wanted to believe in the innate goodness of humanity. I told John that the letter was from an old friend who wanted to meet up and asked if he would be so kind as to take me to the mainland. I would have taken the boat myself but John had told me before that he did not want anyone else using it but him. But at least he did offer to take me across and to pick me up on my return.

I had never visited Wagsale before but remembered that it was a station that I'd passed through on my way to Nabotan. John had a copy of the local train timetable, and I read that there was a train that would get me there well before the two o'clock meeting, as well as one that would bring me home before it got dark. So Sunday came and I took the train to Wagsale. On my arrival, I discovered that it was quite a sizeable market town, with three main shopping streets. I ate the sandwiches that I had brought and afterwards made my way to the centre of worship.

The building was a central landmark in the town, although it was no longer in use and had fallen into disrepair. The café was easy to find and, although I was a little early, I decided to go inside. I walked straight to the counter and ordered a drink, before looking around the room to see if I could spot the person who had sent the letter. The place was quite busy but, at one table, a man was sitting alone. I guessed this must be the person I was here to meet, for he seemed somehow out of place here. He was wearing a long black overcoat and a trilby hat, and reminded me of the two spotters who had accosted me in the bar all those years before.

I walked over, assuming that, as he had his back to me, he

wasn't aware of my presence. As I got closer, I realised he was sitting perfectly still and alert, holding a mug of something. I felt hesitant and slowed my pace a little as I approached, but, without looking around, he spoke, reassuring me:

'Good afternoon, Myrkais.'

He gestured for me to take a seat, which I did with a certain amount of timidity. But as I looked into his eyes I immediately relaxed, feeling enveloped in a strong, loving presence. His smile was warm and reassuring, and the wrinkles on his elderly face gave the impression of wisdom. He began to speak in a soft, hushed tone.

'I imagine you are feeling a little unsure about whether I am a friend or a foe; I admire your courage, Myrkais: it was a risk to decide to come here and face me. That is a sign of just how far you have come in the process of learning to trust your instincts. I want to reassure you that I am a friend who can help you with your journey if you are willing to listen. But let me introduce myself first. My name is Zeus and I too was once a member of the mission. Like you, I am one of the rare few who have left it behind and have not been captured.

'Now, I normally steer well clear of those who choose to leave the mission behind, but when I heard the news of your disappearance something about it really intrigued me. This led me to try to get in touch with you before anyone else found you. I don't know if you fully realised it, Myrkais, but the members of the mission felt that there was something very special about you, and, even though they feared your power, they longed to use it for their own reasons. You created a lot of excitement when you joined them. Now you have left, you pose a very significant threat to the mission due to the power you hold; you are now their most wanted man. It was a wise decision to go and hide on Diarra for it was not easy for me to track you down, Myrkais. But even though it is dangerous for us to meet, now that you are here, I feel that our meeting today is very significant.'

Even though Alamo had told me how rare it was for someone to challenge the programme of success, I had not realised before how important I was for the success of the mission. But I was still curious to know how long he had spent in the mission, why he had chosen to leave and how he had managed to avoid capture. I put these across to him gently.

'I spent nearly 20 years in the mission and had even progressed to the role of teacher. I think I left for the same reason you did: I discovered the hypocrisy that lay at the very heart of the mission. As to your third question, the one thing that allows me to stay one step ahead of those who wish to cage me again is my capacity to live fully from my right hemisphere. You see Myrkais, this is one of the things I wanted to talk to you about today – it will help you escape capture as well – but I will come back to it in due course. To begin with, I need to know whether I am correct in assuming that you've realised the nature of this hypocrisy that I mentioned.'

I felt comfortable telling Zeus about the conversation I had overheard between Dr Small and two other men, and confirmed that, in doing so, I had indeed realised the hypocrisy that was poisoning the mission. Enthusiastically, Zeus picked up on my words.

'Yes, and do you realise, Myrkais, that this hypocrisy has always poisoned every human civilisation that has ever been established in the world?'

I answered that I assumed that this was probably true. Despite my answer, he insisted on giving me his understanding of why this always happened.

'The reason why no civilisation has ever managed to escape this hypocrisy is because the left hemisphere is so powerful. Do you see, Myrkais, that the seed of the mission, like the beginning of most civilisations, was conceived using the wisdom of the right hemisphere. But the difficulty is trying to grow that seed in the harsh conditions of the real world. For, even before the great turning and the start of the modern age, there has never been a time in our history where the right hemisphere of the human brain has held dominion over the world.

'So, in this harsh climate, compromises have to be made in order for anything to grow and flourish. Lofty principles and noble visions are watered down because they do not produce immediate results. When this process begins the seed is very vulnerable to attack from humans who wish to use it for their own selfish agendas. This is exactly what happened when Dr Small became involved in the mission.

'Let me go on to tell you the history of the mission that you will not have been told about. After Krugman left his book in the hands of his female ally she gathered together a small group of men and women that she trusted. Between them, they developed a noble strategy designed to bring about revolution and change. This is the strategy that you were taught to work for during your own training in the mission. However, even after working tirelessly for over ten years, the group were still struggling to have much impact because they lacked the resources needed to recruit new members and to spread the word. This was the moment in the mission's history where they were forced to choose between either upholding their noble principles and having no money or bringing in some money but compromising their principles. And who was it who forced them to take this decision? It was none other than Dr Small.

'Now, the group had always been unsure about what motivated him to become involved in the work of the mission. They had discovered that he had once been a core member of the secret clan but that, after a major disagreement with the Director, he had been forced to leave. After leaving the clan, he learnt of a small group that was plotting a revolution and realised that he could use the work of the mission to get his revenge. Having siphoned off a vast amount of money from the clan, he was extremely wealthy and used this to tempt the rest of the group into accepting him into the mission. Eventually, Dr Small's control and influence became so extensive that the original members of the group felt that they were no longer acting according to Krugman's intentions and disassociated themselves from the mission altogether. From what you've told me, Myrkais, it seems as if you are following in their footsteps.'

I was surprised to hear Zeus say that Dr Small had never met Krugman; I had always been led to believe that they knew each other well. I didn't pursue this but went on to ask Zeus about how control could be wrested away from Dr Small. His answer came as a shock:

'You need to understand, Myrkais, that the mission was doomed even before it started, and, therefore, there is nothing you can to do to save it. To understand this you need to grasp just how powerful the Director and the other members of the clan are. Just think all the time you were a pawn in Dr Small's game, Dr Small was only a pawn in the clan's game.

'The clan have to ensure that society remains stable in order to stay in power. To do this, they have to constantly work on cleansing and purifying any instability to make sure that their systems are functioning efficiently and to stop any elements interfering with this. So, Myrkais, how do you think they remove those people whose beliefs don't quite fit with the system?'

'I don't know,' was my only response.

Zeus suddenly pulled his chair back, reached down to the floor and held a familiar object in front of me: Krugman's book.

'Can't you see, Myrkais? This is the carrot that they dangle before you, but the moment you reach out to grab it you reveal yourself to be the black sheep of the flock. Now, as I have said, to begin with it was a struggle for those in the group to spread Krugman's words as widely as the clan had initially hoped. Then along came Dr Small and they realised that they could use his energy to draw out a bigger group of people who were becoming unstable in the clan's eyes. At the same, the distraction of the mission helped the clan keep Dr Small under close surveillance.'

It was shocking to hear that the clan had been behind the mission all along, but there was still one thing that puzzled me.

'But why has the Director let it get so far? Why has he allowed Small to get so close to the finish line?'

'He wanted to find as many individuals as possible whose views have not been fully purified through the clan's programmes. The Director will strike at the very last moment possible.'

'But what can the Director do?' I asked.

'You have to understand how easy Dr Small has made the clan's job. He has herded all of those people who are a threat to his power into a few locations. This makes it easy for the Director to gather all these people together and punish them accordingly. You see, Myrkais, all of the people in the mission have been asked to go underground and no longer keep contact with friends and family in the outside world. Their disappearance will not be noticed; they have long since disappeared already.'

'So are you telling me that Small's plans for a revolution were all just a myth?' I asked.

'No, not at all. In theory, at least, it is plausible: the clan understood that if Small was going to follow their chosen path it had to look like he was acting of his own accord. Being a member of the clan, he knew about the electronic chip in the second molar, but, naively, he believed that, by removing it, he could live undetected. I know you lived in the commune at Baron, Myrkais. Tell me honestly: did you really believe that such an audacious construction could have been kept secret?

I answered that it had seemed a little far-fetched, but that I had been caught up in the false sense of security that the clan had allowed to develop in the mission. I went on an asked Zeus what would happen when the commune members were caught. He told me bluntly that most would probably be tortured to death. I had been fortunate to leave when I did, he said. My decision had bought me a little bit of time.

'So if I can't save the mission, what can I do to help solve my country's woes?' I asked.

'As I've already mentioned, Myrkais, all you can do is to learn to use the power of your right hemisphere at every moment in your life. You are very wise for someone so young; you couldn't have come this far on the journey if you hadn't learnt how to follow the instincts that come from the heart and into the right hemisphere.

'But, despite these flashes of inspiration, you still have too many moments of weakness when you allow your left hemisphere to get back in the driving seat. I can tell there is part of you that is still working towards solving the question of who you are and how you can find meaning and purpose in life. This part of you is the seeker and as long as you keep on searching you will remain stuck in the dimensions of space and time and one foot will stay stuck in the world of the left hemisphere. Myrkais, you simply cannot discover Satya by searching for it in this way.

'To truly discover Satya you have to be willing to take a leap of faith. Just jump into the ever-present now. This is the fifth dimension that exists beyond our four-dimensional world. When you have placed both feet in this fifth dimension, Myrkais, you will have complete freedom and you will be a tremendous force for good in the world.'

'I understand what you are saying, Zeus, but can't you tell me how you managed to make that leap of faith?'

'Myrkais, you are still trying to reduce the mystery of this vast universe to a meagre jumble of words so that your petty mind can make sense of it. Perhaps a metaphor can help show you how limited your current thinking is. Let's imagine that I've taken a trip north, into the mountainous tundra that lies beyond the Blue Mountains. As I say these words, an image will be coming into your mind of this landscape. But let's suppose you had spent your whole life in the flat marshlands in the east of Arasmas and so had never seen a mountain. You would, of course, be unable to picture what I am describing. So I would use some words and concepts to try to explain what I had experienced and you would start to understand a little bit. But your understanding would be limited by the fact that it is only relative, meaning that when I say that the land rises steeply upwards you would only be able to picture it relative to your understanding of land that does not rise steeply upwards. Therefore, as I have shown, intellectual concepts and language cannot adequately describe personal experience. To understand the true nature of a landscape, you must go there yourself and see and touch it, perceiving it directly. Does that make sense?'

'Well, I can understand the point you are making, but I still cannot grasp what this fifth dimension is.' I replied.

'That is because you are trying to grasp it with your mind, you are trying to trap it and give it a name, and you are trying to reduce it down to a problem that can be solved by the left hemisphere.'

A long silence fell; Zeus's words had touched a nerve. I couldn't think of any way to reply and this left me feeling stuck. Kindly, seeing that I was feeling deflated, Zeus offered me some words of encouragement.

'Don't be downhearted, Myrkais. As I have told you, you are a wise soul who has already had glimpses of Satya. Think about all of the magical and strange coincidences that have happened recently; these are moments when you have been in tune with the power of your intuition. Try to remember the feelings that came with these special moments; use this as a way to help you to stay connected and in the flow.

'There is also one more thing I need to tell you, Myrkais. When you can learn to stay in the fifth dimension you will not have to fear anybody or anything; you will no longer be a fugitive trying to escape from the Director or from Dr Small or anybody else. For in this dimension your intuition will always guide you to where it is you need to be; it will never lead you into danger. Only when you stay, afraid, in the four-dimensional world are you are at risk of being captured and destroyed.'

With that, Zeus got up from his seat and put Krugman's book in his coat pocket. I stood up as well, but, before we said goodbye, he had one final word of encouragement for me.

'I'm getting to be an old man Myrkais. I will not be around forever to preserve this message that I brought to you today. One reason why I took the risk of seeing you was that you are still young; you have a special gift which gives you a chance to carry this legacy forwards. This legacy is something that stretches right back in time to the ancient masters who used to roam the earth offering wisdom and compassion. Although it may appear that today we live in a place devoid of any genuine wisdom, there is still a green shoot, a solitary one in the middle of a vast desert, and it needs tending to. I hope you take my advice to heart and that you are willing to take on the challenge of living by the real light of Satya.'

Zeus took my hands and squeezed them warmly before turning swiftly on his heels and gliding away before I was able to respond. I stood there for a few moments, trying to absorb the effect that his powerful words and inspiring presence had had on me. His confidence filled me with hope. I saw from the clock above the town hall that the train I had to catch was departing soon; I hurried back to the station. John was there to meet me at the train station at Nabotan, as promised, and, with the dusk fast approaching, we crossed back over the water to Diarra.

Chapter Twenty-Nine

Wednesday, 24 March 2032

It was now more than a month since I had met Zeus. I looked back fondly on that day: he had inspired me and reminded me of my inner longing for Satya. But these positive emotions were mixed with feelings of frustration because after returning back to the island, my instincts kept on telling me to wait before leaving. This game of patience continued until late March. Indeed, only after the spring equinox did new inspiration come to me. It happened while I was taking a slow walk around the island on a Wednesday afternoon. It was the most magical time of the season to wander around the island; the bitter winter had now melted away, giving rise to new forms of life that were springing forth all over the island. Even in this remote and barren part of Arasmas it seemed that life could still flourish; the sound of birdsong was heartening for me.

After walking for a while, I found myself a sheltered spot amongst the rocks. There I basked in the warm sunshine, allowing the natural elements to bring life back into my soul. It was while I was lying here that I felt the impulse to go back to the place where my journey in search of Satya had truly begun: on the shores of beautiful Lake Lawdi in the heart of the Blue Mountains. I sensed that I needed to move swiftly; it felt as though I was receiving a warning that my life would be in danger if I stayed on the island much longer. I was also mindful of Zeus' warning that I needed to act on the promptings of my instincts immediately if I wanted to stay one step ahead of my enemies.

Full of a sense of clarity, I immediately started walking back, intending to tell John that I needed to leave. I decided to return to the dishonest tale I had told him upon my arrival, and said that I had been thinking about my wife a lot and felt I had to go back home and try to rebuild my relationship with her. John didn't seem too surprised to hear that I was longing to leave the island, and, in seeing his reaction, I realised that he had probably felt all along that this day would come sooner rather than later. He actually seemed rather relieved, and I guessed that there was a part of him that had always been reluctant to share his life with a stranger; to allow them to see the scars that had resulted from his stubbornness and pride. For I assumed that John must have once been a respected member of society and that he was slightly embarrassed when he thought about his life on the island. Maybe he simply didn't believe that anyone would want to stay and witness his existence for long either. I could understand how difficult it must have been to decide to open his house to me; I couldn't imagine how I would have reacted if a stranger had come to visit during that first winter I had spent living in my rented flat after I had given up my own position in society.

Strangely, after I decided to leave I started to feel bothered by the mixed emotions I felt about the time I had spent living with John. On one hand, I felt grateful to him for opening his home and welcoming me in at a time when I had been badly in need of security and protection. But, on the other hand, there were regrets as I remembered my selfish behaviour during the winter, as well as my failure to truly get to know this man over the nine months that I had lived under his roof. I should have been able to empathise more with him considering that I had once been in that lost state of despair. As I was feeling more balanced, I felt able to face the situation in an honest way. I could now see that John was a man desperately in need of some guidance, and that I had failed to provide any. But despite the temptation I felt to heal these regrets before I left, I stayed quiet on the matter. I guess it didn't feel right for me to open his eyes to the truth as the main reasons I had for doing so were selfish ones.

I left the island just over a week later. In many ways I felt sad about my departure. I realised how much I had relied on John's generosity and support and quickly dropped into a state of insecurity after I left. This was mainly because, having been dropped off in Nabotan, I was finally forced into withdrawing money from my bank account, something that I feared would draw attention to my whereabouts. But Zeus's words were still fresh in my mind and I knew that I needed to stay true to my instincts and to trust that this would keep me safe.

Although it was only a short journey to Lake Lawdi, it was difficult to get there by public transport. It took me the whole of that day, and three connections to get near to it. Even from there I still had nearly 20 miles left to travel on foot. But as nightfall was only a couple of hours away, it made sense for me to try to find a place I could rest in the small village of Curig, one of the few settlements in that area which still had a bus service. However, standing in the village square next to a small hotel with a vacancy sign, I felt a sense of hesitation and, instead, started to walk along the clearly-defined footpath that would take me to my destination. I followed my intuition, but only did so because I assumed that there must be a better place for me to spend the night somewhere else.

However, the longer I walked, the more anxious I became. The path seemed to be leading me out into the wilderness, well away from the main road that ran along the bottom of the valley. There was not a soul to be seen, and it seemed increasingly unlikely that I would find a place to rest. Dusk was falling rapidly, and I felt a wave of panic wash over me. Noticing these warning signs, I stopped immediately, taking a seat at the foot of an old birch tree. I tried to calm my breathing and return to a place of inner peace and stillness. I was grateful for one thing: it was a warm evening, and I was sitting in a sheltered spot. However, although I did wonder whether it had been the right decision to leave the village, the longer I sat the more reassured I felt that I was in the right place at the right time. Not only that, I felt that I needed to stay here and rest until morning.

Night fell. It was a clear night with little light pollution; the skies were filled with bright stars and the full moon bathed the landscape in shimmering light. It reminded me of the evenings I had spent in my forest chalet looking up at the night sky, feeling a sense of wonder at its sheer vastness. I'd no food rations with me, but that night this didn't seem to matter, as I was able to gorge myself on the beauty of the universe. But when I did finally close my eyes, my sleep was fitful as I found it difficult to find somewhere where I would be comfortable and relaxed. The warm evening had given way to a chilly night and many times I woke up shivering. My neck was especially stiff because of the way I had been resting it against the trunk of the tree. I was so uncomfortable that, not long after the first light of dawn, I got to my feet and started moving again. I did some stretching exercises to help get the circulation going before continuing with my journey. As I walked, the only thought that came into my dull and sleepy mind was why it was I had put my body through this experience when I could have found a comfortable bed to sleep in back in the village.

After I had walked for a mile or so, the sun started to rise up behind me, casting a lovely glow across the valley floor. Meanwhile, after following the natural bend of the valley for a while, I caught my first glimpse of Lake Newgo in the far distance. It'd been a sight that I had been longing to see and as it came into full view I could also make out the ominous-looking range of mountains that surrounded the head of the valley on three sides. Eventually, the clearly-defined path that I'd been following rejoined the road at the foot of the lake, exactly where I had parked my car all those years before. As I did so, it struck me that it was almost seven years since I had last come to this spot. It was both incredible and humbling to think how much my life had been transformed in the intervening period. It was at this moment I realised that in a couple of months' time I would also reach the date of my fortieth birthday. This important milestone signified to me that I was moving well into middle age.

Before long, I arrived at the little shop at the far end of the lake. I was glad to find that it was open and serving hot drinks and breakfast. After exerting myself to get here, I was feeling ravished and my body was craving fuel. I recognised the lady at the counter to be the same one who'd served me all those years before. I impulsively asked her whether she knew anything about the old man who I'd met on the shore of Lake Lawdi; I remembered that he had said that he walked in this area nearly every day. Surprisingly, she told me that my description did not fit anyone she knew. This was odd, because I was sure that the man must often have walked past this shop, and if he took this walk every day, as he had said he did, he must be living nearby. Without another word, I paid for the breakfast I had ordered, as well as for the sandwiches I had bought for my lunch.

From the store, I walked up towards the imposing peaks. They looked even more striking this time. I remembered how before Lake Lawdi had only revealed itself to me at the last possible moment, and, even though I was expecting it this time, the moment it came into view I felt the same tingling sensation in my body. It was truly an awe-inspiring sight. I immediately thought of Araya, fondly remembering the tale she had told me about how she had gone out into the mountains and realised that in these landscapes was something very special and mysterious. I noticed that while I spent time in beautiful environments, my left hemisphere, along with all of its petty thoughts and plans, fell quiet. If anything, the scene was even more majestic than before. Clouds had been forming throughout the morning, and moved swiftly through the valley leaving the mountain peaks blanketed with mist. This was a truly moody and sombre sight. Looking up longingly, I wondered whether the very tops of the mountains were above the clouds, as they had been during my last visit. However, at that moment I felt no urge to go and find out; instead I walked down to the shoreline, where I sat down among the rocks as I had before.

After I had taken a seat, I kept looking hopefully to see if the old man would appear in the distance. But, alas, not a soul was to be seen. My mind went blank for a while as I simply sat and absorbed the landscape, watching the dark crags of rock suddenly revealing themselves and then disappearing again into the mist. The wind had also picked up and the water was moving swiftly across the lake, swirling into little eddies. But despite the majestic surroundings, I was soon feeling uncomfortable, tired, restless and quite unable to gather myself together and focus my attention. I took a deep breath once more in order to calm my mind and turn my attention towards my pulsing heart. Trying to be patient, I waited for it to reveal its insights to me. I don't know how long I remained sitting on the shoreline, but it took a while before I was able to settle fully into my body. But eventually, a flash of insight came to me. At first it was just a simple thought, but, once released, it quickly gathered momentum.

It all started after I remembered how I had read about some of the great mountaineers and explorers of the world before arriving here the time before. I thought, with admiration, how strong and courageous they had been, stepping into the unknown to find places where no-one had ever been before. How had these men managed to overcome the feelings of isolation and vulnerability that I was now suffering from, I asked myself. Looking fearfully at the mountains brooding around me, I wondered what it was that had convinced these individuals to make these explorations across uncharted territory. I thought of Lord Namsat who had boldly set sail from the western shore of Arasmas and had become the first person from our country to set foot on Adanac. I was certain that, assuming he was not crazy, surely the only thing that could have led to such an audacious act was if he had been acting from his instincts and living fully in the fifth dimension. The same must have been true for the greatest explorer of them all, Don Mackinnon, who had travelled right across the earth and discovered the mysterious land of Anavrin.

Another thought suddenly struck me like a bolt of lightning. Could Anavrin be the solution to my troubles? I knew that it was a place that everyone living in the four dimensions alone said was nigh on impossible to reach and maybe, just maybe, this was what Zeus had been hinting at when he had told me that if I could access the fifth dimension that I would be able to live freely and without fear of capture. Was it conceivably possible that by living through my intuition, I could find a way of reaching this sacred land?

As I closed my eyes to ponder this new thought, an image formed in my mind of the desert that Zeus had spoken of, with its solitary green shoot that needed tending. When I saw myself standing there with this green shoot I became aware that I was not alone but that I was part of a circle of men and women who were also taking on the responsibility of tending it. Realising this, two choices immediately came to mind. Did I need to go and create this fellowship in Anavrin, or did it already exist there, and all I needed to do was go and find it?

Straight away the answer came to me: this fellowship did already exist. This group were beings of light, working diligently to hold the whole planet in the higher energy frequency of the fifth dimension. These were the real guardians of Satya. I saw quite clearly that the fellowship used spiritual laws to telepathically send energetic healing across the world whenever there was a crisis which threatened to diminish the energy vibration of the planet. I followed this train of thought and began to appreciate that this was not necessarily a fanciful fairytale. After all, these spiritual laws had long been proven to exist by physicists.

Had I just managed to make contact with the fellowship? The idea that the fellowship had established themselves on Anavrin so that they could work in safety and peace was a tantalising one. With civil war in Arasmas apparently imminent it did seem sensible for me to leave the country altogether and to carry out my work of tending to the green shoot from a distance. Apart from the fears of the journey, the only thing that caused me to hesitate was Araya. I wondered sadly whether this decision meant that I would never see her again. Confused by all these mixed feelings, I suddenly felt an impulse to take the notebook and pen from my jacket and write. My writing this time covered only two pages, but, as usual, it flowed naturally, ending at the bottom of each page and starting again at the top of the next.

As I finished writing, I became aware that the clouds were becoming heavier and that a light drizzle was beginning to fall. It seemed that the rain would continue for the rest of the day, and I realised that I needed to decide whether to start the long walk back today or to rest here overnight. My instincts guided me to leave, and taking a moment to feel grateful for the inspiration that I'd received from coming here, I descended back to the valley floor. Fortunately the rain did not become any heavier, but the walk back to Curig was a draining and exhausting one, nonetheless. It was early evening by the time I returned and I calculated that, over the course of that day, I had walked for nearly ten hours.

Arriving at the village square, I was surprised to see that there was a bus waiting, its engine running idle. My pace quickened and, after stepping on board just in time, I was pleasantly surprised when the driver told me that this was the last bus of the day and that it was travelling direct to the nearest railway station in order to connect with the last train, which would depart for Sarum at eight o'clock that evening. The moment the driver told me this, I knew that I needed to board that train.

The train did not arrive into Sarum until the early hours of the next morning, and once I got there, having nowhere to rest, I tried to find a quiet spot to sleep. I eventually settled on a metal bench in the corner of the station. It was not a comfortable place to rest and I was grateful that I had at least got some sleep on the train. The cost of the train ticket meant that I now had no money in my wallet, and it hadn't seemed worthwhile to withdraw some more and to seek out a bed for the night. However, after only a couple of hours rest, I was disturbed by an overbearing security guard who told me that the station was closing for the night and that the police would be called if I did not vacate the station. So, sleepily, and in that transitory state between the real and the dream world, I dragged myself out into the quiet city and started to trudge down the lamp lit pavement.

Instinct drove me towards the beacon of protection that was the old centre of worship; its shadowy and illuminated outline appeared both clear and inviting. As I came to the grassy square that surrounded it, there was not another soul in sight. The gates were closed for the night, but I would not be denied and climbed clumsily over the top, taking great care not to impale myself on their iron spikes. Exhausted, I collapsed in the sheltered doorway of that grand building. I remained comatose there, my head resting on the cold stone floor, until dawn. When the sun rose, it shone brightly on the east side of the building where I was resting and awoke me from my slumber.

It was about six o'clock in the morning when this happened and I sat bolt upright, unsure where I was for a moment. The morning was chilly and my joints had become stiff overnight. Rubbing my bleary eyes, I rose slowly to my feet and again scrambled over the imposing barrier without being seen. I reluctantly withdrew more money and went in search of a coffee house, feeling the need for some warmth. I did not look respectable: I had not changed my clothes for two days and looked out of place among the passing men and women, on their way to work, wearing suits. Standing in the doorway for a moment, it felt strange, and even a little saddening, to see these people reflecting back to me the veil that I had once worn in my attempt to fit in.

After I had ordered a drink and something to eat, I took a seat, knowing that I needed to formulate a plan. Although I was keen to get moving and leave Arasmas behind while it was still safe, I knew that I couldn't just steam ahead and start on this long expedition. To begin with, I needed to eat in order to build up my strength. The diet in the commune and on the island had lacked protein and carbohydrates, and I had noticed on my walk the previous day how weak my body had become. I also needed to go shopping for clothes and other items that I might need for the expedition.

However, while preparations were important, I knew that I would not be able to plot my route to Anavrin in advance, for I was certain that even if I devised the best plan that I could, it would still be formulated within the confines of a four-dimensional world.

Therefore, the most important thing I needed to guide me was my intuition, and all I could do to prepare myself was to make sure that I was in the right physical and mental state to access this guidance. After breakfast I went out and looked at my bank balance, and worked out a budget for how much I could spend making my preparations, then calculated much this would leave me for the long expedition.

I realised that I would only have a very small amount left and instinctively felt afraid. I needed to have faith and trust that there would be money to support me if I really needed it because I had to believe that I would always be safe and secure if I stayed true to my instincts. But I was still learning to believe that I was living in abundance and I was still learning to let go of the inhibiting fears that were arising within my left hemisphere. However, while this time I was able to catch them before they took root, I doubted whether these fears would ever cease completely.

I booked to stay for two weeks at a quiet and small family run hotel on the edge of the city. I knew I was taking a massive risk by staying here in this city for so long and by accessing my bank account. However, I had faith that my presence would not be detected so quickly and that I would be able to make my escape. During those two weeks I made my preparations, eating heartily in order to build up my strength and ticking off all the items on my shopping list. I also booked my passage on a boat that would take two days to sail between the port of Wellington, in the south-eastern corner of Arasmas, and the port of Isanarav, in the north western corner of Aidni.

Many years ago, the easiest and quickest way of reaching Aidni would have been by plane, but shortages of oil had led to all chartered flights being grounded and only those who could afford to buy their own private jet now flew. Fortunately there was a boat sailing on the very day that I was due to leave my hotel and, luckily, there was a berth available at a reasonable price. I did not know where I would go from Isanarav, apart from that I had to continue travelling south-eastwards and that the journey would be a long and treacherous one.

We had learnt a lot about Aidni at school; we had always been taught that this was a poor, overpopulated country that had been stopped from developing by civil wars and harsh living conditions. In addition, I knew from my time in the commune that whilst Satyagraha had given the people freedom from foreign rule, it had not done much to develop the country. The communities here were small, close-knit and tribal. It was a rugged country: the rolling deserts that dominated the southern part of the country offered little in the way of water or shelter, meaning that life could not be sustained there. Meanwhile, the range of mountains that cut across the country from the far south-west to the far north-east used to be heavily populated by nomadic tribes, but I had read that nowadays it was a dangerous place that housed many terrorist cells. This had forced many of the local tribes to drift northwards in search of safety. Those that dared to stay were often engaged in conflict with one another, as they sought to hold on to the best areas of land for their families.

So the only place where people could build a stable life for themselves was in the flat, fertile lands to the north-west of the country. However, we had been taught that the chaos that had beset Sarum around the time of the industrial revolution now besets these towns and cities, which are forced to grow far too rapidly to cope with the incessant influx of people from the south. Shanty towns and slums were constructed overnight and disease was rife. Unfortunately for me, I sensed that I would have to leave the fertile plains and to travel first in the shadow of the mountains, and then to cross them, in order to reach the far side of the country.

After making my preparations, I tried to keep as low a profile as possible by staying in my room for much of the day. Those two weeks seemed to pass like a strange dream. It was almost as if my audacious plan to travel across Aidni into Anavrin hadn't fully sunk in yet. I knew that it would probably not really get through to me until I set sail, or maybe not even until I landed on the western shore of Aidni. In the meantime, I felt that I was being carried along by the demands of the moment, temporarily blinded to the challenges that lay ahead. I became so detached from my emotions that I could not feel one ounce of either fear or excitement in my bones. I would go so far to say that it felt almost as though I was making plans for someone else.

Even on my last day in Sarum, I thought only of the immediate future and the early train that I would need to catch to Port Wellington in the morning in order to meet the boat departing later that evening. The same was true when I was packing my rucksack that afternoon; I don't think I had fully grasped that I was packing it for me and that I would be living out of it for the next few weeks, if not months or even years. Having made everything ready for my departure early the next morning, I slipped into bed at eight o'clock that evening.

<u>Part IV</u>

Chapter Thirty

I was lying across a bench on the top deck of the boat; the cool sea breeze was helping to calm my feelings of nausea. We were due to land in Isanarav the following morning and already I was longing for solid ground. It had been a rough crossing and I was still feeling the ill effects of a powerful storm the previous night which had caused me to be sick. My stomach was now hollow and empty and it was giving me cramps, but I still did not feel strong enough to digest anything but water. It seemed that last minute endeavours to build up my strength for the journey had been in vain, and I was already feeling very weak and vulnerable. It was hard for me to stay focused, and, even though the arduous journey had most definitely begun, I still could not fully absorb the fact that there would be many obstacles to overcome if I was to reach Anavrin and to join the fellowship.

But while I was lying there something strange happened that gave me some welcome reassurance that my intuition was leading me in the right direction. I had been lying there prone for some time, my eyes closed and a hat pulled down over my face. Then, whilst here, I suddenly felt a shadow cast over me and became aware that someone was walking towards me. With a start, I pulled the hat from my face and was met by the sight of an elderly lady. She stood over me, smiling warmly. She reminded me of my own grandmother; she had the same frail appearance and delicate manner. But the light streaming through from her eyes showed me that she was a very wise person; this was wisdom that shone through her decaying form. Seeing me stir, she asked if she could sit down next to me and started to talk to me about the stormy weather. Then, after a long moment of silence, she turned to me and said:

'My intuition tells me that you are looking to travel onwards from Isanarav and that you are considering going even further than Aidni. I am a guide for pilgrims who make this journey and I travel regularly on this ship looking for those who need directions. Is my intuition correct?'

I told the lady that her intuition was correct.

'Now listen very carefully,' she said. 'Once we arrive in the port of Isanarav, you need to make your way across to the north side of the famous river Agnag, which flows down into the sea here from its source in the mountains in the centre of Aidni. Follow the river and you will easily be able to locate Rashmir's guest house; it is a four-storey concrete building standing on the water's edge. Behind the guest house is a network of small streets and narrow alleyways which serves as the city's shopping district. If you climb the steps by the side of the guest house and take the first alleyway on the right and then the second alleyway on the left, you will see a small bookshop with a faded green sign above it. Go inside and, downstairs, you will find a small selection of books written in the familiar tongue of Arasmic. Among this collection you will see a book with a blue cover: an anthology of poems compiled by Graham Calloway. In this book you will find the information you need to continue with your journey. However, it is important that you do not take this book and that you leave it there to help other pilgrims who may follow behind you. Now, are these instructions perfectly clear?'

I told the lady that I understood. But before I could ask whether she knew anything about Zeus or the fellowship, she offered me her best wishes for my journey and left.

The remainder of the crossing was calm. I had felt able to eat again, and had started to regain my strength. The morning we arrived in Isanarav, I stood on deck in order to catch a glimpse of land; eventually I saw it in the distance and I continued to watch as it came nearer and nearer and became ever more distinct. My first impression was that it looked like a hostile and unwelcoming place, but I knew that this impression was influenced by what I had been taught at school about this alien country. We docked smoothly. After walking off the boat and testing my sea legs, what struck me was how intensely hot it was. I had not really noticed the temperature change on the journey because of the sea breeze. But on land, the contrast was stark. Before leaving the port I looked for the elderly lady who had given me directions, but she was nowhere to be seen. I felt alone in a strange country.

The second thing to strike me was how alien the native people of Aidni looked in comparison to the inhabitants of my native land. It was not just that their dark skin was very different from my own pale complexion, but they were so tall and heavy-set that I felt as though I had entered a land of giants. Even the women made me feel like a dwarf. I felt puzzled: these natives seemed so strongly built, yet were also poor and malnourished.

I walked outside the terminal after purchasing some local currency. My immediate instinct was to explore the city by foot. But I had not walked far before I quickly realised that I had not chosen the easiest option. The oppressive heat was one reason. But, even more problematically, my presence was attracting a lot of interest; I couldn't walk far without someone either pestering me for money or trying to convince me to take a ride somewhere on the back of a bike or in one of their rickshaws. I rewarded one driver's persistence by stepping into the back of his rickshaw for an amount of money that, to me, seemed small but which I was sure would support him and his family for a week. I hated the ignominy of being over-charged and it was horrible sitting there knowing that I had allowed my driver to humiliate me by his lack of respect. He could barely speak my native tongue and when I tried to tell him to take me to Rashmir's guest house he told me that it was closed and he would take me to another hotel. I assumed that this was a scam – some way for him to pick up commission – but, after I threatened to get out, he agreed to take me there.

The journey through the city was like no other I had ever

experienced. Describing it as chaotic would be an understatement; I observed that the laws of the road seemed to be loosely adhered to at best and brazenly flaunted at worst. I held on tightly as my driver weaved his way through the throngs of traffic, merrily sounding his horn to tell other road users to get out of his way. The buildings we passed were dilapidated, although, surprisingly, they were made of similar materials to those used in Arasmas. However, as there were no pavements, the buildings simply merged into the street scene.

As well as natives casually walking amongst the traffic, I even caught a glimpse of a docile cow sat in the middle of a dusty road. Even when we came to a roundabout or a junction, the driver did not slow down or stop for traffic coming in other directions; how we navigated through without a collision I will never know. Finally we drew to a halt and my driver pointed me in the direction of the river Agnag. It seemed that he could take me no further.

As I had nowhere to sleep that night, it seemed to make sense to see if a room was available in the guest house before going to look for the bookshop that the old lady had told me about. Again the language barrier made communication difficult but I was able to make myself understood nonetheless and was shown to a room with a view of the river. It was not the cleanest of rooms, but at least it gave some respite from the chaos outside. There was also air conditioning, which gave an immediate and welcome respite from the heat. I decided to take a cold shower before going back outside.

I followed the directions I had been given and easily found the bookshop. It was a dark, musty-smelling place with specks of dust and cobwebs clearly visible in the narrow beams of light that filtered through from outside. The owner was excited to see a foreigner in his shop and tried to lead me over to his best collection of books. Communicating with him was difficult, so I pointed towards a rickety staircase that led downstairs. Fortunately, he did not follow me down and so I had a few moments of peace to look for the book I needed.

I scanned the shelves until I found the section of books that were written in Arasmic. As they were arranged in no particular order, I leafed slowly through until I came across the small blue-leather bound book I was looking for, wedged between two bigger books which had been shielding it from view. The faded print on the spine showed me that it was the title I was looking for, and, eagerly, I pulled it out. I flicked through the first few pages of poems and came across a loose piece of paper that had been left folded inside. Excitedly, I took it out and unfolded it to see what it said. It seemed to be a riddle, for it merely said in bold letters; 'If you be here it will come'. I put the note back and looked through the rest of the book, expecting some further information or maybe even a map. But there was nothing except these seven words. There was nothing else that I could do but go back upstairs, and I left hurriedly before the owner could talk me into buying something that I did not need.

Walking back to the guest house, I tried to work out the meaning of what I had just read. It seemed that the only thing I could take from this riddle was that I needed to stay here and wait patiently for the next clue to emerge. It felt frustrating because I was keen to get going on my journey and to leave the hostile, overbearing city of Isanarav behind.

However, while my mind was longing for the future, my body brought me right back into the present. I had read before coming here that many visitors to Aidni became sick, mainly because of impurities in the water. My diligent precautions were not enough to prevent me from being struck down with the bug too and this, combined with the heat, destroyed my appetite completely. I felt weak, tired, cranky and also a little morose that this expedition was not panning out in the manner I would have liked. Over the days that followed, I did leave the security of my room in order to try and "be here" in the city, in accordance with the words of the riddle.

However, it became increasingly difficult to motivate myself to go outside. Every trip I made brought its own sad tale as I was targeted and led on merry dances by the natives. I found it incredibly difficult to say no and to set firm boundaries. This was challenging because it hadn't been something I had ever needed to do in Arasmas, and these experiences left me craving anonymity.

Meanwhile, money was simply draining out of my wallet, and I felt angry and frustrated with myself because I knew I was letting it fall into the pockets of those who were comparatively wealthy, not into the hands of those who appeared more in need.

When I was in my room my frustration started to boil over; my head was spinning and going haywire. It was as though the chaos and lack of any rules or codes of conduct had splintered my mind and that the left hemisphere of my brain had kicked in to try and create some order and logic for the crazy situation I found myself in here in Isanarav. Unable to find any rationale for my presence here, it had spun out of control, creating all sorts of disturbing thoughts that were laced with fear and judgment. These thoughts kept me in a state of shock; I felt completely paralysed

Strangely, I did still have just enough self-awareness to be able to watch these thoughts emerging, but being able to observe them did not mean I was able to free myself from them. There were thoughts that tried to make sense of this strange and alien environment and there were thoughts that tried to justify the feelings of fear I was experiencing. However, the one thought that kept repeating itself over and over concerned itself with my isolation from civilised humanity and my inability to trust anyone that I met here. I started to bemoan the fact that we, as a human race, had still not developed a universal language for communication. This seemed to show that we had collectively failed, and my mind longed for this situation to change.

However, in my rare moments of stillness, I knew that the problem did not lie in the city of Isanarav or the country of Aidni but within my own heart. For I could see that the fear that lay behind all of my incessant thinking and storytelling was taking me out of the fifth dimension and holding back my progress. I had come far enough to now know that the sickness in my body and the discomforting interactions with the world outside of my room resulted from this fear and nothing else. At this moment it still seemed a wild notion that if I conquered my fear, my situation would change. But I believed this nonetheless, and the only question I was left with was how I could truly "be here".

The answer that came to me was that I must let go of my self-consciousness completely. To help shift my perspective, I would have to put myself in the other person's shoes. I knew that I feared the natives because I was disconnected from them, and I also knew, deep down, that this matter could not really be solved by the creation of a universal language so that we could communicate with each other through words. No, what I needed to do was go beyond that and establish a connection between our hearts, and, by doing so, to break through my feelings of isolation. It was time for me to take the initiative.

I left my room in the guest house and went and sat on the steps that led down to the river Agnag. It was early afternoon and the sun was baking hot so I sat in the shade, watching the swollen river flow past me. A few small fishing boats bobbed past and I watched the small groups of women on the shore, trying to wash their clothes in the dirty water. It seemed to me that life in Isanarav revolved around the flow of this river and I imagined that the daily rhythm must still be quite similar to how it was thousands of years before. The shoreline was lined with traders selling their wares, and there was a lively, bustling atmosphere. But where I was sat I was hidden from view and so I was able to do some meditation in order to help me breathe fully and to centre myself in my body. After a while, I began a visualisation exercise in order to help me understand the experiences and feelings of the natives. It was easy and natural for me to consider the difficulties that the people here faced, and I began to appreciate how precious the training that the clan had given me was.

Yes, the focus on developing the left hemisphere of my brain had held me back from rising above and claiming my sovereignty as a living human being, but at the same time I could see that this had been a necessary stage of my journey. While many of the natives had clearly not developed their left hemisphere at all, this did not mean they had easy access to the power of their right. Feelings of pity swelled up at I realised that instead of rising above the left hemisphere, these people were living in the murky recesses below it.

I returned to my room that evening and realised, with some sorrow, that my meditation that afternoon had not placed me fully in the shoes of these people; I was still too absorbed in interpreting and analysing everything I was observing. I was frustrated that I had so quickly forgotten my training in the commune. There, I had been taught that my only responsibility was to love and accept others, not to solve their problems. But today "I" had still been too much a part of the picture to really reach out and connect with the other.

So the following day I went outside again and again practised my breathing and tried to centre my body. It didn't seem enough to simply visualise a golden light shining on the people I walked past. Something much stronger was needed in order to help me stay grounded in this situation. So this time I sat and tried to observe what was going on outside without any reflecting at all on what was going on inside of me. I started to use all of the power of my heart and found that I was able to begin to reach out and connect in a much richer and more meaningful way. I had found a soft spot in my heart. I felt deeply touched by this; tears sprang to my eyes. I was starting to respond in a compassionate way, breathing in the suffering of the people I saw and breathing out the warm energy of love. Strangely, this did not leave me drained or overwhelmed at all, actually having quite the opposite effect: my sense of self completely evaporated. All that was present was the energy of suffering being mixed with the healing energy of love; it was now impossible to distinguish any boundary between the subject and the object. It felt as if the discomfort was inside of me and that the power to heal this wound also rested deep inside myself.

I continued trying to be compassionate, but it was really put to the test sometimes, in particular when people came up to me and tried to draw me into a power struggle in order to get their needs met. Some tried to sell me things or offered take me for a ride on the river, while others tried to lure me away into a shop or hotel that was paying them commission. At these trying times, I began to discover that being compassionate does not necessarily mean saying yes and going with the flow of things without setting any boundaries at all. I could see that it often did mean saying no, but it was also about discovering the art of saying no without any fear. What I realised was that this meant saying no without any inner resistance or struggle, and, most importantly of all, without needing to think about it afterwards. Dropping the storyline and breathing out compassion seemed to be the message I was receiving that day. And, doing so, I found that the natives stopped bothering me so much and that my body quickly returned back to a state of health.

But, having discovered the secret of staying in the fifth dimension in such a testing situation, I was anxious to continue with my journey to Anavrin. The message I had read in the bookshop was still perplexing me, as I felt I had now learnt how to fully "be here" and conquer my fears.

As I sat on the steps by the banks of the river, a boy came to sit a few feet away from me. He looked sick and malnourished. But he had gorgeously innocent eyes with pupils that were a mysterious and captivating misty blue. His chest was bare and all he wore was a loincloth, wrapped around his waist. The bare soles of feet were cracked from walking on hard concrete. Instinctively, I began breathing out compassion and held his gaze for a moment.

But although I knew that he wanted to beg me for money, he seemed very shy and was obviously reluctant to impose on me. Eventually he inched closer and pulled on my trouser leg, muttering something to himself in the process. Finally he spoke aloud in broken Arasmic, saying; 'come, come.' Strangely, I trusted this boy, and I sensed that I needed to say 'yes' this time. I got to my feet and the boy grabbed me by the hand, before he led me through the maze of narrow streets that spread out to the north of the river. His pace was quick and I followed breathlessly, sweating profusely under the midday sun.

Finally, after half an hour or more, he led me into one of the shanty towns of the city, a place where the air was filled with the stench of raw sewage. I felt doubtful and hesitant about being there, wondering if, by trusting this boy, I had done the right thing. The disorganised mass of streets and homes were strewn across an area of baked mud; I didn't know how my guide was able to lead me so confidently through it. The area was packed with people and, as we pushed through the crowds, it was hard to keep hold of the little boy's hand.

Eventually he came to a halt outside of a building with a corrugated tin roof that was held on with wooden stakes. It looked like a workshop. There were three men and two women inside, busy sifting through bags of rubbish, obviously looking for items that could be reused or sold. The boy motioned me inside and led me to the back of the workshop. I smiled warmly at the five adults but they only looked surprised, obviously because I was a foreigner. I turned my attention back to the young boy and was shocked to see him holding something that looked very familiar to me: a copy of the anthology of poems I had found in the bookshop.

My immediate thought was that this must be the same one I had seen previously, but I thought that this would be an enormous coincidence in such a large city. Since he seemed to want me to read the book, I took it from him and began to leaf through. Inside, was stuck a loose piece of folded paper inside. I opened it and saw not the seven words I had read before, but a map that, on first glance, appeared to show the route I must take to Anavrin. Folding the paper and putting it back inside the book, I showed my gratitude to the young boy by offering him some money. Strangely, he refused to take it. Instead he bowed before me and, taking my hand, took me back through the complex maze.

After the young boy had returned me safely back to the river, refusing a second offer of money, I went back to the guesthouse. I went to my room and lay down on the bed, still dazed by what had happened. I was especially curious to know why it had been necessary for me to go to such lengths in order to get hold of the map I was holding tightly in my hands. My only guess was that this must be the fellowship's way of testing me and ensuring that only those who were truly worthy would make it through to their sacred land. But this thought did leave me wondering what further challenges lay in store for me on this journey.

I opened the map and looked carefully at it. Not only did it offer a drawing but there were also detailed descriptions, written in Arasmic, that'd been neatly added in a small print that was difficult to read. The only words marked in bolder letters were those that offered a warning that while the map pointed the way, it should not be mistaken for the way itself. I could only assume that this was confirmation of what I'd believed before my journey began: namely, that the way existed in the fifth dimension and that no map could possibly convey it through words or symbols.

However, reading through the map, I saw that I needed to take a bus out of Isanarav and head, not south, but eastwards, along the line of the mountain range, towards the distant city of Arga on the far side of the plains. Here there was a large lake that could be crossed by boat. Because this lake was nestled right in the heart of the mountain range, the boat journey helped to reduce the distance that would need to be walked in order to cross over the top. The map informed me that just outside the small port lying in a south-easterly direction, on the other side of the lake, was a statue that had been erected on the top of a mountain that rose directly above the town below. From here I was told to set my compass due east and to walk for three full days. According to the map, this would take me over to the far side to a small village of five homes. From there, I would have to travel due south across the hot desert until I reached the second mountain range marking the border between Aidni and Anavrin. Apparently, I would come to a riverbed, and, by following this into the mountains, I would eventually climb up to the summit. It looked as if this would be my final obstacle; at least from a four-dimensional perspective.

I realised I had a difficult journey ahead of me. But without thinking any further, I decided to rest so that I would be fresh and ready to leave in the morning.

Chapter Thirty-One

The directions to the statue were straightforward to understand but not easy to follow. The journey was a long and tiring one, and I was not helped by the fact that the bus that took me on the first leg was old and rickety, with hard wooden seats. Since most of the roads were unpaved, it was also a bumpy journey. I tried to sleep on the way, but every time I found a comfortable spot, the bus would lurch down into a rut, which would send shooting pains through my lower back. Fortunately, I was not disturbed by the other passengers, although the bus was filled beyond its capacity and I was squeezed between two other people. Once my bus journey finally ended, I caught the boat; this was no easier. Although it was an inland lake, it was as choppy as any ocean, making for a long, uncomfortable journey. The boat was crammed full of people and I had to board quickly in order to get myself a space to lie down on the open deck.

But finally we reached the other side, and I could easily see the statue that stood on top of the mountain that rose up behind the town. To get there, I followed a clearly-marked footpath which took me along an indirect route that weaved its way through a dense forest, before eventually climbing above the tree line. The path finally wound itself around the rock face to take me to the top.

I reached the summit from the south side and looked down to the town and the lake stretched out far below. In all directions were impressive snow-covered mountains. I could easily see now why I had been told to follow this route, for the boat crossing had indeed saved me many days of walking across the mountain range, which was consistently two hundred miles wide. From this point, I guessed that I still had around 50 miles of mountainous terrain to cross before I reached the desert on the other side. On the downside, it did mean that I'd had to take a steeper climb to the top of the pass rather than the more gradual ascent from the fertile plains that lay beyond the horizon.

I took a few moments to catch my breath, and to marvel at the view, and, standing with my back against the statue, I checked my compass to find out which direction was east. Although there was no marked path to guide me across the mountain range, the terrain I had to cross seemed manageable, if a little undulating. I felt grateful that my route seemed to be avoiding the highest mountain peaks and would keep me below the snow line.

The weather stayed fair, and I had sufficient rations in my rucksack to get me through this leg of the journey, which lasted for three days and nights. I was grateful that I had thought to buy camping gear when I was in Sarum as this provided me with overnight shelter. The only things I worried about while walking was the possibility of coming across some of the terrorists and bandits who operated in these mountains. But the area appeared completely desolate and, on the long journey east, there was little sign of bird or plant life. I felt completely alone.

As I started walking on the morning of the third day, I was feeling optimistic; I was confident that, by nightfall, I would have reached the far side of the mountain range and that, hopefully, I would reach the small village I was heading for. But I hadn't walked for long before suddenly, after climbing up a steep slope, I came upon the rim of a grand canyon. Peering nervously over the edge, I looked down over steep cliffs that seemed to drop down to sea level. I could not see how I could possibly descend down. At the bottom, I could just about make out a river that was flowing through the gorge. Then, on the other side of the river, about a mile or two ahead of me, was another sheer cliff face that I would need to ascend in order to continue on my journey.

My immediate response was one of panic. Had I made a mistake and chosen the wrong course, I wondered? I marked the spot where I was standing and followed the cliff edge south in order to see if there was any easier way across to the other side. There seemed to be none. At this point I sensed that I was being tested by the fellowship and that this was my next challenge. Was this the part of the journey that the map had been referring to when it'd given its strange warning? Cleverly, the map did indeed indicate the direction I needed to go in and yet it did this without showing me the way itself. Recognising that this was a test, all I could do was return back to the spot I had marked, and sit and breathe.

But it was difficult to sit there comfortably; I soon felt worried that I would run out of food if I did not continue on my journey. I was tempted to retrace my steps in case I had made a mistake. But, deep down, I knew I hadn't and so I resisted this temptation and continued to sit. Eventually I stood up again and took another look over the edge of the cliff; all that I could see was the grim spectre of death. This was truly perplexing, and I could feel that my fear was pulling me out of a state of inner peace.

Although I had gone through so much over the years, releasing my fears and strengthening my faith, it seemed as if the fear of death was the final knot that I needed to untie in order to achieve freedom. But, strangely, the most powerful feeling that consumed me in this moment was not the fear of my death, but the fear of never again seeing Araya. I now knew that my love for her was strong and true and it struck me that if I was offered the choice between taking a risk and continuing on this journey or seeing Araya again one more time, I would most definitely choose the latter. So was it the hope that maybe I would be able to see her again that was causing me to hold back from the edge?

I continued to sit for some time, but was startled when I saw someone in the distance walking southwards along the edge of the canyon; they were coming slowly towards me. When this solitary figure came closer I was able to see that it was an elderly gentleman and when he got within a few feet I saw that he was beaming at me, a broad smile spread across his face. Although he appeared to be a native of this country I was shocked when he started to speak to me in fluent Arasmic; he was the first person I had heard do so since I had left the boat back in Isanarav.

He asked me where I was heading. I told him that I needed to get to the other side of the canyon and that I was looking for a safe route across. The man smiled and told me, quite casually, that I had arrived at the place where it was safe to do so, and that he knew the route across well. Then, seeing my look of puzzlement, he went on to explain that the reason he could see the route clearly was because he'd been taught over many years to overcome the fears that distorted his perception. Jokingly, he remarked that the body can sometimes see things that the mind knows nothing about.

But when I asked whether he could lead me across he shook his head, reminding me of the graceful art of true compassion, which meant that he could not take on the responsibility for solving my problems. No-one could show me the way to the other side until I was ready, he said. He told me that by telling me there was a way across, he had already said enough.

I nodded my head and smiled warmly, realising what a precious gift the man was offering me. Although I knew that he couldn't lead me across I did ask him if he had any specific advice that might help me to overcome the fears that were stopping me from seeing the route. The man seemed to be enthused by the prospect of sharing his wisdom, and sat down on the ground next to me. He went on to lucidly explain the teachings and practices that had been passed down by his ancestors and which lay at the core of his daily life. He began by concurring with my belief that I needed to face my death if I wanted to overcome all my fears, and went on to say that, in his culture, that they had a particular and unique relationship with the process of dying. He explained:

'Instead of seeing death as the annihilation of oneself, I've been taught to take a much longer and broader view, treating both life and death as part of a continuous cycle that spans across many lifetimes. From this perspective, it is possible to see that death is just the pause between one breath ending and another one beginning and that it is all part of the healthy and natural flow of the breathing cycle. It is the same rhythm that you can see in the changes of the seasons and it is also the process that guides all forms of life. Now, by taking this longer view, I no longer see death as the nemesis of life but as one and the same as life.

'By seeing death and life in this way, I am able to relax a lot more and let go of my fears of death. For let me make clear my fear of death is nothing more than the irrational fear of dropping out of the circle of life and descending into a state of nothingness. Paradoxically, it isn't death that causes the loss of life but the fear of death: it is this fear that causes us to try to halt the natural rhythm and flow of life. So it sounds odd, doesn't it, that the more you try and hold on to something, the more likely you are to lose it. Let me suggest to you that it is this fear of losing something that is hindering your progress across the canyon.'

I listened to this advice intently, but immediately told him that it was not the fear of death that was holding me back but the fear of never seeing my loved one again. The man paused for a moment before responding.

'Death comes in many different guises, not only in the seemingly ultimate death of the human form. When a friend makes a hurtful remark there is death in that and when the clouds dissolve and the rains stop there is death in that too. Life and death are nothing more than the changing circumstances of our lives; only by overcoming the fears we have about death can we find true freedom. You long to be united with your loved one but, if you look deeply into the changing seasons of life and death, you will see that you can never be truly separated because you were never truly attached. It is only because you are holding on to the memory of the time you spent together that you feel fearful.'

I fell quiet as I absorbed this intriguing advice before returning back to the original topic of conversation.

'But how can I trust that I would not be annihilated and disappear into nothingness if I fell down this canyon to my death?' I asked.

'I only know because I have spent many years learning the skill of clairvoyance. But, my friend, you really do not need to step ahead in time to know what will happen to you after death, for you can see the natural flow of the life cycle happening all around you now,' he replied, before pausing reflectively. He continued:

'Perhaps it is time that I taught you a meditation practice that will help you to come face-to-face with death, so that you can loosen the grip that has on you. The essence of the practice is exploring how absurd it is to believe that people live and die separate from the natural rhythm of life. Contemplate and be humbled by seeing how your existence is subject to millions of different causes and conditions within the great web of life. Look deeply and you will see that nothing in your mind or body has been created, by you, out of nothingness. In the same way, when you die you must return to something, for you surely cannot return back to a place of nothingness that does not exist. Through my reflections I've learnt that nothing exists separate from the flow of life and death.

'Just take a moment to think how precious and rare your existence as a human being is, and how much your life depends on the precarious interaction of many variables. You exist in four kingdoms. The easiest one of these to understand is the mineral kingdom; it is relatively simple to understand the relationship between your physical body and the earth out of which it grew. Reflect on the gift that the earth has given to you; it pieced together this physical form from a small seed and, one day, you will return this gift. Then think about the second level: the plant kingdom. As you do so, take a moment to consider that, despite all the advances of modern science, that this kingdom remains beyond our understanding. Life is truly a rare and precious gift that has been bestowed upon you by a blessed force. Again, take time to reflect on the fact that one day you must also return this gift back to its source. Then go a step further; consider the third level, the animal kingdom, and see how precious and rare the gift of consciousness is, something that is beyond our understanding and which, again, must be returned. Then, finally, go a step further and consider the fourth level: the human kingdom. See how precious and rare it is to be a human being who possesses the gift of free will and is thus able to direct his own thinking, and. again see that this is way beyond our ability to possess and must be returned to its source.

'If you are willing to dedicate yourself to this, you may find that you are so humbled by the forces that have granted you the life of a conscious human being that you are able to surrender to them and to let go of any fear of losing your life. For you will gradually come to see that it is impossible to lose something that you never really possessed or controlled in the first place. When you realise this, you will see that there is nothing to fear.'

I listened to his advice, fascinated. As I did so I began to understand that all the while he was inviting me to look again beyond the narrow and petty concerns of the left hemisphere of my brain. This wise man was encouraging me to see that this part of the brain was seeking to convince me that I had the power to control my life. He was encouraging me to, instead, access the vast, mysterious wisdom of the universe by tapping into the wider perspective of my right hemisphere. But whilst I was keen to dedicate myself to this practice as he had advised me, there was still one burning question left: if I am merely subject to the natural forces of life and death, then what is the purpose of my existence?

The man gave the question some thought before responding.

'The challenge is not to be humbled so much that you end up passive in the flow of life. Instead, the question is how to respond to the situations that we find ourselves in. I believe that life is always asking me to stretch and grow so that I can respond with love. This is indeed what it means to dwell in the human kingdom because, as I've already said, we have the gift of free will. This means we can choose whether to grow or to stay stagnant. What this means is that we need to learn to use our free will so that we don't react to situations in the old habitual ways, but are able to see each moment afresh and give it the response it deserves. This clear-seeing response is what we call love.

'So take this situation that you find yourself in: the challenge that faces you of finding a way across this canyon. You've already seen that the power of your consciousness cannot provide you with a simple solution because nothing in your past can help to give you an answer. Indeed your consciousness, which has the responsibility for preserving the life of the organism, is warning you not to continue. It is this warning that is confusing you because, deep down, you know that you are not here by chance and, deep down, you know that this situation is forcing you to stretch beyond the limitations of your consciousness and claim your rightful place in the human kingdom. The practice I have given you is simply one of many different practices that can help you to remove the veil that is blinding you and help you reclaim your sovereignty as a living human being. If you dedicate yourself to this practice you may be able to look at this situation with clear eyes and see the route across that I can see.'

With that, the man said it was time for him to take his leave and continue on his own journey southwards. I thanked him for his advice and he wished me well with my own journey. But, after he had started walking away, he suddenly turned around and gave me one final comment.

'There is one more thing I must tell you. In recognising that death does not mean the end of life, you may feel tempted to drift to the opposite extreme and to act without due care and attention. But as I've explained, it is a rare and precious thing to live in this form as a human being, and, while it is not wise to hold on to it tightly, it is vitally important to respect and cherish your life whilst you have it and to make best use of it in order to learn the lessons that need to be learnt.'

With that he turned away, leaving me to return into a state of meditative silence. I responded to his practical advice by reflecting on the first level of being: the mineral kingdom. As I did so I began to connect with the four elements of earth, air, fire and water and to break down any lingering suspicion that my body was separate from the forces that made up the outer world, or that it was under my control. Instead, I saw that I had grown out of the earth as a result of being nourished by food, water, wind and sunshine and that every part of my body would one day return to the earth. Next, I connected with the plant kingdom and reflected on the mysteriousness of life itself. Whilst I may have some control, in that I could provide myself with the necessary conditions for preserving life, I felt humbled by the realisation that I had no understanding of the switch that creates the spark of life. I moved on to the animal kingdom and in the same way I saw that while I could create the conditions to preserve myself in an alert state of consciousness, I had no way of knowing how to create that spark of consciousness from nothing. As the man had said, consciousness and life were gifts that had been bestowed on me and one day would be taken away and returned back to where they had come from.

But it was when I reflected on the final level, the human kingdom, that I felt truly humbled. I saw very quickly that very few people in the world truly understood the rare and limitless powers which humans can access and I felt fortunate, knowing that my power lay in my ability to reach beyond the left hemisphere and direct and observe my own consciousness. Again though, while I could see that I had some control over these powers, I began to understand that these too were a gift that had been bestowed on me. I knew from experience how rare and fleeting it was for a gift of this sort to come into my possession. It was an act of grace.

Afterwards, I felt as though my mind had been shattered and blown wide open. I enjoyed a tremendous sense of expansiveness and aliveness. In this state I felt naked; it was as though the last lingering, arrogant sense of omnipotence, dwelling in the left hemisphere of my brain, had been discovered and shown up for the lie that it was. Behind this façade I could see clearly the frightened and vulnerable child who understood that he knew absolutely nothing about anything that truly mattered. But, strangely, this humble child seemed infused with tremendous strength and courage, far outweighing the unstable power that lay in my former showy know-it-all self, which had believed that I could live separate to the mysterious laws of life. This was the self that the wise old man on the shores of Lake Lawdi had tried to provoke and ridicule, but it had still taken me seven years to accept his words and understand them fully for myself. However, words could not do justice to what was stripped away from me in that moment; all I could do was surrender to its beauty.

I stood up again and walked over to the edge of the cliff, looking at it with new eyes. I took a deep breath and let my eyes wander freely, without focusing them. Suddenly I saw a piece of rock jutting out of the cliff face that seemed to be deliberately trying to attract my attention. I saw that just below this object there was another rock that was also jutting out, again as though it was trying to capture my attention. Without hesitating for another moment, I slung my rucksack on my back, and started to lower myself down the cliff face. Putting both my hands on the first piece of rock I came to, I found that I was able to lower my right leg down until my foot naturally came to rest on the lower object. I then lowered my left leg down and found that my foot naturally came to rest in a foothold. Patiently, I started to lower myself down into the canyon, finding that there was always a way to maintain at least three points of contact with the rock face.

I felt as though I was descending into the depths of the earth, and time seemed to stop. I had to remain completely focused on each movement of my body, knowing that any lapse of concentration could be fatal. I remembered the last words that the man had spoken to me: how he had urged me to behave in a careful manner. As I descended, I felt the heat rising and observed that the cliff face was transforming. The grey rocks that predominated at the top took on a blood red colour as I descended. It felt as though I was dropping down into another world. Fortunately the descent was not so sheer for the whole duration and there were moments where I could stand and pause in order to rest and take in the rare geological environment that existed in the depths of the canyon. I saw that very little in the way of life could be found down here.

Eventually, I reached the bottom of the canyon, where I found a powerful and fast-flowing river. Strangely, the water was chocolate in colour; this must have been caused by all the silt and mud that it was carrying downstream, I thought. I knew that I needed to cross the river, but the water looked deep and dangerous. But, at that moment, there was still no fear in me, and eventually my eyes caught sight of a series of boulders in the water that looked like they could help me to cross. I walked over to look more closely and, although these stepping stones were unevenly shaped and smoothly polished, I did not stop to consider the risks. Boldly, I sprang from one to the other; there was not a moment where my body was not in motion before I came to rest on the far side.

But my journey was not yet complete; the cliff on the far side loomed large ahead of me. I took a long deep breath and let my eyes wander, trying to find where I should go to take my next step. Once again I noticed a jutting rock that captured my attention and I boldly walked over to place my hand upon it. Ascending was a lot more physically demanding than my descent had been, but, again, I did not have to stretch myself too much to find handholds and footholds. Managing to remain patient, I was able to complete my ascent and eventually I gratefully scrambled over the top and stood again on solid ground. I took one last lingering look back at where I had come from, before checking my compass and continuing on my journey eastwards.

Chapter Thirty-Two

T he remainder of my journey across the mountains was a straightforward one, and soon I caught my first glimpse of the green foothills and the vast desert that lay beyond them. Looking southwards into the hazy distance, I could just about make out the outline of the mountain range that rose up on the far side of the desert; I knew that this was the final obstacle between me and Anavrin. By this point I had run out of food and in desperate need of something substantial to nourish my weary body.

I knew that the hunger and weariness I was feeling were pulling me out of the higher state of awareness that I had achieved while crossing the abyss, and this caused me to reflect that while it was vital that I spent as much time as possible in the human kingdom, I also needed to make sure that I was not neglecting the other three kingdoms that were its essential foundations. I was reminded again that if I was sick in body and mind, I would never be able to live in this higher kingdom.

Feeling weary, and with my state of consciousness slightly dulled, I began to see how difficult it was to hold on to the realm of the human kingdom and to access its vast range of powers. My mind, that had stayed focused for such a long time while I was crossing the abyss, was now roaming beyond my control. I drifted back into the recent past and tried to get some adrenaline flowing by remembering my daring descent down the canyon. My mind seemed to be consumed by a desire to replay these dramatic events over and over again. I was also drifting away into the future; my destination seemed a lot closer now and I was filled with a sense of hope that I had overcome the last significant hurdle and that there

315

would be no more challenges for me to face along the way. I felt that what I'd learnt in crossing the canyon had surely proved that I was worthy of joining the fellowship.

It was hard to let go of these thoughts of the past and the future and to stay grounded in the present moment. Descending down the mountainside, I came into a thick forest. As I pushed my way through the dense undergrowth, it became increasingly difficult to hold a direct line eastwards. But, after crossing a couple of small streams, I came to a clearing, where there were signs of human habitation: it looked like the land here was being used for cattle grazing. I descended further and eventually came to a track; rather than continuing to follow my compass, I decided to follow it, since this meant I would avoid another area of woodland.

When I had got past the woods, I finally saw the village I had been trying to reach, made up of five simple dwellings clustered together in a circle. I was amazed that such a small community was able to sustain itself in such a remote and isolated part of the country. The dwellings were made of canvas and did not look like they had been established permanently. It made me wonder whether the community moved around this area in order to adapt to the different seasons. Had I just been lucky to stumble across them here?

There were cattle grazing in the distance and I could see smoke coming from at least two of the dwellings. Since no-one was in sight, I went up to the first dwelling and called to see if there was anyone inside. A stocky, middle-aged woman peered out, looking at me with curiosity. Her appearance was markedly different from the people who lived on the other side of Aidni; among other differences, her skin was much paler. Although we could not communicate through words, her heart seemed open and warm and she gestured to show that I should come inside her dwelling. At the centre of the room was a large pot, and it seemed that she and another woman were busy cooking broth for the whole community.

I took a seat on the soft sandy floor, and one of the women ladled some of the liquid into a bowl and handed it to me. I accepted their kindness gratefully, savouring every mouthful that passed my lips. Both women were watching me with curiosity; it seemed that they were not used to foreign visitors. As they talked to each other I realised that their language was noticeably different from that which I had heard spoken in Isanarav, and I remained frustrated that I couldn't engage them in dialogue. I had so many questions to ask about their way of life that could not possibly be answered.

Eventually I heard the sound of male voices. I assumed that the men must now be returning from a day's work. But what exactly that work was I was unsure of, and I was still uncertain as to how they were able to sustain their lifestyle here in this harsh environment. My presence in the community seemed to cause quite a stir, and I was touched by the welcome that I received: a young man offered me his bed for the night and chose to sleep on the hard sandy floor. This was not the only act of generosity that I witnessed during my brief stay here. There was a young girl with wild, long hair who seemed fascinated by my presence and who would watch me with her bright blue eyes. I could see from her appearance that she was poorly nourished, something I had noticed among a lot of the younger members of the group.

Watching her closely, I began to realise that sustaining life in this part of Aidni must have become increasingly difficult in recent decades as a result of the changing climate. I imagined that so close to the edge of the desert, drought must be common, whilst, at the other extreme, I imagined that the heavy monsoon rains pouring off the mountain would destroy the nutrients in the soil here. But, despite her malnourishment, several times I witnessed her insisting that more food be put on my plate than her own. This made me think about my selfish behaviour during the time I had spent on the island of Diarra, and I felt humbled by her generosity. I did try to return food back to her plate, but she always stubbornly refused to take it.

However, despite this hospitality, the call of Anavrin was still a strong one, and I was keen to continue on my journey. I drew a diagram in the sand in order to show my hosts where I was travelling to, and intimated that I was ready to take my leave. I offered thanks for their generosity, collected my belongings and quickly set off. However, I hadn't walked far before the young girl came running towards me; she insisted on giving me rations of food and drink to take on the journey. I took them gladly. She then started pulling my leg, insisting that I follow her. Although the direction she was taking me was not the direction in which I had been intending to go, just as with the young boy in Isanarav, I instinctively trusted her.

We walked through the foothills for some time until we suddenly came upon a small group of wild horses that were busy grazing. She held up her hands, showing that I should wait, before calmly walking over to them. I was surprised to see that they did not run away from her. She pulled out a rope from her pocket and gently tethered one by his nose, stroking and patting him lovingly as she did so. The young girl then stood on tiptoes and whispered something into the horse's ear before leading him over to where I was standing. Bizarrely, the horse lay down calmly at my feet; the young girl invited me to sit astride of him before passing over the reins for me to take. She then took a stick and drew a map on the ground, similar to the one I had drawn back at the camp, and, from the way that she pointed her stick at my destination, I knew that she was trying to tell me that this horse would lead me across the desert and would take me where I needed to go. I nodded my head to show that I understood. She then whispered something to the horse to get him to stand up, before waving me off. The horse began galloping southwards.

I had only ever ridden a horse once before, but, as I was not sitting on a saddle, this time it was noticeably more difficult. But my horse was at least gentle and moved us smoothly across the lifeless, desolate plain. I felt glad that I had decided to follow the young girl, for this means of travel would be much quicker, saving me many days walking across this harsh terrain. In the distance, the outline of the mountain range became ever clearer as it dominated the skyline ahead. It didn't seem too long to me before the desert came to an abrupt halt. As promised, the horse had brought me right to the riverbed that my map had been pointing me towards. But, surprisingly, it was not completely dry, for, at the very bottom, was a small pool of water that had not yet evaporated under the heat of the desert or soaked down into the ground. After I had lowered myself to the ground, my horse went to drink from this pool. I walked over to stroke his mane to show my gratitude for his help and left to follow the riverbed into the heart of the mountains.

The climb was shallow to begin with but soon it started to ascend more steeply as the wide riverbed narrowed. I imagined that in the rainy season this would be a rocky stream cascading down the mountainside. But soon I was above the tree line and I could finally start to get a feel for the mountainous landscape and see my route ahead of me. It looked as though I was making for a prominent ridge that stretched out in a line for miles, which I assumed was the border. Although I was keen to make progress towards Anavrin and the fellowship, it was slow and painful going by foot as I negotiated my way through the loose rocks and boulders. Ahead of me I could just about make out a gap in the ridge and eagerly imagined going through and down the other side.

What I had not noticed, however, was that looming behind me was something quite unexpected. This was a rare cluster of storm clouds that had been quietly forming over the mountains. Suddenly, they began pouring lashings of rain down over the landscape. The wind picked up to a gale and the ferociousness of the rain reduced visibility. My clothes were not suited for these conditions and I could feel them sticking tightly to my skin. I tried to continue walking, but this was difficult as my boots were completely sodden. Then, in an incredibly short space of time, water started gushing down the hillside and a beautiful array of waterfalls appeared on either side of me. But of course the rain meant that the stream bed was also starting to fill with water, and the going became tough as I clambered over slippery, dangerous boulders. I had no choice but to continue pushing on, as on both sides there were thick brambles and vines which made the way impassable. Although I was soaked, my spirits had not been dampened by the rain; instead, it was a tremendously purifying experience, being out there at the mercy of nature.

Finally the storm clouds passed and the sun returned, drying my clothes and bringing some much-needed warmth. At this point I only had a few hundred metres left to travel to the ridge. Hurrying through the rocky bed, excited and impatient, I slipped and knocked my knees on the rocks a couple of times, making me wince in pain. But this did not make me stop and I continued striving eagerly towards the end. When I finally clambered up over the last metre and stood on the top, I felt a sense of euphoria, triumph and relief. Would I see a great and vastly developed civilisation on the other side, I wondered, or just a small community like the one I had left behind?

But the answer I received was not one I was prepared for, and it left me in a state of complete shock. For all that I could see below me was empty wasteland. From my vantage point I could see that the land stretched little more than a handful of miles in either direction; the ridge I was standing on curved right around in a semi-circular fashion until it met the ocean and so only a small area of land was left in between. Even from this distant viewpoint I could see that the landscape was completely desolate and my first reaction was one of disbelief. It looked very different from the world that Mackinnon had written about, and it seemed as if the commentators had been correct when they had said that the effects of climate change had destroyed the ancient civilisation that had once lived in this remote and distant land. The next emotion to arise was one of anger as I wondered why I had come all this way when there was nothing to show for it at the very end.

Consumed by rage, I suddenly heard the faint sound of strange music coming from below. I looked down and saw, bizarrely, that there was a man walking along through the shadow cast by the ridge, casually strumming on a guitar as he walked. As the man got closer the situation only became more bizarre: I could tell that he was not native to the area and that he came from the same part of the world as me. As it was unlikely that he would see me from down there, I decided to call to him. Hearing me, the man looked up and smiled, but continued singing and playing his guitar as though it was not at all surprising to see another person in this remote part of the world. Not surprising to see a fellow Arasmasian even. Puzzled, I decided to shout down and ask what had happened to the ancient civilisation of Anavrin. In response, the man turned towards me and laughed.

'You've come too late. Anavrin was destroyed many, many years ago,' he said, casually continuing his walk.

I was so stunned by the sight of this strange man that I could not think of any further questions before he disappeared out of earshot altogether. Instead, all I could do was to take a seat and look down at the emptiness that lay below me. My anger subsided, and as calmness returned, I reflected that there must be something to learn from this situation. It seemed ironic that there were no literal green shoots left in this desert for the fellowship to protect and I was left wondering why, on the banks of Lake Lawdi, I had imagined that there was a community living here.

Sitting and peacefully reflecting, I was able to grapple with this situation. I immediately thought of my conversation with Zeus, and how he'd given me the inspiration to have faith in Satya and in the power of the fifth dimension. But if he had not been alluding to a fellowship in Anavrin when he had told me that I needed to help protect the green shoot of Satya, then what had he meant?

Something struck me at that moment and I quickly realised how foolish I had been. For despite everything that my guides and lessons had taught me, I realised that I had still continued to believe that Satya could be found in the four dimensions of space and time rather than the fifth dimension that exists beyond them. Only now could I finally face my final fear and begin to let it go. Yes, by crossing the abyss, I had already let go of my fear of death, but, despite that, one fear still remained: the fear of Arasmas.

For me, Arasmas, with its multitude of problems, had always

represented the four-dimensional world – one that appeared totally devoid of Satya because of its political shenanigans. By longing to come to Anavrin I had been holding on to a belief that going there would allow me to hold on to the power of Satya much more easily than if I stayed in Arasmas. But it was not only that my longing to hold onto life ended up destroying what was important in it, but my longing to hold on to the light of Satya meant that I was not experiencing Satya at all. This is what the vast emptiness below revealed to me at that moment. Reflecting further, I realised that just as life and death were one and the same, that what I thought could only be found in Anavrin also existed in Arasmas; Satya does live on in the midst of ignorance.

This is what Zeus had meant and I now saw quite clearly how it could be possible for me to be in the world but not of this world. So was it possible, then, for our four-dimensional world to coexist with the fifth dimension? While I had known for a long time that I could access the power of Satya each and every moment, the genuine realisation of this simple truth, which penetrated the fullness of my being, blew away all of my remaining resistance. What happened next took me by surprise: I suddenly found myself bursting into laughter. This was not my normal laugh, however, but, instead, a deep laugh that came from the depths of my being and which resonated all across the mountain range. I continued laughing for such a long time that tears came to my eyes, and I knew that these were tears from eyes that had finally seen the truth. The search for Satya was finally at an end.

<u>Part V</u>

Chapter Thirty-Three

Sunday, 18th April 2032

I awoke with a jolt; the alarm clock beside me was making a monotonous droning noise. Turning over, I looked at the time; it was only six o'clock and the sun had only just come up. My first thought was to wonder why the alarm had been set to go off at such an early time, something I could not quite figure out. My next thought, however, was even more puzzling: where was I? Scanning the room, I could see that the wallpaper was familiar, but my question was only answered when I got up and drew the curtains. For, looking out of the window, I could see, quite clearly, the familiar and homely sight of the spire of Sarum's ancient centre of worship. I looked at the clock and checked the date. I was shocked to see that it was still only the 18th of April; today was the day I was due to board the boat that would carry me across the sea to Aidni. Only then did I realise that this was why my alarm had been set to go off so early, for I needed to go and catch the early train down to Port Wellington and I could see that my bag was packed and ready by the door.

At this moment, I remembered that in some strange way I had just been across to Anavrin and would not need to embark on that journey again. Satya was here with me now and the profundity of it all caused me to burst out laughing. I laughed so uncontrollably hard that tears rolled down my cheeks. When the tears finally stopped I immediately felt the urge to get out my notebook and pen and sit down and write. This time my words covered ten pages and, as before, they flowed naturally, ending at the bottom of each page and beginning again at the top of the next.

When I had finished writing I got to my feet and looked out of the window at the city. It had long been my home but now I felt as though I was seeing it for the first time. It was a marvellous sight and so, with new life pulsing through my body, I bounced out of my room and down the stairs. At the bottom, I bumped into the landlady, and she looked up at me and smiled.

'Good morning. Mr Demeritus. Would you care for some breakfast before you check out this morning?' she asked.

'Good morning to you, Mrs Parsons. I've had a change of plan and would like to stay on an extra week, if I may. Oh, and breakfast would be lovely, too,' I cheerfully replied.

After booking myself in for an extra week, I sat down to savour my breakfast. It was the most wonderful meal I had ever tasted. I lingered over every morsel of food and every mouthful of hot tea before deciding to take a walk through the city.

The street I was walking down was a familiar one, but, because I was walking with a new level of awareness, I wondered for the first time what lay behind the tall brick wall that ran alongside the pavement. It was then that I saw a narrow metal gate, which I had never noticed before. On the gate was a sign reading: 'Sarum Rose Garden: Open'. I decided to go inside to take a look and, in doing so, I realised immediately that it was a magical place. Walking slowly through the network of paths, I savoured a wide array of colours and scents. At each bed I took time to pause and to bend down and smell the flowers before moving on. One bed of roses really caught my attention. Half of the bed was filled with roses that were a deep shade of crimson; the other half was filled with roses that were of the purest white. In the very middle of the bed there stood a solitary pink rose, the most beautiful flower of them all.

When I stroked the petals of this delicate pink flower I received another profound revelation. For I could see that the white rose represented the innocent glory of Satya in its most pure and unrealised state while the red rose represented the ignorance that marred everyday life on earth. On my journey I had been searching for the white rose, and my motive for doing so had been to free myself from the suffering caused by the red rose. For too long I had lived in fear of the red rose; I had been afraid that it would destroy the purity of the white rose.

But the solitary pink rose showed me the higher truth. The white rose was not destroyed by coming into contact with the red rose; instead, it is transformed into something that is much more powerful. By meditating on this, I finally discovered my true purpose in life. My role was not to find or to create a fellowship seeking to preserve the white rose from destruction; it was to tell the world about the way of the pink rose. The only way that I could do this was by living by the power of the pink rose myself and acting as a bridge between these two worlds, enabling them to co-exist. This is what it truly means to live as a human being here on earth.

At this point I realised what my next step must be: I saw that I should dedicate myself to being an artist. I began to see that communication between these two worlds can only take place through the medium of art. However, I did not need to become a great painter, writer or sculptor; I merely needed to practice the art of living and allow the story of my life to become my means of artistic expression. I began to see that art could be expressed and communicated in a gesture or in kind words from a genuine heart, even in the simplest act that is carried out thoughtfully. While doing so, I began to see, quite clearly, that I was unimportant, and that the story was all that mattered.

Crucially, it was a story that suggested that there truly was more than meets the eye in the vast desert of vain opinions and limiting beliefs. Feeling reflective, I felt the urge to open my notebook, which I had been carrying in my pocket, and went to take a seat on one of the benches. I began to write. There was only one page left in the book but, in the end, I only needed to cover this page to bring everything to a state of completion. As I did so, I was struck by the fact that there was a seamless transition between the last line on the last page of the book and the first line on the first page. I took this to be a representation of life, which has no real end or beginning.

After finishing writing, I decided to walk back to the pink rose and to lay the book down next to its stem. While doing so, I suddenly became aware of a presence, one that was very familiar to me, and which, caused me to look around with a start. The gate had opened and a figure had walked in, one that I recognised from the way it glided across the stone path. It was the figure of Araya, and I could see that she was walking purposefully towards me. Warm emotions swept through my body as my eyes settled on her. I do not wish to taint this feeling with words but I would say that this was the energy of the purest love. For I saw that there was detachment in this feeling: there was no pull towards her. I understood now that I could not be separated from her because I'd never been attached.

Instead, as she came closer, I felt a sense of immense gratitude as I saw that she had evidently discovered the light and become free since I had last seen her. I could feel from her energy, and I also noticed how much physically freer she seemed away from the confines of the commune. The lingering pangs of guilt I had felt about abandoning her simply melted away in that moment, and the warm look that was in her eyes as they made contact with mine left me silent. Without a word, I stood up and we embraced for what felt like an eternity.

But then I sensed that a third person was entering the garden, and I let go of Araya. My eyes opened, and I saw a tall, languid figure marching purposefully towards us. His heavy boots were noisy, and he made no attempt to make himself inconspicuous. As he came closer I could see that his gaunt face was twitching nervously, and, with a sudden movement, he pulled a gun from his pocket and pointed it at me.

Strangely, at that moment, I did not feel any fear. I trusted that there must be a very good reason why the three of us had come together at this moment in time. I was able to stay in a loving state. However, I could tell from the way that Araya's body was tensing up that she had not yet fully grounded the power of Satya within herself, and I knew I would have to help her to remain in a state of love. The man had a young face and I could tell immediately that he was uncomfortable using his weapon. His voice when he spoke was shrill, showing his apparent discomfort.

'Are you Myrkais Demeritus?' he asked.

'I am,' I retorted stonily, knowing that he would probably never fully understand what these two words really meant.

'We have reason to believe that you are planning to travel to Aidni today in order to join a terrorist cell that threatens the safety and security of the people of Arasmas. I therefore must ask you to come with me for questioning. If you do not comply with my request, I am under strict orders to shoot.'

I said nothing but could feel that Araya was slowly pulling away from me, seemingly unsure whether it had been wise to try to find me. I squeezed her hand, encouraging her to hold firm. I could tell that doubt and fear were starting to consume her and I knew that this would not help us in finding an effective response to this difficult situation.

As well as supporting Araya, I was also busy sending my love to the poor man standing before me. I don't know how, but I could see quite clearly that he was only in such a senior position because his father was a high-ranking member of the clan and had used his power and influence to help his youngest son. But I could tell that this young man did not belong in this role and that he was only here because he was afraid of his father's wrath. I also had no doubt that he had come here today hoping that we would meekly obey his orders, and I could see that our calm silence was troubling him.

The man suddenly turned his attention to Araya, and sensing her fear, he spoke more firmly to her than he had to me.

'While you are not on my list of suspects I can see that something is not quite right with you either, so I will need to take you in for questioning as well. I must tell you again, if you do not comply with my request I am authorised to shoot.'

I could feel Araya wilting slightly under the man's threats and it was difficult for me to help her hold firm. Eventually I felt her relax as she noticed my calmness and began to trust that I knew what I was doing. When neither of us moved an inch he started to twitch, unsure whether we were resisting his order or whether we were just waiting for him to tell us to move. I knew his training had only taught him to deal with subjects who were consumed with fear and that he didn't know what to do when this wasn't the case.

After a long period of silence his patience finally snapped.

'Why are you standing your ground so calmly and not submitting to my order? Resistance is pointless, so tell me why you are not submitting, before I lose my temper and shoot you both?'

His voice had risen to a nervous squeal, and his last word was spat out. Araya was slowly turning her head towards me, and I knew that she was giving permission for me to speak for her as well. So I responded simply

'Because we choose to.'

Thank you for your purchase of this book.

Author's rely heavily on customer feedback for marketing and promotion of their work. You are warmly encouraged, therefore, to provide a review on the sales channel for this book; on the Amazon website.

About the Author

R.A. Moseley is an English writer currently living in Margaret River, in the South-West corner of Australia, with his wife Melissa and his cat Grace.

His mission in life is to be a spiritual friend; one who uses the power of the written word to illuminate that there is far more going on beneath the surface of our day-to-day human existence.

The Search for Satya is his first publication; preceding:

Tracking Fritz's Footsteps: Meditations on E.F. Schumacher's A Guide for the Perplexed (2013)

The Kingdom of Golf is Within You (2014)

and

Hamartia (2018)

All titles are self-published through Create Space; with print and e-book copies available for purchase through Amazon and other online distributors.

www.ingramcontent.com/pod-product-compliance
Lightning Source LLC
Chambersburg PA
CBHW021043090426
42738CB00006B/159